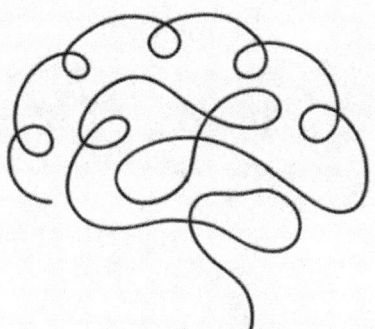

THE SERVICE MINDSET

Dedications and Acknowledgements

Thank you to all of my colleagues, connections, friends and members of my family who have stood by me.

To Thomas and Bobby – thank you for believing in me.

To Suzanna – thank you for your enthusiasm in encouraging me to write this down.

To Jane, Erin, Chloe, Alex and Nellie the Dog – I love you all dearly, thank you for saving me.

To the bullies – you didn't beat me.

To Mum and Dad, thank you for everything.

To Zach – this is who I tried to be.

When writing this book, I used structured tools to help shape and edit my thinking, but the ideas, stories, and content are entirely my own. It's based on my personal experiences and philosophy.

This book was written in a personal capacity, entirely outside of my employment. The views expressed are solely those of the author and do not reflect the views of any current or former employer.

Foreword

Prologue: The Man Who Might Never Have Made It

In 2022, I stood in a grand hall in Mayfair, West London, suitably dressed, as I accepted the award for Outstanding Young Professional at the Economic Crime Awards. Someone once described the Economic Crime Awards (or TECA's) as the Oscars of the financial crime-fighting world in the UK. According to their website, the Tackling Economic Crime Awards (TECAs) are open to anyone working in the UK, operating in the public, private, and third sectors. *The awards recognise and reward individuals, teams, initiatives, and companies involved in tackling different areas of economic crime. The awards are designed to be both independent and inclusive, providing an opportunity for outstanding performers, whether buyers or suppliers, to be recognised and their success to be celebrated.*

This was actually my second award of the night – moments earlier, I had received the award for Outstanding Anti-Financial Crime Leader or Director. The imposter syndrome was hitting me hard – as the award was passed into my hands, I looked around the audience of my contemporaries and simply shook my head.

This was a moment of recognition, a moment of validation. But even as I shook hands and smiled for the cameras, a part of me still couldn't quite believe it. Not because I doubted my ability nor my achievements, but because I remembered a time when I couldn't even remember what day it was.

The very fact that I was able to hold a coherent conversation with anyone was a big enough miracle… The truth is, I shouldn't have been there.

At 18 years old, I was a rising star – academically speaking. I had the world at my feet – near to the top of most of my classes at a solid grammar school in the Kent countryside. Captain of the rugby team, an enthusiastic public speaker, and an Oxbridge hopeful. My life was a carefully laid-out blueprint for success. Then, in a split second, everything changed.

A heavy night of celebration in Tenerife. A wrong step. A fall of 20 feet into an underground car park. A traumatic brain injury. A total blackout. I woke up in a hospital bed, confused, disoriented, unable to recognise the person I had once been.

For the next seven years, I lived in a haze. My short-term memory was shattered - I would ask the same question repeatedly, unable to retain the answer for more than a few minutes. Conversations would slip through my fingers like grains of sand. I lost my confidence, my purpose, my connection to the world. Academia and study – two bedfellows that had come so easily and naturally in the past, were now impossible. Friends drifted away, not knowing how to deal with the shell of a person I had become. I felt like a burden, a ghost of the overachiever I used to be.

Surviving a brain injury is a strange kind of fortune. People look at you and see someone who walked away, someone who "got lucky." They don't see the guilt that comes with knowing others didn't. They don't feel the quiet pressure that follows - the unspoken expectation that because you survived, you must now do something extraordinary, as if mere existence is no longer enough. And outwardly, I suppose I do seem fine. My sense of smell, lost in the aftermath, eventually returned. My speech, for the most part, is coherent once again. I go about my life, but I feel it *every day*. My thoughts are slower, my words more considered - I filter everything before I speak, knowing that sometimes what makes perfect sense in my head doesn't land the way I intend. I see it in the expressions of others when I say something unexpected or slightly off. I feel it in the exhaustion that creeps in after too many days without proper sleep, in the slurring of words when fatigue catches up with me. It's not dramatic, it's not tragic - it just *is*. Perhaps that's the hardest part. No one sees what's wrong. No one would ever guess. Maybe they just think I'm a bit of an arse, but inside, I still feel it. Every day.

At my lowest point, I genuinely believed that the best of my life was behind me. That I had peaked at 18. That I would never do anything of real significance again. I grieved for the version of me that had died in that fall.

But life had other plans.

What followed was a slow, painful, and often humiliating climb back to relevance. I wasn't going to be the same person I was before, but I could be something - and maybe even someone - better. The moment of clarity came not in an epiphany, but in small, gradual lessons. I realised that the more I focused inward - on my limitations, my failures - the worse I felt, but when I focused outward - on helping others, on doing something beyond myself - the noise in my head quietened down.

The Service Mindset wasn't a philosophy I set out to create. It was a lifeline I discovered when everything else had failed me. In finding this book, you have stumbled across a collection of the lessons that I wish I had discovered sooner.

It took me years to discover that the more I helped others, the more I found purpose. The more I led with service, the more opportunities opened up for me. It wasn't about grand gestures or self-sacrificial martyrdom - it was about small, intentional decisions that prioritised impact over ego. And slowly, that mindset reshaped my career, my leadership, and my life.

Perhaps the most important lesson unveiled by The Service Mindset is this: in the dark moments when you feel like you have lost everything, that which truly matters reveals itself.

Fast forward to that awards night in 2022: a brain-injured mess of a man, turned award-winning fraud leader. The trajectory defied logic, but it didn't defy service. This book isn't just about my journey - it's about what I learnt along the way, and how you can apply those lessons to leadership, work, and life.

I've been to the bottom. I know what it's like to feel lost, unworthy, and incapable, but I also know what it's like to come back stronger - not because of raw talent or sheer willpower, but because of a few, relatively simple, shifts in perspective.

In reality, I didn't invent the ideas in this book. In fact, nothing within these pages is truly new. The principles of *The Service Mindset* are built on foundations laid long before I ever had the words to describe them - by ancient philosophers, by thinkers like Adler, by the hard-earned wisdom of those who lived before me. These ideas have existed in different forms, whispered through time, shaping lives in ways seen and unseen. And yet, that does not make them any less mine. Because while I did not create them, I *lived* them.

I wrestled with them in moments of pain, uncertainty, and self-doubt. They guided me through the darkest points of my life, and in doing so, they became part of me. Now, I offer them to you - not as something I have invented, but as something I have *discovered*, tested, and shaped through my own journey. You will recognise echoes of ancient wisdom here, but what matters is not where these ideas began.

What matters is where they can take you.

This book is my way of passing those perspectives on to you – in the hope that they will serve you in the same way that they have helped me to change my life for the better. And because I also know this much: no matter where you are now, you are not finished, and the best way forward is to serve.

Welcome to *The Service Mindset.*

PART ONE

Chapter 1: The Fall and The Awakening

The Accident That Changed My Life

Note to Mum and Dad: if you are reading this, you can relax. I am not going to be talking about my childhood, or my upbringing suffice to say that growing up, for me, was very pleasant indeed.

My parents were the hardest working people. My Dad, an engineer, had left school in his teens and worked his way up to run his own company. My Mum was a nurse, who believed passionately in older people having dignity and care in their old age – and sacrificed long hours, and most of the vertebrae in her spine, to giving them just that.

In many ways, my parents' hard work had given me the gift of privilege and by the age of eighteen, it felt as though I had the world at my feet. I wouldn't call myself academically gifted, but education had aways been a breeze for me – I had always been able to achieve without much in the way of effort.

I was one of the stronger public speakers at my school. A prefect and a leader on the rugby pitch. I had, at one point, been earmarked for Oxbridge, with a future that seemed almost predetermined - one of success, status, and stability - but life, as I would learn, doesn't always follow the script.

It was the summer of 2001 and I had just finished my A-Levels. A couple of friends and I had had the genius idea of spending a week in the sunshine of Tenerife to celebrate the end of our school careers. The plan (like the best plans) was simple: a week of sun, relaxation, and then returning home for the 6th form leavers' ball, tanned and triumphant. Fate, as it transpired, had other plans.

Having been a teenager at the height of hedonistic 90s lad culture, and having never really fit in with it, we arrived in Tenerife determined not to do the whole 18-30s thing. However, travel reps were on us from the moment that we touched down on the island.

"Hey guys, you are going to want to see me for some tickets to some events we are promoting this week!"

"No thanks" we replied defiantly.

*"Don't let this opportunity pass you by guys – you are going to end up doing these things anyway
and it's going to cost you a lot more if you don't buy your tickets from me!"*

Our resolve lasted probably less than 12 hours. The next morning at our hotel's swimming pool, a different guy appeared but the patter was the same: *"Don't miss out on the holiday of a lifetime lads, buy your tickets from me and I will get you into the hottest events this week – it will be a holiday you will never forget."*

As it turned out, it was a holiday that I would never really be able to remember.

And so, on the first official night of our holiday, my friends and I found ourselves sat on a minibus heading into the mountains of Tenerife for a foam party that we never really wanted to go to.

My memories of that fateful night are patchy at best. It was hot and my skin was glowing with having been exposed to too much sun too quickly. Hundreds of people gathered in the foam as the air pulsed with 90s dance music, yet my friends and I – our unmerry band of 3 – sat in an introverted corner staring into our drinks.

Looking back, I think we were probably disappointed in ourselves in having handed most of our spending money to a holiday rep only to end up somewhere we didn't really want to be.

"Come on guys" I said "let's get this party started!" I got up and strode to the bar "3 triple tequilas please!

"*Darling, at this bar, they're all triples*" the bartender replied with a mischievous grin.

I returned to the grumpy corner, only to find that in my time away at the bar, my two friends had struck up conversations with two young women. "Guys, I got your drinks!" I earnestly intimated.

"Ah, its ok mate… we're kind of talking here!" came the reply. The words that weren't being said spoke a volume to me. It wasn't lost on me that at that moment in time, I was the only member of our small group that had a serious girlfriend waiting for me back home. Ironically, up until that night, I had been wearing a silver Saint Christopher around my neck, inscribed with the words *"Love you always..."*

I had taken it off in the hotel earlier that day whilst swimming and never put it back on.

Anyway, there I was, my friends were doing their thing, and I was on a different path to them. I looked down to the three triple tequilas clutched tightly in my hands. A moment later, I had downed them all and had taken the seriously stupid decision to make my own way back to my hotel. Those decisions, taken in that moment, are probably the last decisions that I took with a fully functioning, intact brain.

What follows, is patchy, but somewhere on my way out of the party, I seem to recall that an altercation occurred. I don't remember exactly what was said or done, but I found myself at the bottom of a staircase, picking myself up. Some people approached me in the street and asked if I was ok… I am not sure if I was bleeding or if they had seen me fall down the stairs.

Confused, I stumbled out into the road, narrowly avoiding an oncoming taxi. I grabbed onto a metal barrier in the centre of the road to steady myself, but the barrier wasn't fixed - it collapsed beneath my weight. On the other side of that barrier was a 20 to 30 foot drop into an underground car park.

Darkness.

I would later find out that what happened next was that I lay in that carpark for several hours before employees of the club signed off for the night, discovered me and called an ambulance. However, my next memory was waking up in a Spanish hospital, confused, disoriented, and in pain.

Instinctively, I tried to remove the tubes and wires connected to my body, but nurses restrained me, speaking urgently in Spanish. My next memory is coming to again in intensive care. A doctor stood over me and explained, in broken English, that I had suffered a traumatic brain injury (TBI). In that moment, my overriding thought was to surrender myself completely to the medical professionals watching over me. "Whatever you need doc, whatever you need to do – I consent. If you need to operate, then operate, just keep me alive!"

I remember the doctor chuckling as he explained that surgery wasn't an option. "Surgery in your case," he said, "is like using a machine gun to kill mosquitoes. You need to rest."
And so I slipped back into darkness. I drifted in and out of a coma for the next two weeks, but the true darkness - the one that would take years to escape - was only just beginning.

"Where's mum?!"

I don't really remember coming out of the coma - the order of events or how something emerged from nothing.

I do remember opening my eyes though and there was my dad sitting beside me. My brain was broken and I was very confused, but even so, I knew that it didn't make any sense for my dad to be there.

I knew my dad was in England and yet here he was, sitting in a stiff-backed chair next to the bed, his face lined with exhaustion. He looked like he'd been there for hours, possibly days. There was relief in his expression when I stirred, but also something else - something deeper, a kind of sadness mixed with a silent strength.

I opened my mouth to speak, but my mind was fogged, the words sluggish.

"What happened?" my dad asked.

Thoughts churned through my broken mind like rocks in a tumble drier. Before I could answer my dad asked: "How drunk were you?"

I don't know why, but my first instinct was to lie. "Not very" I replied.

I had never been very good at accepting reality or taking responsibility. For whatever reason, I was deeply afraid of disappointing my parents. So therefore, it was better to lie to them – I could live with them not knowing the truth, but I could not live with their disappointment.

My dad leaned forward. "Is there anything I can get you?" At that moment, I just remember being incredibly thirsty and hungry like I had never been before – God only knows how long it had been since I had last eaten anything.

"Something to drink and something to eat"

"I am not sure if you are allowed" my dad replied as he milled it over in his mind.

"Please dad"

I rolled over and went back to sleep.

Sleep, in those early days, was frequent, but often I would wake up exhausted. I rolled over, opened my eyes and dad was there again, watching over me. There was a drink on the table and a chocolate bar. Dad muttered and slipped out of the room as I devoured the chocolate bar. I didn't hear his words.

I would later learn that my travel insurers, upon hearing of my injuries, had flown my dad out to Tenerife in case someone needed to make funeral arrangements for me. For the duration of my hospital stay, my dad was put up in one of the best hotels on Tenerife – the lucky guy had an infinitely better holiday than I ever did!

I joke of course.

On one occasion, I noticed my clothes folded neatly beside me. They had been washed. That made no sense. I would learn that my dad – upon arriving at the hospital - had scrubbed them clean, removing the dried blood from the fabric, as if by erasing the stains, he could undo what had happened. As if clean clothes could put me back together.

Whilst it was completely unnecessary as I had other clean clothes, I can understand now why my dad had done it – *sometimes when we are powerless and hopeless, we need to do something* – anything – in order to feel useful. To help us believe that we are capable of making a difference.

At the time, I thought little of it - just another practical thing my dad did. But looking back, I see it differently. He couldn't undo what had happened to me, couldn't take away my pain, but he could do *something*. And sometimes, when we feel powerless, the smallest acts of service are all we have.

I did not realise it then, but that action of my father scrubbing my clothes – doing something for another when you are broken inside - was an early encounter with the service mindset in action.

But more on that later.

I had been in the hospital for well over the originally scheduled week. The passage of time was fragmented. I yearned to be at home. One night I would go to sleep and not wake up for a few days. When I did, it was explained to me that a secondary brain injury caused by multiple mechanisms at play in my blood had caused my brain to swell – another period in intensive care followed.

When I regained consciousness in my room, my dad was there. "Hello dad, what are you doing here?" I asked weakly.

"You had an accident, son. You're in the hospital, but you're going to be okay."

"Ah ok… and where's mum?" I asked.

"Its just me, son. They could only fly one of us out to you and your mum had to stay at home!"

I nodded weakly. The words made sense, but only for a moment. Minutes later, I turned to him again, my brow furrowing as the same questions slipped from my lips.

"Hello dad, what are you doing here?"

His face remained calm, patient. "You had an accident. You're in the hospital."

I nodded. Then, another second passed.

"Where's mum, is she with you?"

I looked over my dad's shoulder to the open doorway, half expecting my mum to be there behind him.

Again, the same answer, the same measured tone.

I must have asked him that question a hundred times. Each time, he answered me as though it were the first. There was no frustration, no exasperation - just quiet acceptance that, for now, this was part of our reality.

In the days that followed and, in an attempt to engage my broken mind, my dad tried to teach me how to play cribbage. He shuffled the cards methodically, explaining the rules in the same way he had done when I was a child, but my brain refused to hold onto the information. He would show me a hand, and I would forget it instantly. I saw the flicker of pain in his eyes, the realisation of how damaged I was. Still, we played, moving the pegs along an imaginary board, dealing new hands, hoping something – anything - would stick.

Time would become a meaningless blur. My short-term memory was non-existent. I latched onto whatever stimulus was in front of me. In my hospital room, the only entertainment was a small television mounted on the wall, perpetually tuned to CNN.

I watched it, absorbed in the headlines, fascinated by each story as though it were new. An hour later, the same headlines would return, word for word, image for image. But to me, it was all fresh. The same stories played in an endless loop, and I watched, again and again, unaware that I had already seen them.

I don't know how long I did this - hours, maybe even days. My father watched me watching, his worry deepening, though he never said a word. I imagine he was wondering the same thing I was, though I couldn't articulate it at the time: *Will this ever get better?*

In those weeks in that foreign hospital, I don't recall getting emotional much. I had a minidisk player that I listened to for hours on loop – running the batteries dead and then pestering my dad to find me some more. Younger readers of this book might need this explaining – and I am happy to distract myself from the sadness I experience in recalling these details, to explain.

In the late 20th Century, music was a physical asset – you couldn't just stream it or listen to it – you had to go out and buy it in a physical form that corresponded with your player of choice.

First came records, then tapes, then CDs before eventually, society leapt to digital MP3's the precursor to modern streaming services. Well, shortly before the demise of CDs and the advent of digital formats, someone created the minidisk. The minidisk was a small CD-like disk encased in a hard plastic shell. The sound quality was great and players looked like technology out of the space shuttle – really cool, futuristic stuff.

So, I lay there in my bed listening to *White Pony* by Deftones over and over again.

I have a vague recollection of sharing my broken emotional state with my dad on one occasion. I remember him saying something like "we are going to take those feelings and put them in a box. We are going to seal that box up tight and put it over here on a shelf and never open it again."

So that's exactly what we did.

On the inside though, I was interminably sad. At the time, I was just longing to be home. It was a thought that consumed me completely. I just needed to get home.

I wanted my life back, my autonomy, my future.

Little did I know that when I eventually got home, those things were not going to be handed back to me. Things were going to get a whole lot harder before they would get better.

I was alive. But I wasn't me. Not yet.

Returning Home

For days in the hospital, just like the CNN news cycle, I was also trapped in a loop. Every morning my dad would arrive and plead with me to get up and get dressed – to wash and to do something for myself.

Every evening, he would arrive back at the hospital – exasperated – as he found me in bed, unmoved, undressed – just watching the news over and over again.

I could not tell you precisely what happened, but one morning he wearily implored me to get up and get dressed and the message didn't just dissolve in my injured brain. One day, the message stuck and I knew that getting out of bed, getting washed and dressed – I realised that that small action would make the world of difference to my dad. So that's what I did.

Eventually, my travel insurers sent a specialist neurologist to assess whether I was fit to fly. He had just returned from Australia, where he had been overseeing the rehabilitation of a British man who had broken his neck diving into a shallow pool. I imagine the 90s must have been full of foreign hospitals with British patients - accidents, recklessness, the naive belief that we were invincible.

His job was simple: check me over, make sure I wouldn't die mid-flight, and get me home. We flew back business class, and from the airport, an ambulance took me straight to Queen Elizabeth The Queen Mother Hospital in Margate. My dad had to travel to a different airport to collect his car, leaving me alone with the neurologist for most of the journey.

I felt every bit broken.

The neurologist, however, didn't seem particularly concerned. He talked about how things would *settle down*, how I would need to avoid playing rugby for a while, and how I would, in time, make a good recovery. At one point, as he studied my brain scans, he remarked that my life might get *"a little fruity."*

He was talking about my frontal lobe damage. About the damaged area of my brain that contained what he described as my moral compass. About the possibility that I might struggle to regulate myself, that my sense of right and wrong - of what was *socially acceptable* - might be forever altered.

At the time, I had no patience for this kind of talk. I just wanted my life back. No complications, no setbacks, no warnings about *fruitiness.*

As the ambulance hurtled across the Kent countryside, blue lights flashing, I knew I had to explain to the neurologist just how important it was for me to get home. I had already missed the end of school and my leavers' ball. For the last few weeks, I had felt my autonomy and my freedom slip away completely. I needed to be home, I needed to reconnect with who I had been.

"Listen, doc, you're my get-out-of-jail-free card here."

I was desperate to be home. The last thing I needed was someone deciding I wasn't well enough, trapping me in another hospital, delaying my return.

The neurologist understood.

When we arrived at the hospital, I heard him speaking to the UK doctors in hushed tones, but loud enough for me to catch what mattered.

"Look, this guy's mum is a nurse. He just needs to go home and rest."

That was all they needed to hear. No prolonged assessments, no additional scrutiny. Just a few meaningless observations - blood pressure, pulse, the basics. The UK doctors seemed completely out of their depth. A British teenager with a brain injury acquired in a foreign country didn't really seem to be a situation that was necessarily in their collective wheelhouses.

I lay on the bed, frustrated beyond belief. I was *so close* to home, and yet, somehow, still stuck. Still waiting.

I snapped.

I ranted at the doctors, shouting something about discharging myself. I didn't care about their confusion, their helplessness. I was so *angry*, in a way that didn't even feel like me.

And then I felt it. Another presence in the room.

I turned - and there they were.

My mum. My dad. My two younger brothers.

Standing in the doorway. Watching.

Their faces were frozen, aghast. They saw something I couldn't.

They saw the change before I even realised it myself. The weight of my injury, the way it had altered me. I thought I had made it through, that getting home was the end of the battle. But looking at them, I understood. This wasn't an ending. It was just the beginning of something I wasn't prepared for.

The fight to rebuild myself was only just beginning.

The drive home was silent. The only sound was the occasional rustling of the biscuit packet as I absentmindedly ate my way through it in the back seat. No one spoke. No one even turned the radio on. It was as if they were all afraid of saying the wrong thing, of disturbing the fragile peace that had settled over us. I didn't understand it. I was just me. Why did everyone seem to have a problem with that?

When we pulled into the driveway, my mum turned to me with an enthusiastic smile.

"While you were in hospital, I decorated your bedroom for you."

I wasn't sure how to react. I had barely even stepped back into the house, and already things had changed without me. When I walked into my room, I was met with a shocking burst of colour - bright, yellow walls glaring under the ceiling light. My stomach dropped.

At the time, I could only assume that this was some well-intentioned attempt at helping me to recover. But to me, it felt like an invasion. My space, the one thing I should have had control over, had been taken from me. I was angry, but I didn't have the energy to express it. Instead, I muttered something weak, something dismissive.

"Oh… you didn't have to do that."

I didn't realise then that my mum was, in her own way, practicing The Service Mindset – focusing outwardly on what she could affect - doing what she thought would help, even if it wasn't what I wanted. Doing something to help another when inside she must have felt helpless.

In my frustration, I didn't see it for what it was – my Mum's attempt to help in the only way she knew how. It wasn't what I wanted, but it was what she *could* do. And now I understand: service isn't always about giving people what they ask for. Sometimes, it's about giving them what we *hope* might help.

She urged me into bed, telling me to rest. I couldn't believe it. I had spent weeks in hospital, weeks lying in a bed, desperately waiting to come home. And now, the first thing I was told to do was to get back into bed.

Over the following days, family members I rarely saw before the accident began dropping by. Their visits all followed the same pattern: a lingering stare, a tight-lipped smile, and the same rehearsed phrases.

"God obviously had a reason to keep you here."
"It wasn't your time."
"There must be some higher purpose for you."

I had no idea how to respond. I didn't feel chosen. I didn't feel like I had a purpose. If anything, I felt like I had cheated something inevitable, and I wasn't sure I deserved it.

Then one afternoon, my dad took me to the rugby club. It had been my second home for years.

Every Saturday, I had played there, pushing myself to be the best, to earn my place on the team. The season before my accident, I had even won Young Player of the Year. I should have felt proud to be back.

Instead, I walked into a room full of people who suddenly erupted into applause.

I stood frozen in the doorway, my face burning. The clapping was relentless. They were cheering me for something I had no control over.

I felt like a fraud, as if they were celebrating something I had no choice over. But now, I see what they were really doing. They weren't cheering my survival, they were showing me that they cared in the only way they knew how to - offering their support, making sure I didn't feel alone.

Even so, I hated the attention, the expectation, the implication that my survival meant something more than it did. I hadn't done anything extraordinary. I had fallen, I had been patched up, and I had come home. That was all.

The more people praised me, the smaller I felt. The more they told me I had a purpose, the more I felt like I didn't. I withdrew, avoiding conversations, avoiding people. I spent hours in the garden, wandering aimlessly, unable to shake the feeling that I didn't belong anywhere - not in my home and not in my community. I didn't even recognise the voice in my own head – my internal monologue feeling like it belonged to a stranger.

I started taking my meals alone, away from the dining table. I didn't deserve a seat with people who hadn't broken themselves. I didn't deserve their kindness, their love, their faith in some divine reason for my survival. I was developing an inferiority complex, fuelled by survivor's guilt, and I had no idea how to stop it.

In the weeks that followed my return home, my parents kept me very close. They were watching me carefully, though they tried not to make it obvious - but I could tell. They were worried… and with good reason.

I wasn't myself.

My mood swings were unpredictable. My patience was thin. I made inappropriate remarks without thinking, comments that I knew would have been unacceptable before, but the filter I once had was gone. I could see the concern in my parents' faces every time I spoke out of turn, every time my emotions flared up or shut down entirely.

I was concerned, too.

It started with my sense of smell. Or rather, the complete loss of it. I hadn't noticed it at first - it's easy to overlook the absence of something you take for granted - but eventually, I realised I couldn't smell *anything*. Not food, not the air outside, not my own skin. It was as if a whole part of my sensory experience had been erased. And then there were the intrusive thoughts.

Every time I said goodbye to a friend or family member, a thought would flash across my mind, unwanted and unwelcome. *What if you die in a car crash on the way home?* It wasn't a passing worry; it was persistent. It felt as if my brain had rewired itself to anticipate the worst, to expect tragedy at every turn.

Beyond the immediate concerns, there was the looming question of my future. I was due to go to university in the autumn to study law. My parents didn't say it outright, but I knew they were wondering whether I would be able to live on my own. Whether I would be *safe* living on my own.

We had also planned one final family holiday to Florida before I was due to go to university. I knew my parents were concerned. *Could I fly? Could I go on rollercoasters? Could I live the life that I had always intended to live?*

It was time to get answers.

And so, we went to London to see a neurosurgeon.

He was highly regarded, an expert in his field. He had my scans up on the lightbox as we sat in his office. My parents were with me, hanging on to his every word. I was still clinging to the hope that I would hear something definitive - something that explained why I felt the way I did and, more importantly, how long it would take to *fix* me.

Instead, the neurosurgeon frowned at the images in front of him. He studied them for what felt like an eternity before making a comment that caught us all off guard.

"We need to get you back into hospital"

My jaw hit the floor: *"What?!"*

"Looking at these scans – you appear to be getting worse. Your condition is deteriorating"

My parents were in shock, but I nudged my dad.

"Dad, the scans…" I whispered – my dad looked at me: *"The scans are round the wrong way, he is reading them backwards"*

For a moment, I didn't know whether to laugh or cry. Here was a man - a *specialist* - who was meant to have all the answers. And yet, he had gotten something so fundamental, so *wrong*.

It was tragically hilarious listening to my dad explain to the esteemed neurosurgeon that he was looking at the scans backwards and rather than deteriorating, my condition was actually improving.

"Hmmm…" the doctor mused *"Did you take ecstasy?"*

I was shocked at the directness of the question. *"No, I have never taken drugs"*

The doctor continued *"Given the severe morbidity typically associated with multiple cerebral contusions… what I mean to say is, I have seen these precise injuries in 4 people previously, all in a mortuary setting… all of those 4 people were suspected of having taken ecstasy"*

He trailed off, as if the weight of what he was saying had only just dawned on him. My parents exchanged a glance. I stared at him, trying to piece together what he had just implied.

I was supposed to be *severely* impaired. My level of functioning - my ability to walk, to speak, to think - wasn't what he had expected to see. By all accounts, I should have been in a far worse state.

For the remainder of the meeting, my parents asked questions of the expert but received little in the way of advice or meaningful replies.

We eventually left his office with no more certainty than when we had arrived. My parents tried to reassure me, to focus on the positive - that I was doing better than expected, that I was exceeding expectations, but I couldn't shake the feeling that I was walking a tightrope, balancing between survival and something far more fragile.

The neurosurgeon had had no real answers. His straight-talking assessment had boiled down to one simple truth: I *should* have been dead. Given the extent of my injuries, he couldn't predict what I would or wouldn't be able to do. He wasn't in any position to set limitations on me - his only suggestion was to go out into the world and see for myself.

Just try.

That was it. No restrictions, no medical orders to take it easy, just an open-ended invitation to figure it out on my own.

With no objections from the doctor, the plan remained unchanged. We were going to Florida - one last family holiday before I was supposed to leave for university. A trip that had been booked before my accident, back when everything had been normal. Now, it felt like a test.

I was still struggling. The intrusive thoughts hadn't gone away. I still felt detached from myself, as if I was an observer in my own life and yet there we were, boarding the plane, landing in Orlando, stepping out into the suffocating heat of the Florida summer.

On the first day of our final holiday together as a family, I climbed into bed with my younger brothers and watched *the Karate Kid* on the TV in our motel room.

I could sense my dad's frustration. He had an itinerary – there was stuff to do, things to see, adventures to be had and yet there we were, huddled together in bed, watching a film from the 80s that we had seen a thousand times before.

There must have been something quite reassuring in it for my parents. Seeing me there with my brothers, laughing and joking as we recited the lines of the film together. They left us to it – all plans had gone out of the window. For now, we had a pass to delay the start of the holiday, to enjoy a rare moment of post-traumatic normality.

Eventually, we left the hotel – late, but with a view to getting things back on schedule. Then the Florida summer gave us the mother of all storms… Tropical Depression *Erin*.

It arrived suddenly, thick clouds swallowing the sky, the air electric with tension. The rain came first, relentless and heavy, pounding the pavement and turning roads into rivers. Then the lightning.

I don't remember where we were exactly – a theme park somewhere. As the storm raged all around us, groups of tourists huddled under a large canopy – absolutely terrified as nature revealed her fury all around us.

I don't know what compelled me to go out into it, but I did. While others sought shelter, I stood in the downpour, feeling the energy crackling in the air around me. Every strike of lightning was blinding and hot, followed by the deep, guttural roar of thunder.

I should have been afraid. Any rational person would have been. But I wasn't.
I *wanted* to be there.

I remember standing in an open space, the storm raging around me, sheets of rain soaking through my clothes. The world had narrowed to that single moment - the wind howling, the sky flashing white, the sensation of absolute insignificance in the face of something so vast and uncontrollable.

I danced in the rain as the lightning struck the ground around me, the thunder rolling through my chest like a war drum. My family stood watching from the canopy, horrified, but I barely registered them.

"If it's got your number, it's got your number!" I shouted into the storm, laughing, defiant. Maybe I was testing fate. Maybe I was trying to feel alive. Maybe I just didn't care.

And then, as suddenly as it had begun, the storm passed.

The clouds broke apart, the rain ceased, and the Florida sun came pouring back in, brilliant and golden, as though nothing had happened. As though it had all just been a momentary lapse in the world's perfection.

People stepped back outside, shaking off the rain, laughing at the sheer force of it. The holiday resumed, life resumed - normality was returning to sunlit Florida.

But I didn't move.

I stood there, drenched, rooted to the spot, staring at nothing.

The storm was gone, but inside me, it raged on.

My dad watched, puzzled. We had put all that emotional stuff in a box and *sealed it*. That was the deal. But now here I was, standing in the aftermath, unable to shake the weight pressing down on my chest.

I turned to my mum.

And she knew.

She could *see* it in me.

The rain had stopped, but tears streamed down my face. My whole body felt hollow, like something inside me had been scooped out and discarded.

"I am just so sad, Mum..."

The words broke from me in a sob, raw and jagged. The pain was visceral, heavy, not just in my chest but in my bones, in my heart.

"And I don't know why."

I had survived. I was here. But something inside me was missing. And for the first time, I didn't know if I would ever find it again.

University

I went to university, just as planned. Just as if nothing had happened.

But everything had happened.

Academia, studies – in the past it had all been so easy. Whilst I was never the most popular guy at school – if truth be told, throughout my teens I had been horribly bullied by older boys - I had always had a knack for making good friends.

None of that was true now.

From the moment I arrived at university, I made sure people knew what had happened to me. Every new person I met, I told them that I had a brain injury. That I should be dead. That I wasn't like them. It wasn't exactly a great way to make friends, but university was full of odd characters, and I was just another one of them.

I clung to that identity - not because I wanted pity, but because I didn't know who else to be. Before the accident, I had been bright, confident, capable. Now, I was none of those things. I was someone whose brain didn't work the way it was supposed to. Someone who struggled with things that had once been effortless.

And studying law, even in the best of circumstances, is brutal. For me, it was damn near impossible.

My memory was shattered. I would read a line in a textbook, move to the next, and immediately forget what I had just read. A single page took hours to read and little would go in. I would stare at the words, willing them to stick, but they slipped away like water through my fingers.

There were many calls home to my mum. I'd sob down the phone, exhausted, defeated. *I can't do this.*

She always listened. Always reassured me. Always told me I *could* do it.

But I didn't believe her and I didn't believe in myself anymore… I was broken and hopeless.

At some point, I found a counsellor. He helped me untangle the grief I hadn't even realised I was carrying. It wasn't just that studying was hard - it was that studying had *never* been hard. It was the one thing I had always relied on, the one thing that had always come naturally. And now it was just one of a long list of things that the accident had taken from me.

I wanted to talk about it. I remember calling home after one of my counselling sessions, eager to share what I had learnt, how I was processing everything. But brain injuries are difficult to discuss – it's a very lonely place to find yourself.

Understandably, for friends and family the box that contained my trauma had been sealed.

For me, the box had burst open, and I was drowning in everything I had tried to lock away.

There were definitely the prophesised *fruity* moments. Times when my behaviour was reckless or inappropriate, moments when I did things without really knowing *why*. But mostly, I was just sad. Anxious.

Depression became my closest companion, filling the spaces where my old friends used to be.

And one by one, those friends eventually drifted away.

I was difficult to be around. I could feel it happening - conversations that once flowed became stilted. Invitations came less often. Then not at all. I became someone who was tolerated rather than welcomed.

I felt alone.

And that feeling would stay with me for a long time.

Seven years, to be exact.

Facing the Darkness: Depression, Anxiety, and Identity Loss

Those seven years were hard. I was no longer the person I had been. My memories were fragmented, my thoughts scrambled. It was as if my mind had been reset to factory settings. Here I was, now a man, but with many of those formative lessons of my childhood completely wiped out.

I had lost my sense of smell. My memory was unreliable. The voice in my head - the constant internal monologue that had always been mine - now felt like a stranger's. My past felt like it belonged to someone else. And worst of all, I didn't know who I was anymore.

I had gone from being a young man with confidence and certainty to someone who couldn't trust his own thoughts. Paranoia and mistrust led me to lose my girlfriend. My friendships frayed. A growing distance formed between me and my family. The accident had changed me, but I didn't yet understand how, or if, I could ever reclaim my sense of self.

Depression settled over me like a thick fog. It wasn't just sadness; it was an absence of joy, a suffocating emptiness devoid of hope. Anxiety joined in, bringing with it panic attacks that convinced me I was dying. Every day felt like a battle against my own mind, a fight I wasn't sure I could win.

Well-meaning people told me that I had survived because *"God had a plan for me."* But that only made it worse. *If I was meant to be here, why did I feel so meaningless? If my survival had some grand purpose, why couldn't I see it?*

I was stuck in a cycle of mourning the person I had been, without any idea of how to move forward.

Lost and Unmoored

At my lowest ebb, I was the antithesis of The Service Mindset: lost, without purpose, seeking validation in the most self-destructive ways.

Inside a head injury, reality becomes a distorted maze. Conversations felt like navigating a minefield; I couldn't understand why people reacted the way they did. Every word required meticulous calculation, as if natural speech had become a foreign language. Thinking no longer flowed effortlessly; it was a laborious process, each thought weighed down by the fear of getting it wrong.

Alcohol became my escape. While I wasn't dependent, I relished the temporary silence it brought to the relentless noise in my mind. Intoxication offered a brief respite from the intrusive thoughts and the stranger's voice that had taken residence in my head. However, for individuals with traumatic brain injuries (TBI), alcohol can exacerbate cognitive impairments and increase the risk of seizures. Studies have shown that alcohol consumption after TBI may lead to worsened cognitive recovery and heightened emotional problems, such as depression.

Despite these risks, I drank too much and too often, leading to increasingly reckless decisions. Each night blurred into the next, a haze of faces and places that offered no real connection, only fleeting distractions.

After university, living with my parents became untenable. My unreasonable and erratic behaviour and volatile moods strained our relationship. Eventually, I moved halfway across the country, renting a small room in the home of an elderly couple. For nearly three years, isolation was my only companion.

I remember one night, the weight of loneliness pressing so heavily on me that I could barely breathe. Desperate, I called the Samaritans and wept into the phone.

"I'm so lonely," I confessed, my voice cracking under the weight of my despair.

In that moment, I knew something had to change. *But what? And how?* The path forward was shrouded in darkness, and I was groping blindly, hoping to find a way out of the abyss.

The Turning Point: Acceptance and Growth

The shift didn't happen overnight. In fact, it took years.

There was no clear defining moment, but I do have a memory that stands out - a single conversation - that planted the seed. I was at a friend's house, crying quietly in a corner whilst my friends planned a night out. One friend, frustrated, asked why I was so upset.

I told him: *"Because my brain feels broken. The voice in my head isn't mine anymore."*

He looked at me and asked, *"Can you get a new brain? Can they fix it?"*

"No."

"Then you're stuck with what you've got, aren't you? It's not going to change, so you're going to have to learn to live with it."

At the time, those words stung – they felt deeply unsympathetic, but in the months that followed, I began to realise they contained a truth I had been avoiding and a lesson I probably needed to hear: self-pity wouldn't change anything. *I had to learn to work with what I had.*

My friend probably didn't think of it as an act of service and it certainly didn't feel like one at the time, but now I can look back on it and see that it was. He gave me something no one else had - a truth I needed to hear. Service isn't always gentle. Sometimes, it's a hard shove in the right direction.

But even with that realisation, I didn't immediately act on it. The grief and trauma still weighed me down. I continued to turn inward, allowing my pain to define me. Looking inward served only to amplify my suffering.

At its worst, I was looking inward so intently that I developed feelings of depersonalisation and non-reality. Obsessed with my health and my mortality, I would take my pulse countless times a day – counting out the beats of my heart, literally waiting for them to stop.

Life passed me by in a dreamlike daze. Nothing felt real. I was so completely focused on what was going on inside me that I had totally lost connection with the world around me.

It was only when I started to look outward - to shift my focus to others - that I found a way forward.

This was reinforced when I met my partner, Jane.

It is perhaps remiss to recount Jane's story here – she has lived her own life and may want to write her own book one day. What I will say is that when I met Jane, she was the victim of domestic abuse and had two children from that previous abusive relationship. For the first time in a long time, I felt like I had found my people – people who, in their own way, were a bit broken too – and we needed each other. The happiness of Jane and her children became my responsibility. And for the first time since my accident, I truly lived in service of others.

Through them, I discovered something simple but powerful: *When I thought about helping others, I stopped obsessing over my own problems.* Service became my anchor. By focusing on the needs of others, I found a way to hush the negative thoughts in my own mind.

It started small. Little things. Tiny acts of service that didn't feel like much at the time - offering a hand, being there for someone, listening without expectation - but over time, the needle began to move and for brief moments, the noise in my head quietened.

I began to realise that I felt better – *lighter* - when I wasn't so intently focused on myself.

Maybe I didn't have a purpose. Maybe I would never fully understand why I survived. But I *could* make a difference in someone else's life - and maybe that was enough.

Over time, I built new mental frameworks:

- Depression: I fought it with action - living by the mantra, *the more you do, the more you will feel like doing.*

- Anxiety: I reframed it through stoic logic and pragmatism - *consciousness was just an algorithm, interpreting sensory input – in reality, what was the worst thing that could possibly happen?*

- Purpose: I found it in service. The moment I started helping others, I felt my own pain diminish.

Finally, becoming a father was the moment when everything truly shifted. My daughter, Erin – named for the storm that had almost ended me, came into my life and gave me a reason to find a way forwards.

When Erin was born – actually throughout Jane's pregnancy - for the first time in years, I wasn't thinking about *me*.

I wasn't trying to prove anything. I wasn't drowning in self-loathing.

I was just *there*, present, for my family.

And that was the moment everything truly began to change.

I had spent years believing that my life had lost its meaning. That I was broken beyond repair. That I was just taking up space in a world that was never going to be as good as it had once been.

But in the eyes of these people who had grown to love me, I wasn't broken. I was just *me*.

And actually, its ok to just be you.

That's when I truly began to understand The Service Mindset.

It was about something much simpler than grand gestures, life-changing moments or proving my worth to the world.

It was about *who I chose to be for others, every single day.*

And with that, I began to rebuild.

Key Takeaways from Chapter 1

I used to think service was something extraordinary - something reserved for doctors, teachers, or people who changed the world in big ways. However, now I see that service is often small and quiet. My dad, scrubbing away my bloodstains. My mum, trying to make home feel safe again. My friends, sticking by me even when I wasn't easy to be around. They didn't fix me, but they were there – doing what they could. Maybe, that's what service really is - showing up for people and doing something, even when you don't know how to help.

✦ *Reflection Exercise*: Think of a time when life changed unexpectedly. How did you respond? Did you resist, deny, or adapt? Looking back, how could you have approached it with more acceptance?

✦ *Action Step:* Identify a setback you're currently facing. Instead of focusing on what's lost, list three small ways you can work *with* your new reality rather than against it.

✦ *Service Challenge:* Over the next week, look for one opportunity each day to shift your focus from yourself to someone else. It could be a kind word, a small act of service, or simply being present for someone who needs support. Observe how this changes your mindset.

Final Thought:

This chapter lays the foundation for *The Service Mindset*. The accident didn't just change my life - it changed how I see life. I used to think survival was about fighting against reality, but I've learnt that true resilience comes from acceptance, adaptation, and living in alignment with your intention and values.

The road to that stage in Mayfair was long and hard. I didn't change my life overnight, but I did turn things around eventually. In the chapters ahead, I'll show you how the lessons I learnt along the way can transform your life, too.

Chapter 2: The Roots of The Service Mindset

After my accident, I spent years trapped in my own suffering. I mourned who I had been and felt like a passenger in my own life. The voice in my head no longer felt like mine. The world moved forward, but I remained stuck: angry, lost, and unsure of who I was.

I wanted control. I wanted certainty. I wanted my life back.

However, time only moves in one direction - there's no going back, only forward.

Whilst my time at university was a huge struggle, I did spend some time studying Ethics in the School of Philosophy where I was reintroduced to lessons that I had studied in school before my accident occurred.

As a person with a frontal lobe injury and a damaged moral compass, I relished the opportunity to explore the philosophical foundations of what constitutes "right and wrong" from an ethical standpoint.

During that time, philosophy was often the only thing I could retain. Before we get to what The Service Mindset is, I think it's important to acknowledge the philosophical building blocks that underpin it.

Each of the philosophers detailed herein taught me something vital about resilience, meaning, and ultimately, the idea of service.

Stoicism and Emotional Regulation

The Service Mindset rests on a foundation of emotional discipline. For a long time, I thought there was no choice in the negative emotions in my post-accident brain. It wasn't until I discovered Stoicism that I realised the issue wasn't the emotions I was feeling, but rather my reaction to them.

Stoic philosophers taught that whilst we cannot control what happens to us, we can control how we respond to circumstances. This became an important realisation to me after my brain injury as my emotions: anger, frustration, anxiety, sadness - were heightened, and my instinctive reactions: to panic, to be impulsive, to lash out - were rarely helpful.

So, guided by Stoic philosophy, I employed a simple mental model to help me stay balanced.

Emotional Neutrality – The Swinging Pendulum and Returning to Neutral

Picture a large pendulum in your mind. Each of the two points that the pendulum swings between represent an emotional extreme - euphoria and arrogance on one side, despair and rage on the other. My goal was to keep my mind near the centre, in a neutral, rational space before making any decisions. When something triggered me, I visualised that pendulum and asked: *Am I reacting from the extremes, or can I return to the centre?*

This practice isn't about suppressing emotions. It's a common misconception that embracing Stoicism means becoming emotionless. Instead, it's about recognising your feelings, understanding them, and choosing your response with intention.

📌 **Reflection Exercise**: Recall a time you reacted emotionally and later regretted it. How might a neutral mindset have changed your response?

📌 **Action Step**: This week, when faced with an emotional challenge, take three deep breaths. Picture the pendulum. Ask: Where is the pendulum now? How do I bring it back to centre?

Adlerian Psychology: The Role of Community and Contribution

Whilst Stoicism helped me to manage my emotional world, Adlerian psychology gave me something just as powerful: *purpose.*

Alfred Adler believed humans don't thrive in isolation. Adler taught that meaning comes from contributing to others. He argued that feelings of inferiority are universal, but the way to overcome them isn't through dominance, it's through connection and cooperation.

After my brain injury, I felt useless, disconnected from my old self, but when I stopped asking, *"What have I lost?"* and started asking, *"What can I still give?"* – my outlook began to change for the better.

Adler vs. Freud: Your Past is Not Your Destiny

In many ways, it's a shame that Freud emerged as the dominant theory of approaching trauma in the modern world.

Freud believed that our past defines us. That our behaviour is shaped by childhood wounds and buried trauma. That our past pain informs and guides our present.

Adler – a contemporary of Freud - saw things very differently. He believed that whilst the past influences us, it doesn't determine who we become. Whilst Adler acknowledged that we all suffer pain and trauma, he contended that we were all capable of choosing the meaning that we assign to our experiences and what we do next.

Put simply: *we don't choose what happens to us, but we do get to choose the significance we give to it.*

The Core Divide: Determinism vs. Choice

Freud: *"You are the product of your past trauma"*

Adler: *"You are the product of your choices."*

Freud's model centres on excavation; digging into old wounds to heal. Adler's model is forward-looking: healing comes through the action you take, the contribution you make and the purpose that you find in life in spite of your trauma.

How This Relates to The Service Mindset

One of the greatest traps in life is getting stuck in the story of victimhood. When we believe our pain or past defines us, we become passive. Adler aligns perfectly with The Service Mindset because he taught that:

1. Your past does not dictate your future – Growth is always a choice.

2. Healing comes through contribution – Service restores self-worth.

3. You should focus on what you can control – Let the past inform your present, not imprison you.

Reframing Trauma: Choosing How We Carry Our Pain

We all suffer. Loss, disappointment, grief - no one escapes it. The difference isn't whether bad things happen, it's how we choose to move forward despite what happened.

Tapping into Adlerian psychology, The Service Mindset reminds us that it's we who control the meaning we assign to our pain. Our darkest moments don't have to define us. We can choose to carry them differently and even use them as fuel to drive ourselves forward.

The Job Loss That Lived Rent-Free in My Head

One of the hardest things about getting over a brain injury is in the struggle to find the confidence in your own ability to function in the world once again.

My confidence, in this regard, once took a huge knock when – due to circumstances beyond my control – I lost a job. It wasn't expected. There was no warning. One day, I was called into my boss's office and told to clear my desk and leave immediately. My services were no longer required.

The experience was humiliating, shocking, and deeply traumatic. For a long time, it consumed me. I let it take up space in my mind - reliving the moment, feeling the sting of rejection, questioning my worth.

Worse still, that trauma became a trigger. Every time I received an unexpected email from a boss in future jobs asking to *"have a quick chat"* - my body would react as though history was repeating itself. My heart would race. My breathing would become shallow. My mind would jump to one conclusion only: *I was about to lose it all again.*

The event had passed, but I was still carrying it. I had given it enormous importance in my life. I had allowed it to control me… and it wasn't even a very good job!

Adlerian psychology tells us that it does not have to be that way. That if you can give yourself the space and time to think, you can choose not to allow past trauma to taint the present.

Reclaiming Power Through The Service Mindset

The Service Mindset gave me a new framework, a way to take back control from the stories I was telling myself. Instead of being owned by that experience - the trauma of the past - I learnt to own it.

That change in mindset alone, didn't erase the past, but it certainly helped to loosen the grip that my past had over my future.

I began to break the trauma down into parts I could understand and reframe:

1. Recognising I Wasn't Alone

I wasn't the first person to be blind-sided, humiliated, or broken by life and I certainly wouldn't be the last. Job loss, rejection, failure; these things happen to everyone – and, with the huge social change promised by the advent of AI on the near horizon – we will all inevitably need to make our peace with that feeling of loss.

For a long time, I believed that my suffering was unique and that I was alone in feeling the way I felt. However, as I turned my focus outward, I found that the world was full of people who had similar stories to tell. That realisation didn't take my pain away, but it did make it easier to carry. I wasn't being punished. I was simply another human with a deeply human story to tell.

So, if you are recovering from injury, climbing back from mental health crisis or working for a boss who is desperate to replace you with a robot, turn your focus outward and take comfort from the fact that you are not alone and your suffering is not unique.

2. Accepting Reality Without Letting It Define Me

The job loss happened - it was real - but that single moment didn't have to shape the rest of my life. I had to ask myself: *does this one event get to dictate my future?* The answer was *no* - unless I gave it that power.

It's safe to say that letting go of past trauma is something that's easier said than done. Adler's stance in respect of trauma, was probably harsher than my own personal view – as he would often contend that people would only keep hold of their trauma insofar as it enabled them to live a certain way.

So, returning to that job loss, Adler may have suggested that my symptoms of panic, avoidance, or hypervigilance in future job settings actually served a *secondary function* - not to protect from further trauma, but to *excuse* or *justify* certain behaviours.

In this way, it becomes a way of staying in the safe zone - *an unconscious permission to shrink*. Adler called this the *"yes, but…"* manoeuvre: *"Yes, I'd like to push forward in my career, but I'm scared I'll lose my job again."*

Whilst it can therefore feel harsh to ask yourself why you are holding onto trauma, Adler would not have shied away from pointing out that I was free to choose my own path.

Adler probably would have said something like: *You are not the boy who lost his job anymore. You are the man who survived it and who now gets to choose how he lives.*

Adler believed the courage to be imperfect was the foundation of growth. He'd have wanted me to ask myself:

- *What if I wasn't afraid of being sacked?*
- *What kind of leader could I be if I trusted that I belong, that I was worthy?*
- *What am I avoiding doing under the banner of keeping myself safe?*

Ultimately Adler would say: *live as if you are free to act… because you are.*

3. Reframing the Experience

For a long time, I saw the event as a failure, but what if it was more than that? - a redirection, if you will. That job wasn't where I was meant to be and being forced out had actually made room in my life for something better. Reframing the experience in this way meant that it was no longer something that happened **to** me – but rather, it became something that happened **for** me.

4. Separating Emotion from Reality

In subsequent jobs, I might get an email that read: *"Can I see you for 5 minutes in my office?"*

Any person monitoring my heart rate, stress hormones or blood oxygen levels, would see that my fear response to those words was real. But just because my response was authentic, did not mean it was rational.

Panic would set in every time I got an unexpected email from a manager, but over time I trained myself to pause, to reflect and to remind myself:

- This is a different job.
- This is a different boss.
- There is no evidence that history is repeating itself.

Returning to a neutral mindset - gave me back agency in those moments of panic.

5. Shifting Focus from Self to Service

When I lost that job, I turned inward. I spiralled into self-doubt and fear. But when I turned outwards, towards mentoring, supporting others, and leading with purpose, I realised something powerful:

My value had never been tied to a single job.
My worth came from what I continued to contribute, not in what I'd lost.

My service didn't just help others – by grounding myself in the wheelhouse of what I was really good at, service helped me reclaim who I was.

Letting Go of the Weight We Carry

Trauma is heavy. We carry it in our thoughts, our reactions and our relationships - sometimes without even realising it. When we drag the past into the present, we risk letting old pain shape new fears. But here's the truth: *We don't have to carry it all. Not forever.*

Carrying the weight of that trauma also requires a huge amount of energy and effort – just think of what you could accomplish if you were free to channel all of that energy into the present.

The Service Mindset doesn't pretend that pain doesn't matter. It doesn't ask you to forget. What it offers is a different way of holding it.

It says:

Yes, that happened.
Yes, it hurt.
But it doesn't get to own your future.

It reminds us that our experiences, however painful, are not the whole story. We get to choose whether we labour under them like heavy anchors or use them as stepping stones to move forward in life.

Letting go doesn't mean pretending something never happened. It means loosening our grip on the idea that we are defined by what broke us.

It means asking:

How can I use this?
What might this teach me?
How can I use this to help others?

The truth is, some of our most meaningful contributions that we are able to make will come from the places and times when we've been wounded.

The Service Mindset, takes that pain and turns it into purpose. It transforms what once weighed us down into something that we can use to lift others up.

As we look outwards, and use what we have been through to help and support others, we free ourselves from the pain of the past.

The Power of Contribution Over Competition

We're raised in a culture that glorifies competition. From school grades to workplace promotions, we're taught to compare, to outperform, to win. But what if that mindset is part of what's making us unhappy?

Adlerian psychology suggests something radically different: that fulfilment comes not from climbing over others, but from lifting others up.

Competition isolates us, but contribution connects us.

When we compete, we ask: *How can I prove I'm better?*
When we contribute, we ask: *How can I make things better?*

The Service Mindset is rooted in this shift; from ego to impact and from personal status to service of others.

Success isn't measured by how many people you surpass. It's measured by how many people you help to rise.

That doesn't mean we can't strive for excellence. It means we need to recognise that excellence without contribution is empty. The question we should be asking is not, *"Am I winning?"* it's, *"Am I helping?"*

When we stop comparing and start contributing, we stop treating life like a race to be won and start treating it like it's something meaningful that we're building together.

Service and the Pursuit of Purpose – An Aristotelian View

When people hear the word *service*, they often think of helping others: selflessness, kindness, sacrifice. And while that's certainly part of it, The Service Mindset goes deeper. At its heart, this mindset is about choosing *what* you want to serve in life – and then doing so with clarity, commitment, and care.

That's not a new idea. The roots of this philosophy stretch back over two thousand years to Aristotle and his concept of *eudaimonia* - a life of flourishing. For Aristotle, flourishing wasn't about happiness in the modern, emotional sense. It was about living in alignment with your *telos* - your purpose or ultimate aim - and cultivating the virtues required to honour it.

He believed that a good life wasn't defined by what you possessed, but by how well you lived. That meant asking: *What do I want my life to be in service of?* And then: *Am I living in a way that does that justice?*

Aristotle didn't prescribe what your purpose should be. That was yours to define. What mattered was that once you chose it; whether it was family, work, wisdom, justice, freedom, or something else - you served it with excellence. You didn't just chase the ultimate goal, you built the character needed to overcome the obstacles you encountered on the way to your destination.

This is a foundational idea behind The Service Mindset. It's not about doing what others expect of you. It's about asking yourself what matters most, and then consciously and deliberately giving your time, your energy and your attention to *that*.

Not all service looks the same, but all true service begins with deliberate, strategic intention.

Finding Meaning in Service: The Lessons of Viktor Frankl and Logotherapy

When I was at school, one of my RE teachers introduced us to a book written by a Jewish man who had survived the Holocaust. (He also once wrote on a school report:

"Gareth is a Grade A philosopher. It's just such a shame he's too lazy to ever write any of it down." Well, Sir - this is for you.)

The book in question was *Man's Search for Meaning* by Viktor Frankl, and though it obviously had an impact on me, it wasn't until I suffered my brain injury that its core message would truly resonate with me.

Frankl endured years in Nazi concentration camps. He lost everything: his family, his freedom, his former life, but he observed something remarkable. The people who survived weren't necessarily the strongest. They were the ones who could find meaning in their suffering.

Frankl believed that whilst we can't always choose our circumstances, we can choose our response. He called this *"the last of the human freedoms"* - the ability to decide how we respond, even in the face of unimaginable pain.

That truth would come to resonate with me in ways I couldn't have imagined when I first read his words.

Logotherapy: Meaning as a Survival Mechanism

Frankl's therapeutic model, logotherapy, was built on a simple premise: that the primary driver of human life is not pleasure or power, but meaning.

He identified three ways people find meaning:

1. **Through work or contribution** – dedicating yourself to a cause greater than yourself.

2. **Through love and relationships** – connecting with others in deep, authentic ways.

3. **Through suffering** – finding purpose even in pain, by choosing how to carry it.

Each of these pathways intersects with The Service Mindset because when we stop obsessing over what we've lost, and start asking *what can I still give?* our perspective shifts. We stop being victims of circumstance and instead we become agents of meaning.

With the coming wave of social upheaval that will inevitably accompany the unrelenting advance of AI, it is perhaps more important now than ever before, to remind ourselves of the way Frankl proposed that humans find meaning in life.

✦ **Reflection Point**: Frankl survived the horrors of a nazi concentration camp and kept going. All over the world today there are people who have nothing – they are hungry, in pain and unsafe and yet they choose to endure and survive.

What these harsh realities tell us is that whatever it is that gives life meaning and purpose – it's not something you can possess because it's there in people who are suffering and who have nothing right now. That means it's also there in you right now, its intrinsic – and this is important because if whatever gives life meaning is "in you" from the start, it means that no person or set of circumstances can take it away from you.

No matter how dark it gets, you can endure if you look for the light inside yourself.

Service Isn't Self-Sacrifice. It's Self-Liberation.

For me, service was the door out of my own darkness. At first, I thought I was helping others, but in truth, they were helping me. Every act of support, every quiet moment of being there for another human, reminded me that I still had value and that I still had a role to play.

That's why The Service Mindset isn't about grand gestures. It's about grounding. It's about choosing meaning over misery, action over inertia.

You don't need a big platform and you really don't need to have everything figured out. You just need to serve where you are and with what you have.

There is a healing and restorative power in connecting with other humans and the wider natural world. These things are abundant and freely available to all of us – when we live in connection with something bigger than ourselves, we start to heal ourselves.

Your Challenge: Finding Your Meaning

Viktor Frankl would often ask his patients a pretty confrontational question:

"Why do you not commit suicide?"

It wasn't meant to shock, it was meant to clarify. It forced people to confront what was keeping them going. What gave their life meaning. What, deep down, made it worth continuing.

It's not an easy question to consider, but it is an important one – especially when you think about how closely it aligns with the Aristotelian notion of *Telos* – one's ultimate purpose.

So let me reframe this challenging question for you:

What keeps you going?
What makes your life feel meaningful?
What lines would you not cross?
Who, or what, are you living for?
What would you fight for?

If you don't have a clear answer yet, that's okay. Meaning doesn't always arrive as a lightning bolt. Sometimes it reveals itself slowly, through action, not introspection.

That's why I always return to this: *if you don't know your purpose yet, start by serving others.*

When you serve, you connect. When you connect, you begin to matter again - and when you matter - to someone or to something - meaning isn't far behind.

Meaning is not always something we find, sometimes it's something that we have to build. If you are not sure how to start building something for yourself, The Service Mindset is here to tell you that service is a pretty good place to start.

Bushidō: The Warrior's Code as a Root of the Service Mindset

I've already mentioned the *Karate Kid* films - and I'll stand by this: everyone needs an inner Mr Miyagi.

Growing up, martial arts were always in the background of my life. My brother was a superb judoka, and the discipline of the dojo: respect, control, calmness, left a deep impression on me.

The Service Mindset, in many ways, isn't new. It's a modern expression of something ancient. One of its clearest ancestors is **Bushidō**, the code of the samurai.

Bushidō - literally, *"the way of the warrior"* - was the moral and ethical framework followed by Japan's elite warrior class. The code went far beyond how you conduct yourself in combat, it detailed how you were expected to serve and how you should carry yourself in the world.

Key Bushidō Virtues That Shape The Service Mindset

Let's look at a few of the core principles of Bushidō and how they still speak to us today:

Gi (義) – Integrity and Righteousness

Do what's right, even when it's inconvenient. In business, in your community, in leadership - this is about choosing principle over profit or self-promotion.

Yu (勇) – Courage

Not just physical bravery, but moral courage. The courage to speak up, to challenge wrongs, to do what others won't. Fraud and corruption, for example, thrive in silence, the courage of others to call it out is what often disrupts it.

Jin (仁) – Compassion

Real strength is protective, not destructive. In The Service Mindset, this means using your influence to support others, not dominate them.

Rei (礼) – Respect

Respect for others isn't optional. The way you treat people, especially when they can't do anything for you, defines your leadership.

Meiyo (名誉) – Honour

Honour isn't ego. It's consistency. It's living in alignment with your values so that others can trust you, even when they disagree with you.

Chūgi (忠義) – Loyalty and Commitment

Loyalty to your purpose, your people, your principles. It's what turns a job into a mission.

Bushidō and Service as Strength

The Samurai didn't serve because they were obedient. They served because they believed in something bigger than themselves - because they had a moral code. Their loyalty wasn't to themselves, it was a commitment to a belief that the world could be shaped and changed through their actions.

That's the same choice we have, every day.

Bushidō tells us that to change the world through our deeds, we need to act with integrity, stay grounded in our values, and serve something bigger than ourselves.

The Service Mindset leans into this same energy.

The Hidden Thread: How These Lessons Led to The Service Mindset

Looking back, I can see that these philosophies: Stoicism, Adlerian psychology, Frankl's logotherapy, Bushidō, and Aristotelian virtue ethics, weren't just ideas that my injured brain was interested in - they literally became lifelines out of the darkest points in my life.

Each arrived at different times, and in different ways, but they were all pointing to the same universal truth:

Meaning is not something you wait to receive. **It's something you create by choosing what to serve and then making a commitment to serving it as well as you can.**

At the time, I didn't have language for it. I didn't call it a mindset. I was just trying to survive. Trying to find a way to keep going.

But piece by piece, these ideas began to shape something larger:

Stoicism helped me stop being ruled by emotion, so I could respond rationally rather than reacting emotionally.

Adlerian psychology taught me that fulfilment comes not from dominance, but from contribution to something bigger.

Frankl reminded me that even in pain, we can choose our response and find meaning in our lives even when suffering.

Bushidō showed me that service requires discipline, integrity, and a sense of honour.

Aristotle revealed that a good life is one lived in pursuit of *telos* - a worthy aim - and that true fulfilment lies in cultivating the virtues required to serve that aim with excellence.

It was only very recently that I stepped back and looked at these lessons that have played such an important role in my life and seen that they are all fragments of the same mosaic.

What I eventually came to understand is this:

Service isn't just a moral good. It's a way of choosing who you want to be, and what you want your life to mean.

It's not always about helping others. Sometimes it's about staying loyal to a principle, or devoting yourself to a cause, or committing to a standard of living that reflects who you are.

The Service Mindset wasn't something I invented, it's something I curated – it's the wisdom that helped me at my lowest and kept me going.

The Religious Origins of The Service Mindset

Something strange happened to me in that hospital in Tenerife. Something I've never told anyone before.

One day, I woke up and there was a man sitting beside my bed. He was tall, tanned, dressed in white linen. When I asked who he was, he said he represented a group of people who had been praying for me. He told me I was alive because their prayers had been answered.

Before I could say much more, he handed me a sheet of paper with a Bible verse on it, nodded, and walked out of the room.

I've always been agnostic - rooted in logic and reason. My brain tells me this man was part of a local church or prayer group – or maybe it a figment of an imagination in recovery – although the piece of paper I was handed was real enough.

Whatever your personal, spiritual beliefs, there's no denying that the core of The Service Mindset - living for something greater than yourself - echoes through the world's great spiritual traditions.

Long before modern psychology or business books, people looked to religion for guidance on how to live a meaningful life. And across cultures and centuries, one theme comes back again and again:

We are here to serve.

Hinduism: Dharma – Duty and Righteous Action

In Hindu philosophy, *dharma* means duty: the idea that we each have a moral responsibility to act rightly in the world. It's not about personal reward, but about contributing to the balance and wellbeing of society.

"You have a right to perform your prescribed duties, but you are not entitled to the fruits of your actions." - Bhagavad Gita 2.47

In other words: do what's right, not because it benefits you, but because it's your role to play.

Christianity: Agape – Selfless Love and Service

At the heart of Christian teaching is *agape*: selfless, unconditional love expressed through action.

"Whoever wants to become great among you must be your servant." - Mark 10:43–45

Service in Christianity isn't weakness, it's greatness. It's a redefinition of power, grounded in humility.

Islam: Zakat – Giving as a Moral Duty

In Islam, *zakat* is one of the Five Pillars: an obligation to give to those in need. It's not optional charity; it's a foundational responsibility. Beyond money, the Prophet Muhammad said:

"The best among you are those who bring the greatest benefit to others."

Buddhism: Compassion and Selfless Action

Buddhism teaches that suffering is part of life, but that compassion is the antidote. The Bodhisattva, an enlightened being, chooses to remain in the world to help others rather than seeking escape.

Letting go of ego and self-attachment is key. Service, here, is not about glory - it's about dissolving the self and easing the suffering of others.

Judaism: Tikkun Olam – Repairing the World

In Jewish thought, *Tikkun Olam* means "repairing the world." It's a call to personal responsibility, to use your skills and privilege to make life better for others.

From acts of charity to standing for justice, this tradition is built on the idea that healing the world is a shared obligation.

What This Means for The Service Mindset

Each of these traditions has its own language, rituals, and theology, but the message is strikingly similar:

We're not here to accumulate - We're here to contribute.

We're not here to rise above others - We're here to lift others up.

The Service Mindset isn't tied to any single religion, but it's deeply rooted in the same wisdom: that a meaningful life is one lived in service of something beyond the self.

📌 Reflection Exercise

- Are you living as though your past is dictating your future?

- What would change for you if you focused on what you *can do now* instead of what you've lost?

- Where in your life are you measuring success in ways that don't actually serve you?

- Think of a time when someone helped you with no expectation - how did it make you feel?

📌 Action Steps

- Identify one small way you can step out of self-focus and into service this week. It could be offering support to a colleague, checking in on someone, or simply being fully present.

- The next time you catch yourself spiralling into past regret or fear, pause and ask: *What can I do today that moves me forward?*

- Set a simple daily prompt for yourself: *How can I serve today?* and just notice what changes.

The Deep Roots of Service

Before I ever labelled it *The Service Mindset*, service itself was written into our biology.

From an evolutionary perspective, prosocial behaviour has always been a survival strategy. We are here today not because we were the strongest, fastest, or most ferocious species, but because we were the ones who helped each other. Early humans survived the harshness of nature by forming groups, sharing food, warning of danger, and caring for the vulnerable. The evolutionary reality is that those who could cooperate were more likely to survive.

And perhaps more importantly, they were more likely to matter - to leave something behind. To belong.

It's no coincidence that many of our anxieties stem from isolation, insignificance, and the shadow of death. We are creatures who know we are going to die and so we seek safety not just in shelter or status, but in *significance*. If I serve you, and you serve me, then we are bound to each other. I am not alone - and maybe, just maybe, we will be remembered.

That's why service makes us feel safe. Not in the shallow, transactional sense of people-pleasing, but in the deep evolutionary sense of being part of something greater than ourselves.

Service says: *I exist in relation to others. I have value because I give value to something greater than myself.*

There is also something quietly British about this. Ours is a culture rooted in reciprocity. We pride ourselves on fairness, queues, volunteerism, and "doing our bit." For better or worse, we are a nation of shopkeepers, navigating the world through small acts of trade, kindness, and mutual respect. Our history - steeped in feudal ties, village life, and social responsibility - has shaped a deep, often unspoken, commitment to the idea that we are all, in some way, in service of each other.

We may grumble about it. We may pretend we don't care. But when things go wrong: a flood, a pandemic, a neighbour in need, it's remarkable how often we quietly step in to help. Service is not something new we need to learn. It's something old we need to remember.

Final Thought: Your Future is Yours to Build

Adler taught us that we are not chained to our history.

Frankl showed us that we can find meaning, even in suffering.

The Stoics taught us to respond with discipline, not impulse.

Bushidō reminded us that service is strength, and that honour matters.

And Aristotle asked the question that brings all of this into focus:

What are you here to serve?

Not just who, but what. Not just in action, but in purpose.

The Service Mindset is not about self-sacrifice or self-denial. It is not about being endlessly agreeable, or putting others first for the sake of moral points. It is about *choosing* - deliberately, honestly and with intention - what you want your life to be in service of - and then serving it with care, with character, and with courage.

That purpose – what Aristotle called your *telos* - must be worthy of you. It cannot be a shallow pursuit of status, or an endless chase for approval. It must be something that brings you into alignment with your better self. Something that asks more of you than indulgence or instinct.

Something that requires the cultivation of virtue.

This is perhaps where The Service Mindset finds its sharpest edge. It does not tell you what to serve, but it does demand that you choose something. That you choose consciously. That you serve with discipline, not drift. With principle, not convenience.

And perhaps - just perhaps – there is something liberating in that – a freedom we didn't know we needed, because when you know what you serve – when you find your telos - maybe then you are free to stop chasing and worrying about everything else.

You no longer live by accident, or by comparison.

You stop looking outward for worth, or upward for validation, or backwards to a trauma that holds you back.

You begin moving forward – anchored to a sense of purpose, not drifting through life but tied to intention with the freedom that comes with living on purpose.

Most people's suffering, dissatisfaction, or burnout doesn't come from laziness or lack of drive - it comes from **conflict**.

They are serving multiple, competing masters.

Or they are serving something they don't truly believe in.

Or they haven't chosen at all, and life is choosing for them.
The Service Mindset recognises a quiet truth: **we all must serve something.**

However, in the modern world, we're pulled in a thousand different directions.

We're told to chase everything: money, followers, power, perfection.

And so we try – and often fail - to serve all of them, half-heartedly, until we're stretched too thin to even begin to feel fulfilled.

So how do we choose what to serve and what to give meaning to?

The Service Mindset says that that decision must be **a moral one** as well as a practical one. It's not just about what feels good. It's about what *makes you good*. What stretches you. Strengthens you. Connects you to something bigger than yourself.

A worthy *telos* will ask more of you, not less - but it will also give you more in return: The freedom of living on purpose.

📌 The Telos Test

What are you serving? And is it worthy of you?

To help bring this reflection to life, I want to share a memory and then offer you a tool.

When my Grandad was alive, he once sat me down as a child and explained that everybody has one thing that they are good at – a talent that I remember him calling a God-given gift.

I remember my Grandad saying that you can do anything you wanted to in life, but perhaps the worst sin you could commit was to squander, or waste, the talents that you had been gifted.

In the aftermath of my brain injury, I found myself falling back on the things that I was once good at. Feeling competent, being in the zone with your gifts, gives you the space to grow in confidence.

When we serve the correct telos in life, we become the best version of ourselves. Our passion cancels out our effort. We grow and blossom as people, as our confidence, through intentional service, increases.

Unfortunately, there will be times when jobs, people, relationships or situations will either look to exploit your talents or fail to give you the space to flourish.

As I type these words, I am reminded of the Foo Fighters song "Best of You" which, in its chorus, repeatedly asks the listener: *"is someone getting the best, the best, the best, the best of you?"*

I have devised the following test to help you to explore what your telos might be in life and to help you to consider your answer to the Foo Fighters' refrain. The first part asks questions to help you to explore what call in your life might currently be going unanswered.

The second part of the test then asks you to consider whether the thing that you are serving is worthy of your service.

When I was looking to rebuild my life following my brain injury, my family and fatherhood found me. Quite suddenly, I felt like I was doing what I was put here to do and there is no question that my family – the people that I choose to serve – are completely deserving of my devoted service.

This test is ultimately designed to help you find clarity before you commit to moving forward.

Use it to reflect honestly on your values, your priorities, and the purpose you feel most drawn towards. Then put that purpose to the test.

And if you discover that what you're currently serving is not worthy of you, take heart. That clarity is a gift. You now have a chance to choose better.

Part One: Look Inward – What do you already know?

Question	Your Reflections
Forget what you have been told to value - What really matters to you and what do you truly value?	
When have you felt most alive, connected, or at peace? What were you doing when you were at your best?	
If all rewards vanished: titles, applause, money, followers, influence - what would still feel worth doing?	
Imagine yourself at the end of your life. What would make you proud? What would you regret not having given yourself to?	
What pain or conflict are you feeling between competing priorities? What does that reveal about the choices you have made?	
If you had the courage to choose one thing to build your life around, what would it be?	

When are you at your best? Are those talents being put to their best use or are they going to waste?	

Once you've reflected on what truly matters, Part Two of the test invites you to ask whether it's worthy of your service.

Part Two: Test It – Is it worth serving?

Question	Yes / No / Maybe	Notes or doubts?
Think about where your energy is currently going and who or what is getting the best of you… Is it virtuous? Does it cultivate honesty, courage, humility, integrity?		
Is it life-giving? Does it foster growth, connection, and contribution - for you and for others? Does it enable you and/or others to flourish?		
Is it sustainable? Will it nourish your soul long-term, or just feed short-term cravings?		
Is it chosen freely? Are you pursuing it by choice, not pressure, fear, or habit?		
Is it grounded in reality? Does it engage the real world, or is it based on image or fantasy?		

What is Important?

I was raised to have a pretty strong idea about what was important.

Working hard, doing well at school, achieving in my career – these are just some of the things that were programmed into me as being important by virtue of my upbringing.

So, I have two questions for you.

Firstly: *what is important to you?* – go ahead, list all of the things in your life that are priorities and that are important.

Then we turn to the next question: *how many of these things did you actually choose for yourself?*

I ask this question because often, so many of the things that we are told are important are **given** to us. How many of the things that are *important* did you actually choose for yourself?

Sometimes, it's the moment when we lose something, that we ask ourselves for the first time whether it was actually important at all. That job your clinging onto, that person you are trying impress, that number you are trying to reach on the scale – are those things really important to you? Did you choose them for yourself?

This is the thing about telos, and about life more generally, **you** get to decide what is important – not your parents, not your social group, not your school and definitely not your boss… **you!**

So consider what's important to you and choose it well because if you don't – somebody else is likely to choose for you.

Final Reflection

Ask yourself:

What is the one thing I now feel most called to serve and am I willing to serve it well?

Is someone getting the best of you?

If your answer isn't perfect or complete, that's okay. What matters is that you're asking the question and that you're starting to choose with care.

Because once you choose your telos, the rest of this book will show you how to serve it well.

In the next chapter, we'll explore how these principles form the foundation of the core tenets of The Service Mindset and how you can apply them to your own journey toward meaningful success.

Chapter 3: The Core Tenets of The Service Mindset

TENET 1. Acceptance as a Starting Point

Of all the tenets, none is more foundational than acceptance. Before we can serve, lead, or create change, we must first make peace with our reality. Without acceptance, we waste energy fighting circumstances we cannot control instead of using what we *do* have to make a difference.

I learnt this the hard way. My brain injury didn't just disrupt my life - it shattered everything I thought I knew about myself. I resisted for years, mourning the person I had been, convinced I could somehow claw my way back to who I was. But no amount of frustration or denial could undo what had happened. Only when I stopped fighting the unchangeable, only when I accepted reality, did I begin to move forward.

The moment I embraced what remained, rather than what had been lost, everything began to change for me. And that is why acceptance sits at the foundation of The Service Mindset: because it's the key that unlocks momentum, impact, and meaning - whatever your circumstances.

Working With What You Have

You can only play the cards you've been dealt. The Service Mindset begins with accepting your reality then making the best move possible from where you are.

After my brain injury, I spent years measuring myself against an ideal that no longer existed. I clung to a version of myself that was gone, believing that if I just pushed hard enough, I could get **him** back. It wasn't until I fully accepted my new reality that I began to build something meaningful.

Acceptance isn't about giving up. It's about recognising that progress only starts when you stop fighting what *is*.

The Service Mindset demands brutal honesty about your circumstances. You might wish you were taller, thinner, more confident. You might wish your career had gone differently or that your parents had shown you more love than they did. However, the more energy we pour into wishing things were different, the less we have available to change what's actually in front of us.

Rather than ruminating on what we could do *if* life were different, The Service Mindset challenges us to ask:

What can I do with what's real now?

Acceptance is not Passive Surrender

Acceptance is often misunderstood as passivity - as if accepting something means giving in or giving up. But true acceptance isn't surrender. It's a strategic act. It means recognising reality clearly and deciding how best to move forward within it.

The Service Mindset demands that you stop wasting energy on battles you can't win and start focusing on the ones that matter.

A personal example: we suspect that my daughter, Erin, may be autistic. As her mother, Jane, and I began to understand more about her experiences, we noticed how she struggled with things most people take for granted: certain fabrics against her skin, the chaos of a noisy room, even the taste of some everyday foods.

At first, we saw these as challenges to be overcome, but the more we learnt, the more we realised that the true nature of the problem was that the world wasn't built with Erin's needs in mind.

With this reality at the forefront, we set about changing what we could.

One small example: Erin hates strong mint flavours. Whilst researching sensory sensitivities, we questioned something simple: *do we even like mint toothpaste, or have we just accepted it by default?* That question led Jane to realise she didn't like it either. Now, there's a peach-flavoured toothpaste in the bathroom, and everyone's happier.

It's such a small shift, but it changed how I saw the world. How much of our discomfort comes from tolerating things that were never designed with our needs in mind in the first place?

Acceptance isn't about forcing yourself to like what makes you uncomfortable. It's about giving yourself permission to change what you can, whilst letting go of what you can't. Erin didn't just teach us how to support her - she helped us question the invisible assumptions we all live with at times.

Accepting and Embracing the Present: The Buddhist Truth of Suffering and the Power of Now

One of the hardest truths to accept is this: *suffering is inevitable.*

Buddhism teaches the First Noble Truth: *that all life involves suffering*. Not because life is cruel, but because pain, loss, disappointment, and struggle are part of being human. If we live trying to avoid suffering entirely, we create even more of it: anxiety, denial, frustration.

This truth may feel bleak, but it's actually liberating. When we accept suffering as part of life, we stop resisting it and start finding meaning through it.

After my brain injury, I didn't just lose memories or my sense of smell - I lost my sense of self. The voice in my head no longer sounded like mine. What once felt instinctive became laborious. I wanted it all back. I clung to the hope that things might return to how they were.

But they didn't.

And the longer I resisted that fact, the worse things got. It wasn't just grief, I was torturing myself with the refusal to accept what had happened. The turning point came when I let go of that resistance. I stopped demanding that life return to what it had been and started again, on different terms.

The Trap of Living in the Past or the Future

For many of us, the hardest thing to do is to live in the present.

We convince ourselves that happiness lies elsewhere:

- "I was happier back then… if only I could go back."

- "I'll be happy when I lose weight… when I get promoted… when life finally settles down."

- "Things will improve soon - I just have to get through this rough patch."

But that mindset robs us of the only thing we truly have: this moment – the now.

The past exists only in memory.

The future exists only in imagination.

The present is the only time we can act, feel and live.

We often chase happiness as if it's some distant milestone, but happiness isn't out there, it's found in the now. If we don't train ourselves to be present, we risk missing out on happiness altogether.

Finding Happiness in the Now

If you want to be happy – you have to create happiness in the moment.

That doesn't mean pretending everything is fine or denying the difficulty of life. It means training ourselves to be present, to notice what is real and meaningful in the moment we are actually living in. When we stop chasing the illusion of perfect circumstances and start appreciating what's already here, we begin to experience real contentment.

We often imagine happiness as something grand - some major achievement, milestone, or breakthrough, but in truth, happiness usually comes in small, fleeting moments:

- The warmth of a loved one's laughter.

- The quiet peace of a morning walk.

- The satisfaction of completing something meaningful.

- A familiar song playing in the background when you least expect it

If we rush through life in search of "more," we miss these small moments that are often, in and of themselves, enough. If we can just slow down and pay more attention to the moment, we find that happiness was never out of reach - it was always with us in the now.

Living with an Open Heart

The Service Mindset draws heavily from the Buddhist principle of acceptance - not as a passive surrender, but as a gateway to peace, compassion, and presence. It teaches us that life isn't about escaping suffering, but about learning how to live with it: openly, honestly, and wholeheartedly.

To do that, we need to live with an open heart.

That means:

- **Allowing ourselves to feel** – not numbing the pain, but acknowledging it and continuing to move forward anyway.

- **Practising gratitude** – not for perfection, but for the small moments of light that show up even in dark times.

- **Serving others** – not because we're perfect, but because giving to others breaks the cycle of self-absorption and softens our own suffering.

- **Letting go of control** – recognising that we can't change everything, but we can choose how we respond to circumstances.

Living with an open heart doesn't mean being naïve or overly sentimental. It means choosing to engage fully with the world, even when it's imperfect. It means being present with compassion and with a willingness to act.

When we approach life this way, we stop waiting for perfect conditions before we start living. We accept what is, give what we can, and open ourselves to the quiet beauty of the present moment.

Accepting Peaks and Troughs: The Natural Rhythm of Life

We're often led to believe that life should be a steady climb - that progress is linear, that success builds without pause, and that motivation should be constant. But real life doesn't look like that.

Life moves in waves. There are moments when everything flows: when you feel focused, energised, and in control, and then there are times when things stall, energy dips, and progress slows.

It took me a long time to understand that nothing is meant to stay at full speed forever. The dips aren't problems to be solved, they're part of the natural rhythm of life. Resisting them only makes things harder. Accepting them makes space for rest, reflection, and recovery.

Here's how I like to think of it: *"when there are always biscuits in the tin, where's the fun in biscuits?"* The good stuff only feels good because it's not constant. The peaks exist because the troughs do. One gives the other its meaning.

You don't have to love the slow patches, but when you stop fighting against life when it naturally slows down, it does get a whole lot easier.

The acceptance of this reality is something that we will all have to grow more accustomed to as we move into a future where AI and robots inevitably do more and more of the traditional work in society.

If you struggle to find peace in the moments when there is less to be done and work is scarce, then the Service Mindset is here to say: fill your time with service.

📌 **Reflection Exercise:**

Where in your life are you expecting constant forward motion? How might you see things differently if you saw rest and stillness as necessary - not as something to feel guilty about?

Why Resistance Creates Suffering

So many of us make life harder than it needs to be - not because we're failing, but because we're resisting the natural rhythm of things.

We convince ourselves that we *should* always be achieving, always be energised, always be making visible progress. But that mindset is exhausting and, more importantly, it's unrealistic.

I once heard someone say that the hardest part of swimming the English Channel isn't the cold, or the distance, it's the tide. At a certain point, the current turns against you. You can swim as hard as you like, give it everything you've got… and still make no progress. You're stuck in place, waiting for the tide to change.

The key isn't to fight harder - it's to stay steady. To trust that the current will turn, and when it does, your progress will return.

Life works the same way. There are times when you're doing all the right things, but it still feels like nothing is moving. That doesn't mean you're failing. It means the tide hasn't turned yet. Stay patient and true to your values and trust that progress will eventually come.

The people who thrive long term aren't the ones who sprint endlessly, they're the ones who understand these cycles. They push when it's time to push, and rest when it's time to wait. They don't waste energy resisting stillness, they learn to work with it.

📌 **Key Insight:**

Resistance doesn't protect you, it burns you out. There is wisdom, peace and resilience in learning to flow with life's natural rhythm.

Finding Your Own Rhythm (Especially When it's Hard)

Once you accept that life moves in peaks and troughs, you can begin to work *with* that rhythm, rather than against it.

But let's be honest, this is not always easy. It's one thing to *understand* that rest is part of the process, it's another to *accept* it when you feel like you're stuck in quicksand, when your mind is heavy, and every task feels like you are climbing a mountain.

Sometimes, when you're in a trough, you know what you "should" do, but the energy just isn't there. And when your motivation slips, self-doubt inevitably creeps in. That's when you need self-compassion the most.

Here's how to work with your rhythm - *especially when life feels hard*:

1. **Stop feeling guilty for the quiet times.**
   Rest isn't failure. Fatigue isn't weakness. Sometimes, not giving up is the most courageous thing you can do.

2. **Recognise when you're in a trough and adjust your expectations.**
   This isn't about giving up, it's about being realistic. Maybe you can't deliver your best work today. That's okay. Focus on doing *something*. Even if that something is just getting out of bed, replying to one email, or taking a walk.

3. **Start smaller than small.**
   When everything feels too much, shrink the task. Can't write a page? Write a sentence. Can't cook a meal? Make toast. Can't face the world? Open a window. Small acts rebuild momentum - and momentum rebuilds motivation.

   Tell yourself: *"The more I do, the more I will feel like doing!"*

4. **Remember: this isn't forever.**
   No trough lasts forever. The tide *will* turn, even if you can't see when it will happen. Don't measure your worth by how productive you are right now. Survival is progress too.

5. **Be kind to yourself.**
   If you saw a friend struggling like you are, you wouldn't yell at them to *"just get on with it."* You'd sit with them. You'd reassure them. You'd remind them they are not alone. So do the same for yourself.

✦ Key Insight:

The Service Mindset isn't about relentless performance, it's about sustainable presence. Serving others doesn't mean being perfect, it means being real - and sometimes, the most powerful act of service you can offer is giving yourself permission to be human.

Accepting and Owning Your Mistakes: A Lesson in Integrity and Growth

When I was younger, I broke a stack of plates at my mum's house. Not just a chip or a crack - a proper disaster. I panicked. Instead of owning up, I slinked off to bed and hoped, somehow, it would all go away.

The next day, I stayed hidden. I knew I was in trouble, but I thought if I kept my head down long enough, maybe I'd avoid the fallout. When I eventually saw my dad that evening, it was clear I hadn't dodged anything, I'd just made it worse. He wasn't furious about the broken crockery. He was disappointed that I hadn't come clean. That was what stung.

He sat me down and said something that's stayed with me ever since:

"Real men own their mistakes and apologise."

That moment sticks in my mind, not because he shouted (he didn't), but because I realised the real issue wasn't the damage itself - it was the fact that I'd tried to dodge responsibility. That, more than anything, taught me a lasting lesson about integrity.

It's one I've carried into leadership, relationships, and everyday life: people don't expect perfection, but they do expect honesty.

Integrity is the label we attach to a person that reflects the true nature of reality and behaves in a way that is consistent with their values.

My behaviour when I broke my mum's plates lacked integrity because I pretended it hadn't happened and then I hid when I should have apologised.

In demanding acceptance, The Service Mindset is telling us that we must act with integrity.

Accepting Failure as a Stepping Stone, Not a Dead End

The Service Mindset asks us to face an unavoidable truth: **everyone gets things wrong.**

We all make poor decisions from time to time. We say things we regret. We fall short. That's not failure in the final sense, it's part of the fallibility that makes us human.

What matters isn't the mistake itself, but what we do afterwards. Do we ignore it? Bury it? Pretend it didn't happen? Or do we own it, learn from it, and carry on?

Too often, people treat mistakes as a definitive full stop when perhaps the kinder, more compassionate thing to do is to see them as a comma – an opportunity to pause, take stock, adjust, and keep going.

If you're never making mistakes, you're probably playing it too safe. Real growth happens on the edge of your comfort zone, and that's also where things can go wrong. That's not something to fear; it's something to understand.

The Service Mindset doesn't expect perfection. It calls for courage, honesty, and the determination to keep going and this is especially true after we've fallen short.

Owning our mistakes, apologising when necessary, and learning from them is what allows us to move forward.

When we acknowledge our shortcomings with humility, we build trust. When we take responsibility instead of deflecting blame, we show strength of character. It has always amazed me how politicians from all walks of the political spectrum will never say "sorry" or "I got that wrong!" When The Service Mindset calls for acceptance, we have to accept the true nature of reality. Part of the true nature of our existence is that there are no infallible humans – everyone has a mistake in them and our politicians might do well to understand that there is great strength in saying "sorry" when people expect you to say it.

This is the essence of The Service Mindset: facing reality, learning from it, and choosing to grow.

Opportunity in Disguise: Accepting Reality and Moving Forward

One of the biggest obstacles to personal growth is disappointment. When things don't go as we hoped, it's easy to become so fixated on what we wanted that we miss what's right in front of us. The Service Mindset demands rapid acceptance of reality and the ability to pivot quickly from frustration to purposeful action.

The Story of an Opportunity Missed

Early in my career, while working in a junior role, a person from another company came to visit our office. He was curious about anti-fraud processes and wanted to know more about what we did. He started at the top, requesting meetings with senior leaders, but one by one, they declined: too busy, not interested, or didn't see the value.

Eventually, he made his way down to me - someone with no title, no real authority, and very little influence. When he asked if I could talk to him about fraud, I said yes. I spent two hours walking him through the basics, followed by a friendly drink and a chat.

That conversation led to an unexpected job opportunity. It turned out to be one of the most important and rewarding career moves I've ever made.

The lesson? Most people don't recognise opportunity unless it comes dressed the way they expect it. The senior leaders saw the meeting as a distraction. I saw it for what it was: an open door.

Accept Reality Quickly - Then Work With It

On another occasion, a colleague found themselves assigned to a project they hadn't wanted. They had been hoping for something more aligned with their strengths - something more exciting, more strategic and they were disappointed when what they were offered did not align with their hopes and ambitions.

What they didn't see immediately - because their disappointment masked it - was that the project they'd been given had far greater potential than anyone realised. There was plenty of low-hanging fruit and a chance to make a real impact. If they embraced it and delivered results, it would set them up for even more significant opportunities in the future.

The faster we can move from *"this isn't what I wanted"* to *"what can I do with this?"* the faster we start gaining momentum. Those who thrive are rarely the ones who get exactly what they hoped for - they're the ones who accept what is and make the most of it.

How to Turn Setbacks into Success

When things don't go your way, it's easy to get stuck in frustration. But the Service Mindset offers a different path - one that turns disappointment into progress by shifting from resistance to action.

Here's how to move forward when reality doesn't match your expectations:

1. Recognise the Emotion… Then Let It Go

It's natural to feel deflated when things don't work out. Allow yourself a moment to acknowledge the feeling, but then, gently let it go. Holding onto frustration won't change the situation - it only drains your energy.

2. Ask: Where's the Opportunity Here?

Sometimes, setbacks contain hidden opportunities. Maybe it's a chance to develop new skills, build relationships, or demonstrate resilience. Instead of asking, *"Why is this happening to me?"*, ask, *"What can I build from this?"*

3. Take Action Quickly

Momentum matters. The faster you engage with your new reality, the quicker you start to regain control. Don't waste weeks stewing over how things *should* have gone. Act on what *is* now.

4. Trust That Mastery Leads to More Opportunities

Excelling in any role, even one you didn't choose, builds credibility. People notice when you consistently deliver and it is through delivery that you earn trust and influence, which opens the door to the next opportunity.

Final Thought: It's Not About What Happens - It's What You Do With It

Disappointment isn't the end of the story. It's just the turning point. If you accept your reality, commit to doing something useful with it, and keep moving, you'll find that success often grows from the very places you least expected.

There's a quiet strength in acceptance - not the kind that shouts or demands recognition, but the kind that quietly says: *"This is where I am. This is what I have. Let's begin."*

It's easy to get caught in the loop of *"why me?"* or to fixate on what could have been, but that loop keeps you stuck and unable to progress. The Service Mindset asks a different question: *Given where I am, what can I do next that brings value?*

When we accept our circumstances - truly accept them - we create space for growth. We stop mourning the life we thought we should have had, and we start building the one that's still in front of us.

Practical Steps Toward Acceptance

Be honest about your reality
Acceptance helps you separate what's within your control from what isn't. Focus your energy on what can be changed, and let go of what can't.

Question what you've accepted by default
Just because something is "normal" doesn't mean it's right for you. Ask yourself whether long-held habits or expectations still serve you.

Adapt your environment where you can
Rather than forcing yourself to endure discomfort, make small changes that support your wellbeing. Even minor adjustments can make a big difference.

Stay curious about your discomfort
When something feels wrong, don't just put up with it - explore it. Often, our discomfort is a signal that something needs our attention, not something to ignore.

📌 Reflection Exercise:

What's one part of your life that you've been resisting?
Is it something you can change, or is it time to accept and pivot?

📌 Action Step:

Write down three ways you could adjust your mindset or environment to better align with your current reality. Focus on small, constructive changes that move you forward, rather than resisting what is.

TENET 2. Serve with Intention

When Life Loses Its Anchor

After the brain injury, my life slowly came apart and I allowed myself to drift in a quiet and dangerous way.

One moment, I had a future and there had been a plan: university, law, a career. A life of meaning – though much of it had been chosen for me – the plan gave my life direction. I had structure, expectation, and a path that kept me tethered to something.

And then it was gone.

In the years that followed, I became untethered. Not just from ambition or success, but from meaning. I lurched painfully between depression and anxiety. Some days I was too numb to feel anything at all. Other days I felt everything all at once and wanted to run away from everything.

Life became a series of emotional reactions: panic, despair, anger, fear - and all of it felt like it was happening to me, without any say in the matter.

When you are robbed of purpose, a vacuum opens inside you. And like any vacuum, it tries to fill itself - often with the wrong things.

I made poor decisions. I neglected relationships. Friends and family drifted away, and if I'm honest, I let them. I didn't invest in those connections because I didn't feel like I had anything meaningful to invest.

I began taking risks with my health and my life. Drinking. Promiscuity. Neglect. None of it felt good, but all of it felt better than facing the void. I wasn't chasing joy - I was chasing the absence of emptiness.

Even rugby, which had once been a source of discipline and pride, began to slip away. I had been good. I trained, I played, I competed hard. At one point, I even lived my life with a steadfast belief that one day I might play for England. After the injury, I went back to the pitch. Partly because I was stubborn, partly because I wanted to prove I still could - but mostly because it gave me a thread of purpose to cling onto.

Eventually, I had to accept what I didn't want to face: I couldn't play anymore. The physical toll of the hardest game in the world was affecting my cognition. The damage was too real to ignore.

So I stopped playing, but for a while I didn't stop going to the club.

I could still drink in the bar.
I could still flirt with a woman and pretend I was fine.
I told myself I was still in it - still part of the game.

But deep down, I knew: I wasn't there for rugby anymore. I was there to fill the silence.

That's what happens when you live a life without *telos*.

You stop choosing, and life starts choosing for you… and most of the time, without any input from you, it chooses badly.

We All Must Serve Something – The Myth of Neutrality

For a long time, I thought I wasn't serving anything at all. I wasn't going to university, I wasn't chasing a career, I wasn't chasing anything, really. I was just trying to get through each day. I thought that made me neutral. That I was on pause, but I wasn't.

I was still serving something - I just hadn't chosen it.

Most of us think that if we're not chasing a grand ambition, we're somehow sitting it out, but life doesn't work like that. Whether we mean to or not, we're always in service of something. It might be comfort. It might be fear. It might be the need to feel safe, or wanted, or in control, but something is guiding our actions, even if we're not conscious of it.

I wasn't driven by purpose in those years after the accident. I was driven by avoidance. I was in service to the path of least resistance. Anything that helped me forget or escape

- even briefly - got my attention. Alcohol, promiscuity, distraction, detachment. These were the things I turned to, not because they were meaningful, but because they were there.

Looking back, I can see that my life wasn't neutral.

I was living in service of the wrong things… things that temporarily took the pain away when what I really needed was to find purpose and meaning.

That's what most people don't realise: if you don't choose what to serve, the world will choose for you.

It will offer you a version of success built on image.

It will push you towards things that look good from the outside but leave you hollow inside.

It will reward you for chasing the wrong things: status, approval, performance - because those things are easy to sell.

And you'll find yourself exhausted, achieving things you never really wanted, wondering why it all feels so empty.

The Service Mindset starts with a simple but difficult truth:

We all must serve something.

The question is not *whether* we're serving, but *what* we are serving.

And whether it deserves us.

What Makes a Telos Worthy?

It's not enough to say "live with purpose" and leave it there.

People can live with purpose and still end up miserable.

Plenty of people pursue their goals with intensity - that doesn't mean the goal is good.

Some people live in service of wealth, some live for their reputation. Some are entirely driven by revenge, or resentment, or the need to prove someone wrong.

The truth is, if you apply discipline, focus, and drive to any of those things, you'll probably get them, but you'll succeed in the wrong direction.

So we have to go deeper.

We don't just need a purpose - we need a *worthy* purpose - a telos that brings out the best in us, not the worst.

The ancient philosophers knew this. Aristotle didn't just talk about choosing a goal, he talked about *virtue*. About character. About becoming the kind of person who deserves to flourish - that's the test we have to apply:

Not *does this give me what I want?*
But *does this make me who I want to be?*

If the thing you're serving is making you smaller, harder, more anxious, more selfish - then no matter how shiny it looks from the outside, it isn't worth your life.

So here's what I've learnt to ask myself, and what I encourage you to ask yourself too:

- Is this pursuit making me more honest, more courageous, more compassionate?

- Is it giving something back, not just to me, but to the people around me?

- Is it something I can sustain, or is it burning me out?

- Did I choose this freely, or am I serving someone else's expectations?

- Is it grounded in the real world or is it built on fantasy, fear, or the need to be seen?

These aren't easy questions, but they are necessary ones, because your energy, your time, your one life on this planet – it's all going somewhere, so we should make sure it's going somewhere good.

When I lost my job all those years ago, it lived rent-free in my head for far too long.

It shaped how I approached every role after that. I clung on desperately and often to the point of exhaustion in every role I served thereafter.

I equated security with value. I told myself *I couldn't let go*, no matter what the cost to my health, or my family, or my sense of self.

The Service Mindset – in telling us to serve with intention – challenges us to ask ourselves: *is this thing helping me to flourish? Is it worthy of my service?* And when we do that, we start to realise that maybe the job you're clinging to isn't worth the cost.

That maybe the relationship you're exhausting yourself to maintain isn't serving either of you.

That maybe the version of yourself you're trying to protect is already gone.

When you see that clearly - not emotionally, but *ethically* - you become free.

Free to stop being performative.
Free to stop trying to prove yourself.
Free to walk away from things that are not aligned with the person you want to be in the world.

And that, more than anything, is what choosing your telos gives you: permission to move forward with purpose.

Choosing a Telos – With Courage, Not Clarity

One of the common mistakes people make when talking about purpose is imagining it will arrive all at once, fully formed. We think there will be a moment of clarity - some blinding realisation that shows us exactly what we're here to do. In my experience, it doesn't work like that.

Purpose is rarely loud. More often, it shows up quietly, in the background of your life. You notice it in the things you keep coming back to. In the work that still feels meaningful, even when it's difficult. In the people you're willing to support, even when no one's watching. These aren't dramatic moments but they signal where something valuable might be growing.

The truth is, most of us don't find our purpose - **we choose it**. Not once, but repeatedly. We choose to care about something - we decide to commit to it - and we do that, not because it's easy or obvious, but because deep down, we sense it matters.

That choice doesn't require absolute certainty. It requires courage. Courage to stop drifting. Courage to step away from things that no longer fit. Courage to take a step towards something that might not have a guaranteed outcome, but that feels more aligned with who you are.

I didn't arrive at my telos through a grand plan. It came through experience - through mistakes, regret, and the slow process of learning what mattered. I began doing things that felt useful: mentoring younger colleagues, supporting people who were struggling, listening more carefully. Not because I had some grand mission in mind, but because those things resonated with me and deep down those actions felt worthwhile.
Over time, a thread began to emerge - something steady, something real. A sense of service. A desire to lift others. A growing commitment to justice, integrity, and doing things that made the world even slightly better. That thread gave shape to my work in fighting fraud, and eventually, it gave shape to my life.

That's the point. Purpose doesn't land in your lap, complete and clear. It unfolds over time, through the act of choosing. You decide what matters and then you serve it well.

The Freedom of Commitment

There's a strange idea that freedom means keeping your options open. That the more you avoid commitments, the more choice you'll have and the happier you'll be.

What we call freedom often ends up as paralysis. The constant weighing of options. The endless pursuit of something better. The quiet anxiety that comes from never quite knowing what you stand for, or where you're headed.

Real freedom isn't the absence of commitment - it's choosing what to commit to.

Because when you choose something worthy of your service; something that aligns with your values, that builds your character, that brings something good into the world, you no longer need to keep looking over your shoulder. You're no longer spread too thinly across a dozen half-lived lives.

You're anchored, and when life inevitably gets difficult (and trust me – it will), that anchor will hold you and keep you steady in the storm.

For a long time, I thought commitment meant being trapped. I worried that if I chose one path, I'd lose all the others, but what I've come to realise is that **not choosing** is its own kind of trap. It keeps you in limbo. You drift. You react - and you wake up years later wondering how you ended up so far from where you thought you'd be.

Commitment, when it's rooted in the right *telos*, gives shape to your days. It narrows your focus in a way that brings clarity, not limitation. It helps you say *no* to things that don't matter, so you can give more of yourself to what does.

It's not about grand declarations or melodramatic decisions. It's about choosing, today, what you want to serve and then just doing your best to serve that thing well.

Not everything deserves your energy and not every pursuit deserves your loyalty, but when you find something that does - something that makes you more honest, more human, more useful to others - that's where a better life begins to unfold.

That's where the Service Mindset begins, too.

📌 Reflection Exercise

Take some time to think honestly about what you are currently serving.

Not what you *say* you value.
Not what you *wish* you were doing.

But, what your time, energy, and attention are actually going towards each day.

- What's getting the best of you right now?
- Does it reflect who you want to be?
- Is it helping you flourish, or just helping you cope?

If your answer unsettles you, don't panic. It's never too late to make a different choice.

But you do have to *choose*. Because what you might not have realised is this: **not choosing is still a choice.**

📌 Action Step

Revisit **The Telos Test** at the end of Chapter 2.

Pick one *telos*: a purpose, a cause, a value – that you feel drawn to. It doesn't have to be perfect, just something that feels honest.

Then, for the next week, give it a little more of yourself.

That might mean protecting time for it.

It might mean having one brave conversation.

It might mean saying *no* to something that doesn't serve it.

Watch what changes when you stop drifting and start deciding.

TENET 3. Stand Beside, Not Above.

At the heart of The Service Mindset is a simple but unwavering truth: **every human being is equal in worth.**

People may carry different responsibilities, wear different uniforms, earn different salaries, but none of that changes their intrinsic value. Titles don't make someone more important. Status doesn't make someone more deserving of respect. We all come into the world the same way, and we all leave it the same way. What we do, in between those two points, is what counts.

The Service Mindset begins with the rejection of superiority. It challenges the idea that value is something to be earned or proven through competition, status, or achievement. Instead, it sees value as something already present in every person - something that needs to be recognised, not bestowed.

Society conditions us to rank each other: by wealth, intelligence, job title, or social standing. But these are surface-level distinctions. Beneath them, what we share is far more powerful than what separates us.

Yes, this principle matters in leadership. Leaders who act superior create resentment and those who serve create loyalty, but it goes deeper than that. It's about how we treat the waiter, the receptionist, the person struggling just to keep it together. It's about how we speak to others when no one's watching. It's about choosing to stand beside people - not above them.

The Service Mindset isn't just a philosophy for leaders. It's a way of seeing the world. A way of saying: *I am no better than you. You are no less than me. Let's start there.*

The Intrinsic Value of Every Human – Kant's Moral Imperative

The belief in human equality is a moral and philosophical cornerstone.

Immanuel Kant, one of the most influential thinkers of the Enlightenment, argued that people must never be treated merely as tools or stepping stones, but always as ends in themselves. In other words: every person has an innate value, not because of what they can do or what they achieve, but simply because they are human.

In a world obsessed with status, performance, and hierarchy, this idea can feel radical. We're taught to measure ourselves and others by output, by title, by income, by influence. But the Service Mindset rejects those measures. It doesn't deny that people have different roles or responsibilities, but it insists that no role or title confers greater *worth*.

If you truly believe in service, then you must start with respect - **for everyone**. Not because of what they can offer you, not because of what they've achieved, but because of who they are.

That means:

- Seeing people as individuals, not just roles or functions.
- Valuing relationships over transactions.
- Speaking to an apprentice with the same care and consideration you'd show to a CEO.
- Letting dignity lead the way.

Kant's philosophy wasn't abstract to me - it became real the moment I could no longer define my value by what I did. When my identity and output crumbled, I had to ask: *what's left?* The answer, it turns out, was the beginning of everything that came next.

The Trap of Superiority – And How I Escaped It

Before my brain injury, I wouldn't have said I thought I was better than anyone, but I did believe I was going places. I was sharp, confident, and moving fast and in subtle ways, I measured my worth by how far ahead I was of the person next to me.

And then everything stopped.

The injury shattered the version of me I had taken for granted. Suddenly, things that had once been easy became uphill battles. My memory slipped. My ability to process information faltered. I second-guessed every thought, every decision. The voice in my head - once clear and self-assured - now felt foreign and uncertain. I swung between feeling utterly inferior and frantically trying to prove I was still someone - still valuable, still ahead, still better.

But the more I scrambled to reclaim my old place in the race, the more exhausted I became.

Because that's the thing no one tells you about chasing superiority: **it never ends.**

There's always someone else to overtake. Always another benchmark. Always another reason to feel like you're not quite there yet - and as long as you see life as a hierarchy, you will always be climbing and never arriving.

What the brain injury did, what trauma and recovery forced me to realise, is that the whole race was a trap.

True peace, true presence, comes when you stop measuring yourself against others and start seeing people as they truly are: fellow travellers on the road through life. We are all made of the same stuff. We may be at different points in our journey, but none of us is more or less worthy. We all stumble. We all carry burdens… and we all matter - **equally.**

I had to lose my place in the pecking order to realise that the pecking order itself was the real problem.

Superiority vs. True Leadership – A Workplace Contrast

Nowhere is the rejection of superiority more visible, or more important, than in the workplace.

Over the years, I've worked with many types of leaders. Some led from ego. Others led from service. The difference was night and day.

The Ego-Driven Leader
- Speaks more than they listen.
- Leads with authority, not empathy.
- Claims the credit, deflects the blame.
- Measures success by status, not impact.

The Service-Driven Leader
- Listens first, speaks with purpose.
- Empowers others instead of controlling them.
- Shares success, owns mistakes.
- Measures success by the growth of those around them.

Superiority pushes people away. Service pulls them together.

Ego demands compliance. Service earns trust.

The most impactful leaders I've worked with didn't chase admiration - they built it by consistently demonstrating humility and intent. They didn't need to prove they were above you. You went with them because you felt that they stood beside you.

The Role of the Sensei – Finding a Mentor Who Guides, Not Controls

Everyone needs a Mr Miyagi in their life - someone who guides with patience, wisdom, and quiet strength, rather than demanding obedience or status.

One of the most powerful ways to practise service and reject superiority is through mentorship.

Not all mentorship is created equal. The best mentors don't lecture or dominate. They don't hoard knowledge to preserve their status. Instead, they teach like a **sensei** - guiding with quiet confidence, sharing wisdom without ego, and focusing not on how important they are, but on how much you can grow.

A true sensei-style mentor will:

- Challenge you without belittling you.
- Offer insights freely, without expecting praise.
- Encourage independent thinking, rather than creating dependence.
- Help you surpass them, rather than keeping you in their shadow.

In contrast, poor mentors can't help but make it about themselves. They expect admiration. They subtly compete. They view your growth as a threat instead of a legacy.

I've been lucky to learn from people who understood that teaching is a form of service. Their goal was never to stay ahead of me, but to help me rise, and I've carried that mindset forward into my own role as a mentor.

If you find yourself with a mentor who demands loyalty instead of encouraging progress, you haven't found a mentor, you've found an ego looking for applause.

True mentorship is never about superiority. It's about walking alongside someone as they grow, not standing above them while they struggle.

From Mentorship to Shared Humanity - The Wisdom of Burns

The principles of mentorship and equality aren't confined to the workplace. They echo through every aspect of how we relate to others. When we embrace The Service Mindset, we begin to understand that leadership, connection, and meaning all stem from recognising one simple truth:

We are more alike than we are different.

This isn't just a modern idea. It's a truth that's echoed throughout history - perhaps nowhere more powerfully than in the words of the Scottish poet, **Robert Burns**.

Every year on **Burns Night**, people from all walks of life gather to celebrate poetry, community, and shared humanity. The tradition is striking not because of how elite it is, but because of how levelling it is. Whether you're a CEO or an apprentice, everyone sits at the same table. Titles don't matter. What matters is connection (as well as an ability to drink copious amounts of whisky).

In his poem *A Man's a Man for A' That*, Burns wrote:

*"The rank is but the guinea's stamp,
The Man's the gowd for a' that."*

In other words: **status is surface-level - it's character that counts**.

Burns came from humble beginnings. He wasn't interested in pretence or posturing. His work endures because it reminds us of a truth that we often forget: **the person in front of you has the same worth as you do**, no matter their background, bank account, or business card.

When we lose sight of this, we become trapped in a constant need to compare and compete - but when we remember it - when we honour the shared humanity in each of us - we become capable of real service.

Not service as performance.

Not service as superiority.

But service as **equality in action**.

How This Ties to The Service Mindset

To live The Service Mindset is to make a daily, conscious decision: **stand beside others, not above them**.

This means:

- **Leading with empathy** – choosing to understand rather than judge.

- **Offering grace** – recognising that everyone is a work in progress, including yourself.

- **Lifting others up** – because success isn't about winning a race; it's about helping others finish it too.

- **Choosing mentors who teach through humility** – not ego.

- **Treating every person as inherently valuable**, regardless of title, experience, or status.

When we reject the need to be "better than," we create space for connection. And when we lead, serve, and live from that place - side by side - we don't just uplift others, we become better, too.

At the end of it all, people won't remember your job title or your salary.

They'll remember how you made them feel.

They'll remember whether you saw them, valued them, treated them as equals.

That's the legacy of service.

★ Reflection Exercise:

Think of a time when you felt the urge to prove your superiority: in a meeting, a conversation, or a moment of comparison. What would have changed if you had seen the other person as your equal? How could you have approached it from a mindset of service rather than competition?

★ Action Step:

This week, make a conscious choice to support rather than compete. That could mean helping a colleague without expecting credit, acknowledging someone else's success without comparison, or simply listening more than you speak. Look for chances to stand beside others, not above them.

📌 **Mentorship Tip:**

Identify someone in your life or field who embodies wisdom without ego - a mentor who serves rather than controls. Reach out to learn from them. If you're already in a position to guide others, ask yourself: *Am I lifting others up or holding them back?*

TENET 4. Find Strength in the Simple Things

Why Simplicity Matters More Than Ever

Modern life is complicated. We're bombarded with information, surrounded by choice, and constantly pulled in multiple directions. In our efforts to optimise, maximise, and achieve more, we often lose touch with the things that matter most.

The Service Mindset pushes back against this. It says: **simplify.**

Strip away the noise. Let go of unnecessary complexity. Stop chasing things that don't serve your purpose.

Simplicity isn't about laziness or minimalism for its own sake. It's about clarity. It's about creating space - in your head, in your heart, and in your diary - so that you can focus on what actually matters.

That might mean making space in your diary instead of filling it. It might mean walking the dog without your phone. It might mean saying *no* to something that might impress, so you can say *yes* to something that might make a difference.

When we choose simplicity, we make room for service - not just to others, but to what matters to ourselves.

Epicureanism and the Strength in Simplicity

The pursuit of simplicity is not a modern concept – it is a lesson from history, embedded in some of the greatest philosophies of human thought. Amongst them, Epicureanism offers one of the clearest arguments for why simplicity is not just practical, but essential for a fulfilling life.

Epicurus taught that happiness does not come from wealth, power, or status, but from removing the unnecessary and focusing on what truly matters. He believed that most suffering comes not from what we lack, but from chasing things we do not need.

He divided desires into three categories:

1. **Natural and necessary** – food, shelter, friendship, peace of mind.
2. **Natural but unnecessary** – luxury, indulgence, excessive pleasure.
3. **Neither natural nor necessary** – fame, status, power, material excess.

But there's one need Epicurus may have understated: **belonging**.

Belonging is more than friendship or affection. It's the sense of being part of something larger than ourselves - of having a place in the world that is secure, meaningful, and recognised by others. Without belonging, all other comforts feel hollow. We are social beings, wired not only to survive, but to connect. Yet, in the modern world, belonging is often treated as optional - something nice to have, but not essential.

In truth, **belonging is as necessary as food or shelter. Without it, we don't just suffer - we wither**.

And here's where The Service Mindset offers something transformational: **service is the gateway to belonging**. It's the act of saying, *"I matter here, because I contribute here."* When we serve others, we embed ourselves in the community. We create trust. We earn our place, not through superiority, but through usefulness.

We often think we need to be impressive in order to be valued, but it's not admiration that creates belonging - it's connection - and connection comes from service.

So perhaps Epicurus was right to highlight the danger of chasing status and indulgence, but maybe he missed something too. Maybe he didn't quite grasp that in the end, **belonging isn't a luxury - it's the whole point.**

Enter Sisu: Simplicity in Action

If Epicurus taught us to strip life back to its essentials, the Finnish concept of sisu teaches us what to build in its place.

Sisu has no perfect English translation, but it loosely means *grit*, *determination*, and *a quiet, stubborn resilience*. It's not about dramatic displays or endless optimism - it's about doing what needs to be done, without fuss, without validation, and without overcomplication.

You don't need to feel ready. You don't need the perfect conditions. You just begin… and then you keep going.

That's the essence of sisu: *uncomplicated strength*. A refusal to be beaten down by obstacles, fear, or fatigue. While the world spirals into over-analysis, a person with sisu simply gets on with it.

In a world obsessed with feeling motivated, sisu is about doing what needs to be done, even when you don't feel like it.

Sisu is simplicity in motion. It doesn't waste time overthinking or spiralling in doubt. It doesn't need a perfect morning routine or a motivational playlist. It just puts one foot in front of the other - again and again.

You see it in the nurse who turns up for the night shift even though her body aches. You see it in the single parent doing the school run, then the shift at work, then the bedtime stories. You see it in people who quietly carry on - not for applause, but **because someone is counting on them.**

And this is the critical link: **sisu is not just strength, it's service.** It says: *I'll keep going, not because it's glamorous, but because someone needs me to.*

When you act with sisu, you are embodying The Service Mindset. You are cutting through complexity, shelving ego, and saying: *"What needs doing? Right… I'll do that."*

That's why sisu fits so naturally into The Service Mindset - because true service, the kind that lasts, is rarely glamorous. It's turning up when you don't feel like it. It's doing the work without needing applause. It's putting others first, not because you feel amazing, but because it's the right thing to do.

Sisu is simple, it is quiet and it is powerful.

It aligns with The Service Mindset in three core ways:

Sisu is Simple – It cuts through the noise. No theatrics, no overthinking. Just clarity and action.

Sisu is Present – It doesn't dwell on what went wrong or worry about what's next. It focuses on what needs doing *now*.

Sisu is Service-Based – It's not about ego. It's about endurance - often for the sake of others.

You don't need to wait for motivation, you don't need to feel ready, you just need to begin.

When You're Lost, Get Lost!

Sometimes the best way to find yourself is to get off the path entirely.

Not metaphorically… literally. Walk a different way home. Turn left instead of right. Climb over the fence. Follow the trail that disappears behind the hedge.

Modern life teaches us to crave structure and predictability. We walk the same streets, drive the same route home, scroll the same feeds. We tell ourselves it's efficient - that routine brings stability and sometimes, it does. But when you're stuck, when your mind is heavy or your heart is tired, familiarity can become a trap. You don't need more of the same, you need to get lost.

That was the lesson I didn't know I needed until a small, apricot-coloured, dog wandered into our lives.

It started, as most good things do in our house, with a PowerPoint presentation from Erin. She'd decided we needed a dog - and in her mind, the evidence was overwhelming. One slide simply read: *"Without dog, we are sad. With dog, we could be happy."*

I was sold.

Jane was… not.

But while she was working a long shift at work, I made the unilateral decision to bring home a Maltipoo puppy.

If you are reading this thinking it might be a good idea to surprise your partner with a puppy – I can only advise you that it is not, and that there is a price to be paid. It took two weeks of stony silence before Jane forgave me, but in time, we both came to realise it was one of the best decisions *we've* ever made.

We called her Nellie - and almost every day since, I've walked with her through the forest - no agenda, no destination, just movement. In doing so, I began to see the forest for what it really was: a place to reset. To let go. To be.

There is something deeply honest about being in nature. Trees don't perform. Paths don't pretend. The forest doesn't ask you to be productive or clever or fine. It just exists - wild, still, present.

And, if you let it, it can bring you back to yourself.

I remember one day in particular - years before Nellie, deep in the thick fog of an episode of depression. I'd forced myself out for a walk, no plan in mind, just a desperate need to escape the four walls of my flat. The sky was clear, and the sun was shining when I left - so I dressed appropriately in shorts and T-shirt. About forty-five minutes in, without warning, the heavens opened.

Torrential, icy rain soaking me to the skin in seconds. And then, in the middle of nowhere, dripping and freezing and exhausted, I looked up at the now bright blue sky and I laughed.

For the first time in weeks, I felt something. The coldness, the absurdity of it, the utter unpredictability - it cracked something open in me. I wasn't healed, but I was aware, and that felt like a start.

Then there are other memories - smaller, but just as vivid. Like those long, hot primary school days when the teacher would say, "Let's do the lesson on the grass today." Those were the best days. Sitting cross-legged in the sun, the warmth of the earth beneath us, learning felt different. Less like instruction. More like discovery.

What both memories have in common - the storm that came from nowhere and the lesson on the hot school field - is presence. A sudden jolt out of routine. A change in environment that shifted the way I thought, the way I felt, the way I was.

Nature does that - it resets us because it just *is*.

And when you spend time in it, really *in* it - not just passing through on your way to somewhere else - it gives you space. Space to breathe. To see clearly. To come back to yourself without expectation or judgement.

That's why, in The Service Mindset, nature isn't just scenery - it's a teacher.

It reminds us:

- That discomfort can wake us up.

- That control is often an illusion.

- That presence is found in sensations like the wind on your face, the mud on your boots, the tension in a dog lead as a tiny dog pulls you relentlessly towards a café where she knows that biscuits are waiting.

It teaches that service isn't always about doing more. Sometimes, it's about stopping. Listening. Reconnecting with what's real.

So when you feel stuck, overwhelmed, or numb - don't rush to fix it. Don't fight to get back on the track. Instead, try getting lost.

Take the path that disappears into the trees.

See what's around the corner.

Let the world remind you that it's bigger than your inbox, your worries, or your well-worn route to work.

Because sometimes, the best way back… is through the wild.

Simplicity as a Discipline

Simplicity isn't about doing less. It's about making space for what matters most and often, what matters most, is connection.

We don't just *want* to belong. We *need* to. It's a fundamental human requirement - right up there with food, sleep, and safety. However, in a world of constant noise, that need is easily hijacked.

Modern life offers endless simulations of connection: emails, notifications, online approval, digital validation. They feel like belonging, but they're not. They prey on our instincts, offering a quick dopamine hit in place of something deeper. So, we fill our lives with noise, mistaking activity for intimacy, and stimulation for meaning.

A full inbox isn't the same as a full heart.

A hundred likes aren't the same as being truly seen.

A busy schedule isn't the same as being needed - not really.

We don't need more digital feedback loops. We need something real.

The thing is, real belonging doesn't have to be complicated. Sometimes, it's as simple as **stepping outside**, feeling the wind on your face, and remembering that you are part of something vast and timeless.

That's why nature matters in The Service Mindset.

It grounds us.

It nourishes us.

It gives us something bigger than ourselves to belong to - not through effort or performance, but simply by *being*.

When we return to that space - when we reconnect to what's real - we serve better. We lead better. We live better. Not from exhaustion or ego, but from clarity, presence, and rootedness.

✦ Reflection Exercise:

Where in your life are you mistaking noise for connection? What parts of your routine are simulating belonging instead of fulfilling it?

✦ Action Step:

Choose one small way to reconnect with something real this week. Take a walk. Touch the earth. Sit in stillness. Let it remind you of where you truly belong.

TENET 5. Regulate your Emotions – Don't Let Them Take the Wheel

The Truth About Emotional Strength

There's a common misconception about what it means to be emotionally strong. People imagine calm leaders, unflinching decision-makers, or stoic individuals who somehow don't *feel* things the way the rest of us do. As if strength means silence. As if feeling less is a mark of personal or professional development.

It isn't.

You don't get to choose what you feel. Emotions arise uninvited - hard-wired, fast and automatic. You don't sit down and decide to feel ashamed, or anxious, or angry. Those signals emerge from parts of the brain that evolved long before logic, strategy, or conscious intention.

So, the goal is not to stop the feeling. The goal is to create space after it arrives and then to choose what happens next.

That space - between stimulus and response - is where emotional regulation lives, and it's one of the most important skills a person can develop. Not just for your own wellbeing, but for the people around you. If you're always reacting, you're always pulled along by your first emotional wave and that means you're not really in control - your feelings are.

This is where the Stoics were right. They didn't preach emotional suppression - they preached observation. Step back. Name the feeling. Acknowledge it - but don't hand over the keys. Don't let the emotion take the wheel and drive.

Marcus Aurelius, the Roman emperor and philosopher, put it plainly:

"You have power over your mind - not outside events. Realise this, and you will find strength."

You can't control what happens to you, but you can control how you meet it.

That's the foundation of emotional discipline and it's essential to The Service Mindset.

The Service Mindset demands steadiness. It demands that you don't inflict your own chaos on others, especially when they're looking to you for clarity or reassurance. Whether you're a leader, a parent, a partner, or a friend, your emotional presence matters.

This doesn't mean becoming a robot. It doesn't mean pretending not to feel. It means building the discipline to *respond*, not *react*. To stay grounded when everything around you feels shaky. To feel it and to still choose wisely.

Emotions Are Signals, Not Commands

Emotions get a bad reputation. People talk about being "too emotional," "overreacting," or "not thinking straight" but the truth is, there's nothing wrong with emotion itself. It's not weakness. It's not failure, it's part of our biology.

Emotions are signals. That's all. They're part of an ancient internal system designed to help us survive - to keep us safe, connected, and alert to danger. They're not rational, but they're not meant to be. They're fast, instinctive, and deeply embedded in who we are.

That's the point - you don't get to control what rises up inside you, but you do have control over how you interpret it **and** what you do with it.

Whilst emotions are real, they're not always right:

Fear doesn't always mean danger.
Anger doesn't always mean injustice.
Excitement doesn't always mean something is a good idea.

Your body might be reacting as though you're being chased by a lion, when in fact, someone just hasn't replied to your message. Your heart might be racing as if you're under threat, when all that's happened in reality is that someone has asked your availability for a meeting.

Your nervous system is doing what it's evolved to do - trying to protect you in a world that's no longer built for instinct.

But here's the problem: if we treat every emotional signal as a command, we stop choosing, we stop living intentionally and we start reacting. We lose our ability to pause and assess, and we hand over our agency to a passing wave of adrenaline, cortisol, or shame.

In the context of service, that's dangerous, because service demands presence. It requires us to think not just about how *we* feel, but how our responses affect the people around us. When you're in service to others - at work, at home, or in your community - your reactivity doesn't just impact you, it ripples outward.

That's why emotional regulation isn't about numbing yourself. It's about being aware of what you're feeling and being able to ask yourself: *"Is this useful?" "Is this true?" "Is this what I need right now?"*

It's the difference between hearing the fire alarm and assuming the house is burning down... or pausing to check whether someone just burnt the toast.

The Service Mindset doesn't ask you to ignore your feelings. It asks you to *investigate* them. To treat them with respect, but not surrender. And above all, to hold onto this simple truth:

Emotions are information, they are not an instruction.

Returning to Emotional Neutrality

Back in Chapter 2, we introduced a simple mental framework to help make better decisions: A visualised swinging pendulum.

It's worth bringing it back here - not to repeat it, but to show how it applies when emotions are running high. The truth is, when you're caught in a moment of intense emotions - whether that's panic, anger, elation, or fear - you're no longer thinking clearly as you find yourself at the extreme arc of the pendulum.

Picture it again. A large swinging pendulum.

- The left side is where we act from negative emotional extremes: anxiety, shame, anger, despair, fear.

- The right side is where we act from overly positive extremes: euphoria, impulsive excitement, inflated confidence.

- The point in the middle is where rationality and emotions meet. That's the space where you have the most clarity. That's where service becomes possible again.

Emotional regulation isn't about eliminating the pendulum altogether and it not really about not avoiding emotional extremes. It's about having the emotional discipline to recognise when you are close to the edges and then bringing yourself back to emotional neutrality before making a decision as to how to act.

That's not always easy - especially in the moment.

I once found myself hurtling along the wrong side of the pendulum, and I wasn't just being emotional - I was driving a car.

I'd entered a roundabout, indicating right, when another driver suddenly pulled out in front of me without looking. I braked hard. Hit the horn. Flashed my lights. My blood boiled.

As fate would have it, we both exited the roundabout onto the same road. The moment turned into a chase. I pushed the accelerator down. Sixty. Seventy. Eighty. I was no longer driving, I was *raging*. Completely hijacked by adrenaline.

And then, just as quickly, it hit me.

What the hell am I doing?

If the police had clocked me, I'd have been done for dangerous driving - and what exactly was I planning to do if I caught up to the other driver? Give him a lecture? Start a fight?

I eased off, but the lesson lingered.

What almost caused a crash that day wasn't the other driver - it was *me*. Or rather, it was my unregulated emotion, running the show.

That's the danger of the extremes of the pendulum.

You're not just a risk to yourself, you're a risk to everyone around you and this is why emotional neutrality matters so much in The Service Mindset. Not because it's some Zen ideal or a performance of calm, but because it's *safer*. Smarter. Kinder. You make better decisions from the centre. You do less damage. You stay available.

You won't always catch yourself in time, I didn't, but the more you practise noticing when you're at the edge, the more you build that muscle of *returning* to neutral and the more you reclaim your power.

So the next time you feel yourself speeding up or shutting down, ask:

Where am I on the pendulum's swing?
Am I reacting - or responding?
Do I need to come back to centre before I move forward?

The Speed of Emotion – A New Way to See the Pendulum

Not everyone thinks in pendulums. For some, picturing a mental pendulum is helpful, it gives a visual cue to return to the emotional centre-ground. But there's another way to understand what's happening in those intense moments. One that might feel even more familiar.

Think of a speedometer.

You're driving along - not literally this time, but emotionally. And at a steady 30 miles per hour, you're doing alright. You can see what's ahead. You've got time to react to obstacles. You're not crawling, and you're not speeding. You're in control.

But emotions don't always let you cruise.

Sometimes, you hit the accelerator. Excitement builds. Adrenaline surges. You get an idea, a buzz, a burst of anger or drive and suddenly you're doing 60, 70, 80. You stop thinking ahead. Everything becomes about the next second. Reaction replaces strategy and like speeding on the road, your margin for error gets smaller with every second.

Other times, it's the brakes that hit. Fear, shame, anxiety - they don't speed you up, they slow you down. You hesitate. Stall. Doubt yourself. You sit at the crossroads for so long that opportunities pass you by. Paralysis replaces progress.

In both cases, racing or stalling, your emotional speed is distorting your judgment.

And that's where this metaphor becomes useful. Because just like with real driving, the goal isn't to be static, and it isn't to race and lose control. It's to find that optimal cruising speed - the place where you're responsive, aware, and moving forward with clarity.

So next time you feel yourself caught in a wave of emotion, try asking:

What's the speed of my emotion right now?
Am I racing too fast to see clearly? Am I stalled and unable to move? Am I travelling at a pace where I can respond to something that might appear in the road ahead of me?

This reframing won't make the emotion disappear, but it gives you a gauge to check before you act.

When you're serving others - as a friend, a colleague, or a leader - your emotional speed matters because it affects the people around you.

Drive too fast, and you create panic.

Drive too slow, and you create frustration.

But drive steady and people will be happy to travel as passengers in your car.

Premeditatio Malorum – Facing the Worst Without Falling Apart

The Stoics had a practice with a name that sounds like something out of a Defence Against the Dark Arts Lesson: *premeditatio malorum* - the premeditation of evils.

It sounds bleak, but it's a practical emotional tool that has helped me to manage anxiety.

The idea is simple: imagine the worst. Picture the thing you fear most - not to wallow in it, but to make peace with it. To look it in the eye and say: *"If this happens… I'll survive."*

It's the opposite of catastrophising.

Catastrophising is what happens when fear takes over and your imagination races away from you without permission. A delayed text means rejection. A headache means a tumour. A quiet boss means redundancy is imminent. It's your imagination going to a place of dread but in an uncontrolled way.

Premeditatio malorum puts structure around that fear. Instead of spiralling, you get specific.

You ask:

"What if the worst did happen? What would I actually do?"

And more often than not, the answer is: *cope*. You wouldn't enjoy it, but you'd manage. Life would carry on. You'd adjust. The sky wouldn't fall in.

This type of thought exercise allows you to reclaim your agency as you stop being ruled by *"what if…?"*

When you start making decisions based on what *is* happening – as opposed to the worst case scenario, you become more available: emotionally, mentally, even physically. You're not consumed by imagined futures. You're grounded in the present, where real life actually occurs.

It reminds me of a joke by the comedian Tim Minchin. In one of his shows, he describes sitting on the sofa watching a film with his wife, when she suddenly says, *"I'm just going to go check on the baby."*

And without missing a beat, he replies:

"Darling, let's suppose the worst has happened and the baby has died - you're not going to be able to do anything about it, but you will have ruined a perfectly good movie. So why don't we wait until the film's over and then go check?"

It's outrageous. Dark… but brilliant.

The joke exposes the absurdity of panic-driven thinking. The truth that we often ruin perfectly good moments trying to prevent things that haven't happened - and may never happen at all.

That's the real damage of catastrophising. Not just the fear itself, but what it steals from you. It robs you of the now. It pulls you out of presence and into fiction. It demands emotional energy for events that haven't even occurred.

The Stoics understood this. They didn't recommend *ignoring* hardship - they just wanted you to meet it with a steady hand and a calm head.

That's where The Service Mindset builds on Stoicism. It understands that you can't serve well if you're spiralling. You can't make wise decisions from inside a future that doesn't exist. The only place you can act - the only place you can help anyone - is here and now.

It's something I get asked a lot when facing the coming wave of AI and technological advances: *"What will I do if AI comes for my job?"*

Let's face it, there aren't many jobs in the future that AI won't able to do and that means there is not going to be a huge amount of traditional work around. Maybe new jobs will emerge, maybe we will all become creatives or entrepreneurs.

Those of us who practice premeditatio malorum are already picturing ourselves in that situation and trying to imagine what we might do. When that time comes, and it probably will, we will endure, and perhaps more importantly, we will survive.

Emotional Hijacking – From Manipulation to Inner Voices

When your emotions are heightened, you're easier to influence.

Fraudsters, marketers, manipulative partners, they know this and they all use the same trick. They don't come for your logic, they come for your *feelings*. They create urgency, fear, excitement, guilt. Once they've stirred up that emotional response, they can get you to act before you've had time to think.

Click here or your account will be locked.
Buy now - this deal won't last.
If you loved me, you'd do it.

This emotional hijacking works because it shortcuts your ability to regulate.

When you're afraid, you rush.
When you're ashamed, you surrender.
When you're flattered, you lower your guard.

However, it should be noted that not all manipulation comes from outside.

Sometimes, the most convincing manipulator is the one inside your own head.

That quiet inner voice. The one that tells you you're not good enough. That you're fat. That you're going to fail. That everything is about to collapse, and it's all your fault.

I know that voice. I've lived with it for years.

After my brain injury, it became relentless. I'd lie awake at night, waiting for disaster. Checking my pulse. Bracing for panic. A single unkind thought would spiral into hours of anxiety, or, worse still, a full-body shutdown where I'd lie on the floor, unable to move, paralysed by the sheer weight of the impending, imagined catastrophe.

For a long time, I believed it. That's what made it so dangerous. I didn't even question it. The voice *sounded* like me - so I assumed it must be telling the truth… It wasn't.

Eventually, I learnt that just because a thought shows up in your mind doesn't mean it belongs there.

You don't have to obey it. You don't even have to believe it. You can learn to talk back to it with calm, grounded defiance.

"That's not helpful. I hear you, but I don't need to hear that right now"

As you practice talking back to your inner critic, you will find that over time, that voice loses its power.

Give Others the Space to Regulate Too

We don't live in isolation. Our actions, tone, timing, and presence affect other people, just as theirs affect us. And yet, we often forget that emotional regulation takes time - not only for ourselves, but for the people we rely on and the people who rely on us.

Too often, we throw emotional grenades into someone's life and then expect an immediate response.

A difficult email. A loaded question. A piece of bad news dropped in the middle of the day.

Then, almost without thinking, we follow up with: *"So… what do you want to do about it?"*

It's not fair and The Service Mindset asks us to be more thoughtful than that.

It asks us to recognise when someone else isn't in a position to think clearly and to give them the same thing we would ask for ourselves: space.

This isn't about walking on eggshells. It's not about avoiding difficult conversations. It's about timing. It's about respect. It's about being emotionally literate enough to know that people need time to process their feelings before they can be useful.

If you've just delivered difficult feedback to a colleague, don't expect a detailed solution on the spot.

If your partner's in shock, don't push them for emotional availability.

If your child's having a meltdown, don't demand logic or rationality.

If someone's gone quiet in a moment of stress, that silence might not be avoidance. It might be restraint - the space between reaction and response playing out in real time.

Giving someone the time and space to regulate their emotions is ultimately an act of service.

Final Reflection - Calm is a Discipline

There's a temptation to think of calm as a personality trait. Some people are just naturally composed, we say. They don't get rattled. They don't overreact. They're wired that way.

However, true calm - the kind that holds under pressure - is a discipline we are able to train ourselves in the way of.

It's the result of small choices made again and again: to pause instead of snap. To breathe before speaking. To let the moment settle before you act. It's the habit of checking your emotional speed before you hit send, or walk into a meeting, or respond to someone you care about.

It's not always easy - especially in a world that wants you to be reactive. Algorithms on social media are designed to provoke an extreme response, some workplaces can seem to reward urgency. Our culture also treats emotional intensity like proof that you care.

The Service Mindset rejects the idea that you have to match the chaos around you. It says: steady yourself first, align with your values and then serve.

You won't get it right every time. You'll still get angry, flustered, panicked. That's human, but if you apply these lessons to your life, you'll find that you recover faster. You'll pause more often. You'll start to notice the gap between emotion and response and, with practice, you'll learn to spend more of your time there.

Think clearly, then move deliberately, but ultimately - serve well because you've learnt how to feel without falling apart.

That's composure.

That's what keeps you in the service of others and out of the grip of your own chaos.

📌 **Reflection Exercise**

Think of a time recently when you reacted emotionally: a message, a meeting, a moment that got under your skin.

Now ask yourself:

- *Where were you on the emotional speedometer?*
- *What might have helped you return to centre sooner?*
- *What would the calm version of you have done differently?*

📌 Action Step

Over the next week, when you feel your emotions rising, whether you're speeding up or shutting down, pause and ask:

"What's my speed right now?"
"Is this the time to act, or the time to wait?"

Then give yourself a few minutes before responding. Let the intensity drop. Let clarity return.

📌 Key Thought

"You are not responsible for your first feeling, but you are responsible for what you do next."

TENET 6: Lifting Others – The True Measure of Leadership

A leader's success should not be measured by how high they climb, but rather by how many people they help to rise along the way.

Too often, insecure leaders suppress ambition in others, seeing it as a threat. The strongest leaders recognise that great people will rise eventually and, when they do, they should see you as someone who helped, not hindered, their growth.

Leadership is not about power. It is about service - and service means lifting others; helping them to reach their potential, supporting them when they struggle, and giving them what they need to succeed in their own right.

This is often one of those things that is easier said than done. Many of us, whether we are in leadership positions or not, feel the urge to compete with, rather than, to elevate others. We do this because it often feels natural to protect our own status rather than encouraging others to surpass us.

The Service Mindset rejects this insecurity and says that it's important to understand that life is not a race to be won, but a journey to be shared.

The Three Core Practices of Lifting Others

If you want to become the kind of person who elevates others, these three principles must be at the heart of how you conduct yourself:

Lifts others - don't hoard credit, share it.
Don't fear other peoples' ambition - encourage it.
Don't guard the ladder - lower it, again and again, open doors, offer guidance, and help others in their climb.

If you commit to these three things, you will not only build stronger teams and better relationships, you will also find meaning in your own journey.

Lifting Others Doesn't Mean Losing Yourself

One of the biggest misconceptions about *lifting others* is that it requires self-sacrifice. That, in order to help someone else's rise, you have to diminish yourself.

That couldn't be further from the truth.

Lifting others isn't about giving away your own success; it's about helping people realise their own potential. And often, the most impactful ways to do this don't require major sacrifices or dramatic actions.

Think about it:

- A simple conversation can give someone clarity on a problem they're struggling with.

- A word of encouragement at the right time can give someone the confidence to take a leap they were afraid to make.

- A genuine acknowledgment of someone's talent or hard work can be the validation they need to push forward.

None of these requires huge effort - just awareness and intention.

The best leaders, and the best people, understand that lifting others is not about losing yourself in the process. It's about creating an environment where everyone has the opportunity to succeed.

Because when the people around you grow, so do you.

✦ **Reflection Exercise:** Think about a time when someone lifted you up. Was it a grand gesture, or was it a small act that had a big impact?

📌 **Action Step:** Find one small way today to help someone realise their potential. It could be encouraging them, offering advice, or simply recognising their effort.

Lifting Others is a Path to Meaning

In *Man's Search for Meaning*, Viktor Frankl argued that meaning is not something we find, but rather it is something we create through how we respond to life's challenges.

His philosophy aligns with The Service Mindset in two critical ways:

1. **Acceptance** – We do not control everything in life, but we control how we respond.

2. **Lifting Others** – The surest way to find meaning is through service.

Frankl's First Lesson: Acceptance Over Resistance

One of the most liberating realisations in life is that we don't control everything, but we do control how we respond to what we cannot change.

Frankl was imprisoned in a concentration camp, stripped of everything: his family, his career, his freedom and yet he endured because he accepted that whilst he had no control over his suffering, he did have control over how he framed it.

Most of us will never face suffering on such an extreme scale, yet we often allow far smaller struggles to consume us.

- We resist reality, wishing things were different.

- We dwell on the unfairness of our circumstances.

- We let resentment and bitterness dictate our actions.

But acceptance is not surrender. It is acknowledging what is, so we can move forward productively.

📌 **Reflection Exercise:**

Think about a challenge you've faced in life. How much energy did you spend wishing it wasn't happening rather than accepting it and moving forward?

Frankl's Second Lesson: Meaning Through Service

Frankl argued that the deepest fulfilment comes not from focusing inward, but from turning outward toward others.

This is why *The Service Mindset* is not just a philosophy, it's a practice. It requires action.

When we stop fixating on our own struggles and turn our attention outward, we not only help others, we also heal ourselves.

A Decision That Defined My Leadership Philosophy

There was a point in my career when I was headhunted. Another company approached me and offered me more money, more seniority, and what seemed like an exciting new challenge.

At first, I was flattered. It's always validating to be noticed, to have your work recognised to the point that another company actively tries to recruit you.

But once the initial ego boost faded, I found myself in a state of uncertainty. I wasn't actively looking for a new job. I wasn't unhappy where I was. So what should I do?

Puzzled, I sent an email to my boss, not to negotiate, not to play companies against each other, but to be honest. I explained that I had received the approach, had been offered better terms, and genuinely didn't know what to do because this wasn't something I had solicited.

At the time, my boss was on holiday in a foreign country. Yet, despite being on vacation, he immediately scheduled a phone call with me.

He listened. He reassured me that I was valued.

That should have made my decision easy, but I was still unsure. Everyone says you should never accept a counter-offer, that it's a mistake, a sign that you should leave anyway. I put this to my boss, expecting him to say something about why I should stay.

Instead, he said something that I have never forgotten:

"If you are ever unsure of where to go or what to do, you should go to the place where you can do the most good."

That single sentence changed the way I think about leadership and career decisions. It reframed everything. It made me shift my focus away from salary, titles, or prestige, and towards service, impact, and meaning.

The more I thought about it, the more I realised that this wasn't just about where I could do the most good at work. It was about where I could serve best in my life.

The new role would have required extensive travel - constantly moving between different offices, long days on the road, and time away from home. I would have been serving my career, but I wouldn't have been serving my family.

And that was the real deciding factor.

It wasn't just about where I could lead a team or make a difference professionally - it was about who I wanted to be present for in my life.

On that advice, I rejected the advances of the other company and stayed where I was because there was meaningful work to be done, both at work and at home.

Because I framed that decision with service, I am able to look back on that episode without a shred of regret. I did what was right, I chose to serve in the most effective way.

Mentoring: How Lifting Others, Lifts Us

After my accident, I spent years feeling adrift, disconnected, and uncertain of my worth.

I was trapped in my own thoughts, dwelling on what I had lost rather than focusing on what I could still give.

Even after coming to the realisation that I had much left to offer, there have been times in recent years where I have felt insecure in my position and uncertain about the future. In one particular uncertain and unsettling moment, I started mentoring a colleague.

My colleague is very sharp and has a huge bright future ahead of them, but for whatever reason, they found herself at a point in their career where they were struggling. It's fair to say that in that moment, my colleague lacked confidence, felt lost in their career, and wasn't sure where to go next. I helped them to navigate challenges, build resilience, and see their own potential.

But something unexpected also happened: as I lifted them up, I started to rise too.

I realised that in helping others grow, we reaffirm our own value. Lifting others isn't just about them, it transforms us too.

📌 Challenge for the Reader:

If you are struggling to find meaning, start with service. It doesn't have to be life-changing; it can be small:

- Take time to mentor someone who could benefit from your guidance.
- Support a friend who is struggling.
- Do something for your community, no matter how small.

Frankl's Final Lesson: The True Path to Success

Frankl wrote:

"For success, like happiness, cannot be pursued; it must ensue."

We don't find happiness by chasing it.

We don't discover meaning by waiting for it to arrive.

Instead, we cultivate it through action, through acceptance, and through service.

The Service Mindset is a commitment to meaningful action.

The more we live by it, the more we realise that helping others is not just an act of kindness - it's the key to our own fulfilment.

📌 Reflection Exercise:

Think of a leader or mentor who lifted you up. What did they do differently? How did it impact you?

📌 Action Step:

Identify one person in your workplace or community whom you can actively support in their development this week.

A Tiny Flash of Light in the Darkness

In the grand history of the universe, 14 billion years of stars being born and dying, galaxies colliding, and entire worlds forming and vanishing, your life is infinitely small.

A tiny but brilliant flash of light in an infinite yearning void of darkness.

Your time here is fleeting: a moment, a breath, a heartbeat and then it's gone.

But within that small flicker of existence, you have a choice.

What will you do with the tiny moment you've been given?

You could chase power. You could hoard wealth. You could fight to be remembered in a world that will, eventually, forget you.

Or, you could spend that fleeting moment doing something that matters.

Something that lifts another person up.

Something that makes the short time you have, mean something beyond yourself.

A Second Chance - But What For?

I've often thought about why I survived my injuries when so many others have not.

The fall should have killed me. The doctors thought it would. The survival rate for injuries like mine is devastatingly low.

Yet, here I am – living, breathing, writing – albeit weirdly!

For a long time, the world would have me believe that I had been given a second chance - a chance to live differently, to be a better version of myself, to prove that my survival meant something.

But over time, I started to ask myself a different question.

What if the second chance I was given wasn't just about me?

What if it wasn't about becoming a better version of myself, but about helping others become better versions of themselves?

I don't believe in fate. I don't believe that my survival was for some great purpose, but I do believe in choice.

And if I waste the time I've been given by keeping that second chance to myself, then what was the point of surviving at all?

So, I choose to lift others.

I choose to serve.

I choose to use whatever time I have left to make others stronger, braver, and more fulfilled. I wrote this book, not for profit or glory, but to help.

Not because I was meant to, and definitely not because I think I am special, but because I can.

And if I can, why wouldn't I?

The Moment You Choose Who You Are

If you embrace the Service Mindset, then one day, someone will think back on the moment you changed their life.

It may not be a moment you even remember.

It may have been a single conversation, a small act of encouragement, a simple act of belief in them when no one else saw their potential, but to them, it will have meant everything.
It was the moment they found the courage to take the leap.

The moment they stopped believing they were alone.

The moment they realised they mattered, and you… you will have been the reason why.

That's what it means to lift others.

That's what it means to live in service.

And when it's all said and done, that's what counts.

The Service Mindset: Choosing Others Over Ourselves

To embrace The Service Mindset is to make this choice to place others before ourselves, again and again, not because it is easy, but because it is right.

It is a commitment to the idea that true success is not measured by what we accumulate, but by what we contribute.

It is the understanding that in a universe where we are given so little time, the greatest thing we can do is to use that time to lift someone else.

Not out of obligation. Not for recognition - but because this is who we choose to be.

In the context of an infinite universe, the decision to help others is more than just noble; it is a declaration of the kind of person you really are.

📌 **Reflection Exercise:**

If you knew your time was running out, what act of service would you want to be remembered for?

📌 **Action Step:**

Choose one small action today that will make someone else's journey easier, brighter, or better.

Closing Thoughts: Why This Matters

Lifting others is not just about mentorship or leadership.

It is a way of living.

It is a daily commitment to making the world around you better: one conversation, one action, one act of kindness at a time.

And the best part?

When you lift others, you lift yourself.

By embracing The Service Mindset, we reject fear, competition, and insecurity and instead, we lead with confidence, generosity, and purpose.

📌 **Final Thought:**

Your legacy won't be measured by the titles you held or the wealth you accumulated. It will be measured by the people you lifted up along the way.

TENET 7. Act with Integrity – Do What's Right, Not What's Easy

What Integrity Really Means

It might not surprise you, given that I've spent much of my career fighting fraud, that integrity sits at the very core of The Service Mindset.

It is arguably the single most important principle in this book.

Integrity isn't about looking good. It's not about being seen to be righteous, or about claiming some moral high ground. It isn't something you declare. It's something you live.

It's there in the quiet moments when no one's watching, when there's no applause waiting, when the easiest path is the one that betrays your principles just a little bit. Integrity is about what you do in those moments. Not what you say, not what you think, but what you **do**.

It's tested when the truth is inconvenient, when honesty might cost you something, or when you could get away with doing the wrong thing and nobody would know. That's where character is forged. That's when the kind of person you really are becomes clear.

And here's the uncomfortable truth: there are hundreds of moments like this in your career and your life - maybe as often as every week. Examples include:

- A shortcut you know you could get away with.

- A tough conversation you choose to avoid.

- A compromise you make to stay popular, or profitable, or safe.

Each one on its own might seem minor, but they add up. In this way, integrity is built, or broken, in the thousand small choices we make when no one's keeping score.

So why does this matter?

Because integrity is not just a moral ideal - it's the foundation of trust, and trust is the only currency that holds its value over time.

When people believe in your integrity, they believe in your judgement. They listen when you speak. They trust you with responsibility. They lean on you in difficult moments. But the opposite is also true: when integrity slips, trust collapses - and when trust is gone, everything else becomes harder.

So ask yourself - not once, but often:

What kind of person do I want to be when nobody's watching?
Am I making decisions I'd be proud of if they were played back on camera?
Do my actions match my values, even when it's inconvenient?

The Day I Walked Away

In the early years of my career, I worked in the legal profession, helping injured people get access to support and compensation. Many of the clients I worked with had been through traumatic events: car crashes, workplace injuries, serious accidents that had left them unable to work and unsure how they would get through the next month, let alone the rest of their lives.

Because I'd lived through my own trauma, I carried a quiet empathy into the role. I knew what it felt like to be disoriented, afraid, and unsure of your future. So, the work felt meaningful. I wasn't chasing money or prestige, I was trying to help people find their feet again.

However, over time, The legal profession I'd entered gradually morphed into something else. The pursuit of justice was replaced with sales targets. Scripts replaced empathy.

Call centres replaced qualified professionals. The work became transactional. Mechanical. The injured were no longer people with stories - they were leads. Metrics. Opportunities to close.

I tried to ignore the changing dynamic. I told myself I was still doing good, still helping - but ultimately I stayed too long in a role that was slowly losing meaning.

Then one day, I reached a line I could not cross.

The auto-dialler connected me with a woman. As usual, I followed the standard script:

"Our records show you may have been involved in a road traffic accident. You might be entitled to compensation..."

There was a pause on the other end of the line. Then her voice broke.

She explained that it wasn't her, it was her son. He had been in an accident. He hadn't survived.

She had been receiving call after call like mine. Cold, scripted, relentless. Each one forcing her to relive the worst day of her life.

And now here I was, just another stranger prodding at a wound she just wanted to heal.

She cried down the phone. I didn't speak. I just listened. And then I said, softly:

"I'm so sorry. I'll make sure your details are removed from our systems. You won't be contacted again."

I ended the call.

Moments later, the sales director arrived at my desk. She'd been listening in.

"What are you doing?" she asked.

"Get her back on the phone and close the deal."

I looked her in the eye and replied, calm and clear:

"I'm not going to do that."

"It's your job."

"Then maybe I don't want to do this job anymore."

I took off my headset, stood up, and walked out. I never went back.

There was no applause. No grand speech. Just a quiet refusal to do something that felt wrong. A decision, made in real time, to walk away from a job that had stopped aligning with my values.

That moment has stayed with me because it was just so ordinary. It didn't feel heroic. It just felt necessary.

That's the truth about integrity: it rarely announces itself. It doesn't arrive with fanfare. It's usually quiet. Inconvenient. Costly.

And that's exactly why it matters.

Integrity vs. the Easy Option

When I walked out of that job, I didn't have a plan. No safety net. No idea what I'd do next. I just knew I couldn't stay in a place that asked me to silence my conscience.

And the truth is, I nearly didn't walk at all.

It would have been so easy to stay. To shrug it off. To tell myself I was just doing my job, that I needed the money, that someone else would have made the call if I hadn't. Those thoughts were all there. I could feel them - ready to offer comfort, justification, an excuse.

That's what the easy option looks like. It doesn't announce itself as wrong. It whispers. It reasons. It gives you an out.

But I knew, if I stayed, I'd be taking the first step down a path I didn't want to follow. I wouldn't just be giving up a job, I'd be giving up something internal. A sense of who I was. And once that's gone, it's very hard to get back.

That moment taught me something simple but essential: integrity isn't tested when things are easy. It's tested when doing the right thing comes with a personal cost.

And here's the catch: most of those tests don't arrive as big dramatic showdowns – they sneak in unannounced:

A chance to take credit for something that wasn't yours.
A moment where you could stay silent and let something wrong slide by.
An invitation to soften the truth because it's more convenient that way.

They don't feel like betrayals - not at first - but they accumulate - and every time you choose the easy path, the voice in your head that knows better, gets quieter.

This is the very real cost of training yourself to ignore your values – when you are lost and don't know which way to turn, that voice in your head, and in your heart, that you have been ignoring, isn't there anymore.

What makes integrity hard is that it rarely rewards you straight away. You don't often get a pay rise for being honest. You don't get a round of applause for walking away. Sometimes, you don't get anything but the quiet knowledge that you did the right thing.

But I guess, if nothing else, that knowledge is the foundation of self-respect.

It's what lets you look in the mirror without flinching and over time, it becomes the bedrock of credibility - the one thing people can't fake and the one thing others can feel.

When your integrity has secured others' trust in you, you don't need to convince people or shout in some performative way. When other's trust your integrity, you just need to speak.

The Currency of Credibility

When people talk about leadership, they often focus on intelligence, experience, or strategic thinking, but none of those things matter if people don't believe you or your ability to deliver.

Credibility is what turns a good idea into a plan others will follow. It's what allows you to lead change, manage risk, and carry people with you through uncertainty. The strange thing about credibility is that it doesn't come from being clever, it comes from being consistent.

I learnt this early on.

At one point in my career, I had to deliver a message that nobody wanted to hear. We were about to see a spike in our numbers - not because performance was slipping, but because we were clearing a backlog of long-outstanding cases. It was the right thing to do, and it would make our long-term performance stronger, but in the short term, the data would look worse.

It was tempting to bury the story and to fudge the messaging in order to soften the blow.

Instead, I took the honest route. I told the business what was coming. I explained why it was happening, and how we'd emerge from it stronger. I said the numbers would worsen before they improved, and I gave a timeframe for when we'd see results.

And then I delivered on that plan.

The reaction was telling. At first, there was pushback, but as things unfolded exactly as I'd outlined, people changed in their demeanour towards me. People started to trust that when I said something would happen, it would.

There's a simple framework I still use to this day:

1. Tell people what's going to happen.
2. Make it happen.
3. Do it consistently.

People often overpromise to please others, or spin the truth to avoid short-term discomfort, but every time you do that; you spend a little credibility and it's a currency that's slow to earn and fast to lose – and when it's gone, it's hard to get back.

That's why I have always told the teams that I have worked with this:

If you want people to trust you:

- Be honest in your messaging - even if it's uncomfortable.

- Be clear in your intentions – don't let there be any room for doubt.

- Deliver with precision. No excuses. Just results.

In the end, credibility isn't about impressing people. It's about giving them a reason to believe in you and a track record to back up what you assert.

The Slippery Slope of Justification

I've spent much of my professional life studying fraud, and one of the patterns I see again and again is that very few people who are caught committing fraud think of themselves as dishonest. They don't see themselves as criminals. They don't even think they've done anything particularly wrong.

Instead, they explain it away:

- "I'm just borrowing the money. I'll pay it back later."
- "The company underpays me anyway."
- "No one's getting hurt."
- "It's not fraud – just bending the rules a bit, playing the game"

Criminologist Donald Cressey examined this behaviour in devising what he called *The Fraud Triangle*: a theory that explains the three forces that must be present for most people to commit fraud:

1. **Pressure** – Often financial or personal stress. A sense of desperation.
2. **Opportunity** – A weakness in the system. A loophole. A gap.
3. **Rationalisation** – The mental gymnastics that make the behaviour feel okay.

So, rationalisation is a key ingredient when it comes to committing fraud, but it's not just criminals who do this.

We can all do it in smaller ways:

- We hide a mistake and say, *"It's not worth flagging."*
- We tell a half-truth and say, *"It's for the greater good."*
- We justify a decision that benefits us and say, *"Everyone else would've done the same."*

These aren't massive betrayals but they do quietly erode our integrity.

That's how integrity begins to break down and once you start to make peace with a little dishonesty, the next time gets easier. Then easier still. Until, eventually, you no longer recognise the person you've become.

Which is why *self-awareness* is one of the most important tools for preserving integrity.

You have to be willing to stop yourself and to ask:

- *Would I be comfortable explaining this decision to someone I deeply respect?*
- *Am I doing this because it's right, or because it's convenient?*
- *Am I spinning a story - to others or to myself - to justify something I know doesn't feel quite right?*

We should ask ourselves these questions, not to try and make ourselves perfect, but minded to catching the justifications we might be making to ourselves *before* they start to shape our behaviour.

Integrity and Service Are Not Submission

One challenge that people could raise about The Service Mindset is this:

"If we're supposed to serve others, does that mean we have to tolerate everyone - even those who treat us badly?"

Absolutely not.

Service is not the same as submission.

It's not weakness, it's not silence, and it's certainly not obedience.

You don't serve someone by enabling their poor behaviour. You don't serve someone by abandoning your own values to appease them - and you definitely don't serve someone by shrinking yourself so they can feel taller.

Sometimes, the most powerful act of service is saying *no*. Drawing a line. Refusing to comply with something that isn't right.

I've worked with people who assumed that kindness meant pliability. That if you were respectful, you must also be passive. That if you showed humility, you must be willing to roll over.

They were mistaken.

True service is grounded in strength, not submission.

The Service Mindset doesn't ask you to shrink yourself to keep others happy. It asks you to stand firmly in your values, to act with quiet strength, and to know when to say, *"No, that's not acceptable."*

So how do we live this in practice?

By staying true to your values.

That means:

- **You can be clear without being cruel.**

- **You can be firm without being aggressive.**

- **You can walk away from toxic dynamics without guilt.**

When someone treats you with disrespect, tries to manipulate you, or demands something that compromises your ethics, the right response isn't to placate them - it's to hold your ground.

Not in anger, not in defensiveness, but with calm, rooted certainty.

Service doesn't require self-erasure. It requires discernment. The ability to see clearly what someone really needs, and sometimes, what they need is accountability.

If a colleague is behaving unethically, you do not serve them by protecting them.

If a client is abusive, you do not serve them by tolerating their abuse.

If a boss is asking you to compromise your values, you do not serve them by complying.

You serve them by holding a mirror up, by being the one person who tells the truth, who refuses to play along, who demonstrates that decency still matters.

In the end, The Service Mindset is not about always saying *yes*. It's about saying *yes* to the right things… and *no* to the wrong ones.

Aligning with the Right People and Environments

Integrity doesn't live in isolation. It's shaped, tested, and either supported or eroded by the people and systems around us.

You can have the clearest values in the world, but if you're in an environment that routinely asks you to compromise them, you'll either walk away or be worn down.

That's why **who** you choose to work with, and **where** you choose to spend your energy, matters as much as any single decision you make.

You don't need to be perfect, but ultimately you will serve the best when you are surrounded by people who value your honesty and respect your authentic self. These people won't pressure you into grey areas and wouldn't rather you say something convenient over the truth.

The reality is, some environments reward manipulation. Some leaders quietly reward those who cut corners but hit targets. Some companies say all the right things about values and culture, but act very differently under pressure.

In places like that, doing the right thing will always feel harder because you'll be the exception, not the rule.

The opposite is true of environments that value integrity. Doing the right thing is the norm and you don't have to explain why honesty matters because it's a given.

The same applies to your colleagues, your partners, your friends. You become like the people you spend time with. So, if you want to preserve your integrity, start by protecting your environment.

Ask yourself:

- *Do the companies you work for truly align with your principles?*
- *Do the people around you lift your standards or drag them down?*
- *Are you part of a culture that supports clarity, fairness, and honesty, or one that rewards outcomes at any cost?*

This doesn't mean only working with people who think exactly like you, but it does mean finding common ground on the fundamentals - on what matters when no one's watching.

Personal Story – Failing on Your Own Terms

There was a point in my career when I interviewed for a high-profile role at a company.

The kind of position that looks great on a CV: bigger title, more responsibility, more visibility.

I took it seriously. I did my research, studied their values, and read through their leadership frameworks. I wanted to show that I was what they were looking for.

One line stood out in their material: *"We only hire the best people."*

It sounded good on paper, but instead of reading it as a call to integrity or character, I interpreted it as a challenge to impress - and that's where I went wrong.

In the interview, I wasn't myself. I presented what I thought they wanted to see; confident, polished, assertive. I packaged up the version of me that ticked all the right boxes. The problem was, it wasn't real.

When the feedback came in, it was pretty hard to take. They told me I'd come across as arrogant. Not authentic. Not a cultural fit.

It stung obviously - not just because I didn't get the job, but because I knew they hadn't rejected *me* - they'd rejected the version of me that I had manufactured for the interview.

I hadn't failed by being true to myself. I'd failed by pretending to be someone else.

That taught me something that's stayed with me ever since: success that's built on inauthenticity is fragile, and failure that comes while pretending is the worst kind of loss.

At least when you fail whilst being true to yourself, you're still whole… intact. You can learn from it. Build on it. Try again without compromising who you are.

But when you fail as someone you're not? You lose twice. You lose the opportunity, and you lose a little piece of yourself in the process.

The irony is, had I simply brought my real self to the table - flaws and all - I might have had a better shot. People can smell when you're performing. They respond to sincerity, even if it's imperfect.

That's the choice integrity gives you: the freedom to fail with your self-respect intact. The ability to walk away from a rejection knowing that you didn't bend yourself out of shape to try and win approval.

Because real credibility, the kind that lasts, isn't built on playing a part. It's built on being honest about who you are.

Integrity in a Disruptive World

We're living in an age where truth itself feels under siege.

Deepfakes, manipulated media, AI-generated misinformation, it's becoming harder and harder to know what's real. Leaders bend reality to suit their agendas. Companies spin stories to protect profits. Social media rewards those who perform, not those who are honest.

In that kind of world, integrity can feel like an outdated virtue. Something slow. Something naive.

You see people cutting corners and being rewarded for it, and it's tempting to follow suit.

But when everything around us is noisy and uncertain, integrity becomes more important, not less.

That's because when the world becomes louder and more chaotic, the people who stay grounded in truth become anchors for others. Their clarity cuts through the fog of nonsense – the AI slop!

If people know your word means something - if they know you'll do what you say, not just when it's easy, but when it's hard - they'll seek you out.

Ultimately, people who build their lives on what's real are the only ones who are building something capable of endurance and are the only ones with any hope of a legacy that outlives them.

Final Reflection – Integrity as a Way of Living

Returning to the job that I walked away from and that poor woman who had lost her son – I guess she had no way of ever knowing that her story ended my career in that law firm. She never knew that, through her grief, she reminded me who I was, and who I refused to become.

That's what integrity often looks like. Quiet. Unannounced. It doesn't need a spotlight. It just needs a line you won't cross and the strength to walk away when that line is tested.

In a world where so much is curated for applause, the person who stays rooted in their values becomes something rare.

You'll still make mistakes. You'll still face doubt and pressure and moments where doing the right thing feels like the harder road, but you'll know, deep down, that you're not building your life on shifting sands.

And that knowledge - that quiet, grounded confidence - is worth more than any promotion, praise, or perception of success.

You'll sleep better. You'll lead better. You'll serve better - because when people know they can trust you, they stop needing to second-guess your intentions. In a world of fakes, masks and post-truth messaging – that authenticity is a gift.

Integrity is not a badge you wear. It's a decision you make, over and over again - especially when it's inconvenient.

So remember to ask yourself, not just once, but often:

- *Am I doing the right thing, or just the easiest thing?*
- *Would I be proud to explain this decision to someone I love?*
- *Am I becoming the kind of person others can rely on?*

The Service Mindset begins and ends with trust - and trust begins and ends with integrity.

📌 Reflection & Action

- **Reflection:** Think back to a time you compromised a value. What was the cost? And what would it have looked like to act with integrity instead?

- **Reflection:** Who in your life do you trust completely? What do they do that earns that trust?

- **Action Step:** Write down your five core values. Keep them visible for a week. When a decision arises, big or small, check your actions against them.

- **Action Step:** Notice the small justifications/rationalisations that creep into your day. Challenge them. Choose clarity over comfort.

TENET 8: Let Go of Perfection – The Power of Imperfection in Service

For as long as I can remember, I have been chasing *best*.

I was raised with the idea that I should always try my best. Somewhere along the way, that idea was warped, twisted into something it was never meant to be. "Best" stopped meaning *effort* and started meaning *flawlessness*. If something wasn't the best, then perhaps it wasn't worth doing at all.

I don't know exactly when that shift happened in my mind. Maybe it was in school, where I learnt that second place wasn't as celebrated as first. Maybe it was in my career, where mistakes could be costly and expectations were always high. Or, maybe it was just something that took root in my own mind, growing unchecked and unabated.

What I do know is that in a pretty unhealthy way, perfection became my measuring stick.

It became the thing I waited for, planned for, and convinced myself I needed before moving forward – and, like all impossible standards, it held me back.

The Illusion of the Perfect Moment

If there is one moment in my life that I could describe as perfect, it was the moment Erin was born.

I will never forget the way she looked at me, the way her tiny fingers wrapped around mine.

That moment is indelibly etched into my mind, something that will stay with me for as long as I live.

And yet, if Jane and I had waited for the *perfect* moment to have a child, we would still be waiting.

At the time, my employment was unstable. My earnings were poor. We had yet to find our place in the world and we were surrounded by uncertainty.

When I think back to that moment - when I held my daughter for the first time - not a single one of those imperfections mattered.

Had we waited for perfection, I would have missed out on the most perfect moment of my life.

For me, most of the time, perfection arises from imperfect moments.

The Paralysis of Perfectionism

We often think of perfectionism as something admirable: high standards, commitments to excellence. However, if we are not careful, our pursuit of perfection can hold us back.

This is because there is often a fallacy in our notion of perfection - that if something is perfect, it is immune from failure, from criticism and from disappointment. It is the idea that if we can just get everything right, everything else will fall into place.

Perfectionism is often not a pursuit of greatness, but rather a fear of getting things wrong.

For years, I held myself back from taking action, from finishing, from sharing things with the world because they weren't *ready yet*. They weren't *right yet*. And, if they weren't perfect, what was the point?

Perfectionism does not make us better.

It makes us *slower*, it makes our output *smaller* and sometimes, it makes us miss the moments that matter.

The Trip That Was Supposed to Be Perfect

Years ago, before we had any suspicion that Erin might be autistic, I saved up for what I thought would be the perfect family holiday.

I wanted to give her an *unforgettable* experience, something magical, something *big*. I took her to Florida: theme parks, fireworks, music, all the things a child is *supposed* to love.

From the moment we arrived, it was clear that this wasn't the dream I had imagined.

The crowds, the noise, the extreme heat, the constant changes in routine, she found it overwhelming. Where I had pictured excitement, I saw exhaustion. Where I had expected joy, I saw stress. She didn't love it, and that was hard to accept.

A year later, we took a much smaller trip. A long weekend in Hastings.

I had built it up in my head as something unimpressive. Hastings was a town I had loved as a child, but - like many coastal towns - it had become run-down and tired. I lowered my expectations. It wasn't Florida, after all.

When we got there, something strange happened. We explored the smugglers' caves, wandered through the aquarium, and sat on the beach eating absurd amounts of ice cream.

There were no fireworks. No giant parades. No characters in costumes - but Erin loved it. She still talks about that holiday to this day.

And that was when I realised something…

The Beauty of Imperfect Moments

Some of the most powerful moments of my life have come from times of uncertainty, chaos, and even fear.

I remember the great storm of 1987. It was terrifying… the wind howling, trees crashing to the ground, the power flickering out.

However, what I remember most vividly is not the storm itself.

I remember being huddled under blankets with my parents, eating sweets by candlelight, feeling warm and safe despite the chaos outside. It is one of my fondest childhood memories.

Years later, something similar happened.

My family was staying in a gîte on a French farm when one of the worst storms in over a hundred years swept through the region.

The gîte flooded, the roof was ripped apart, and in the morning, the farm was devastated.

The following morning our family came together with the farmer's family, helping collect scattered roof tiles, salvaging what we could. That evening, the farmer invited us to his home for dinner.

We sat at their farmhouse table, drinking wine, breaking bread, and sharing stories – in spite of the language barrier. With my GCSE French, I played translator, helping us to connect despite our differences.

It is important to remember that often, close to perfect moments arise in the most imperfect of circumstances.

Moreover and in my experience, perfection is only ever recognised in hindsight.

It is not in the places we expect, nor in the moments we plan.

It is only when we look back that we realise: *That was perfect. Just not in the way I thought it would be.*

Why Perfection is the Enemy of Service

This is where The Service Mindset comes in.

If I had spent my time chasing a *perfect* holiday, I would have missed the actual perfect moments. And if we spend our time chasing: *perfect work, perfect ideas, perfect timing*, we risk missing the *actual moments that matter*.

How often do we wait until something is fully polished before we share it?

How many times have we delayed taking action because the plan wasn't quite there yet?

Who have we *not helped* because we were waiting for a perfect version of ourselves to arrive?

Perfectionism is not about making something better. It is about delaying action in the hope that fear will disappear.

The Power of Progress Over Perfection

If perfection is an illusion, then progression is the only thing that's real.

I spent years believing that success was a fixed destination, that I had to reach a certain level of competence, achievement, or recognition before I could feel like I had *arrived*.

However, success isn't something you reach, check off a list, and then hold onto forever. It is something that unfolds in increments, in slow and steady progress, in one step after another.

The most meaningful progress happens when we set realistic goals and allow ourselves to improve consistently instead of constantly measuring ourselves against an impossible ideal.

This is something I've had to learn in my own life.

There were times I set expectations so high that the reality could never measure up. So, I had to train myself to let go of those expectations and when I allowed myself to find joy in progress rather than chasing perfection - I started to appreciate things as they were, rather than as I thought they *should* be.

This was especially true in the aftermath of my brain injury. I made the mistake of seeing being *perfectly fixed* as my ultimate destination, when – in truth – I would have been best served by focusing on the progress I was making rather than getting frustrated by the reality that my brain was not perfect.

In this way, there are times when we can all become so fixated on a rigid vision of success that we miss out on the joy in what is actually happening.

I've also found that some of the best moments in life have not come from things going exactly as I planned.

They have come from surprises. From adapting. From seeing value in the unexpected.

They have come from moments like sitting in a run-down seaside town eating ice cream, from making a home in the middle of a storm, from letting go of what *should have been* and embracing what *was*.

So, if you're waiting for perfection, waiting for *the* moment where everything finally feels flawless - stop waiting!

Set a goal and make progress!

And if things don't turn out exactly as planned? Look for the joy in what happened instead.

Done is Better Than Perfect

There is something in your life right now that you are holding back on. Maybe it's a project you haven't finished, a conversation you've been overthinking, a decision you've been postponing.

If you are anything like me, it might be a book that you always thought you could write, if you only had the right words.

Ask yourself:

What's stopping you?

If the answer is *because it's not quite perfect yet*, then ask a different question:

What impact could it have if I just did it anyway?

The truth is, the world has never been changed by perfection.

It has only ever been changed by people who did something, even when they didn't feel ready.

If you wait for the perfect moment, you will wait forever.

If you wait for the perfect conditions, you will never begin.

And if you wait until you feel ready, you will never move.

The truth is, the world is changed by imperfect people taking imperfect action.
And I promise you, none of them did it perfectly.

Ambition vs. Purpose

Ambition is often seen as a virtue. From an early age, we're told to aim high, push forward, stay hungry. In many ways, ambition can be useful - it gives us direction, keeps us moving, fuels a desire to improve.

But at its root, ambition is often about one of two things:

1. The need for validation - to be seen, praised, recognised.

2. The need for superiority - to be better than others, to win.

Neither of those things align with The Service Mindset.

When I was younger, I was ambitious. Not just driven - my upbringing turbocharged me to succeed. I wanted to move fast. Progress quickly. Get ahead. In my early career, I was the kind of person who always had their foot on the accelerator. What I didn't realise at the time, however, is that speed comes at a cost.

When you move too fast, you miss things.

You miss the warning signs. You miss the subtleties. You stop responding thoughtfully and start reacting instinctively - always chasing the next thing, never really seeing where you are.

It's no different from when you are driving. When you're flying down the road, everything blurs. Your reactions shorten. Your field of vision narrows. You don't see the full picture, just what's directly ahead, in the moment, and that can often lead to bad decisions being made.

That was me: always in motion, but rarely moving with intention.

It took years - and a few hard lessons - to realise that the people who make the best decisions aren't the ones going the fastest. They're the ones who slow down long enough to see things unfolding. The ones who act with clarity, not urgency.

That's where purpose comes in.

Where ambition is about chasing success for yourself, purpose is about serving something bigger than yourself.

When you trade ambition for purpose, you stop needing to prove yourself. You start asking different questions: not *"How can I get ahead?"* but *"What's the right thing to do here?"* Not *"How can I win?"* but *"How can I help?"*

The Service Mindset doesn't ask you to stop progressing. It asks you to progress with direction. To go after meaningful goals, not just impressive ones. To stop measuring your life in trophies and victories and to measure it instead in terms of your contribution.

The world tells us that ambition is everything, but there is a reason they call it *blind ambition* – and that's because of its potential to rob us of clarity.

Perfectionism doesn't just hold us back - it can hold others at arm's length, too. When we delay helping because our offer isn't polished, or when we expect others to get everything right before they're worthy of our time or trust, we lose something vital. We miss the chance to connect in the messy middle - the real, human space where people grow, stumble, learn, and try again. That's where service lives. Not in flawlessness, but in the willingness to step in anyway.

And in a strange way, this is one of the big risks of the coming AI wave. There is a danger that we end up living in a world that's trying so hard to be perfect – a world where every email is rewritten by AI and everything is done perfectly at the first time of asking – that we lose sight of the fact that it is often in the messy middle space, where our human imperfections come together, that we find happiness.

Final Reflection – Presence Over Perfection

If there's one thing I've learnt through all of this, it's that service has never been about getting everything right.

It's not about crafting the perfect moment, saying the perfect words, or waiting to become some ideal version of yourself before you step in.

It's about being there: fully, honestly, without trying to impress.

I think back to that storm in France. The broken roof. The wrecked gîte. The laughter over bread and wine with people we could barely speak to. It wasn't perfect, but we were there together - and that made it matter.

I think of Hastings - a tired seaside town, a few fish in an aquarium, a bit of sun, and far too much ice cream. No fireworks. No big moments. Just me and my daughter, side by side, making a memory neither of us knew would last.

The truth is, the people we remember aren't the ones who had it all figured out. They're the ones who were there when it counted. Who gave what they could, even when the best laid plans had gone sideways.

In the end, service doesn't require you to be perfect, it just asks you to be present.

Not polished. Not impressive.

Just there.

And that's what turns ordinary people into unforgettable people.

📌 Reflection Exercise:

Think of a time when something didn't go to plan - a holiday, a conversation, a project - but ended up being meaningful in ways you didn't expect.

- *What surprised you?*
- *What stayed with you?*
- *Would it have been better if everything had gone 'perfectly'?*

📌 Reflection Exercise:

What's one area of your life where perfectionism might be holding you back - from finishing, sharing, or helping?

- *What are you waiting for?*
- *What would "good enough" look like instead?*

📌 Action Step:

Take one small step this week on something you've been delaying because it's not quite ready.

- *Send the message.*
- *Share the idea.*
- *Start the thing.*

Not because it's perfect, but because it matters.

📌 Action Step:

Practise presence.

- Set aside ten minutes in your day to simply *be where you are* - no distractions, no multitasking, no self-critique.

- Whether you're with family, colleagues, or just on your own - let that be enough.

TENET 9: Drive Your Own Car

The Near-Accident

You might remember the story I shared earlier - the moment I narrowly avoided a car accident. At the time, I used it to talk about emotional regulation, about how quickly we can lose control of ourselves when something jolts us into a strong emotional response.

There was something else I took from that moment - something that stayed with me, quietly shaping the way I think about roles, responsibility, and the strange things we carry that aren't ours to hold.

After the initial shock of the near miss wore off, I found myself thinking about what had actually happened - not just externally, but internally. And I asked myself a simple question:

What was *my* job in that situation?

My role was to drive my car safely from A to B. To follow the rules of the road. To protect my passengers. That was it. That was my task.

But that wasn't how I had responded. My mind had leapt straight into outrage, indignation, judgement. I wanted to teach the other driver a lesson. I wanted to correct them. I wanted to make them realise how careless they'd been.

In short, I wanted to drive their car.

That's when the realisation hit me.

It wasn't my task to teach them how to drive. It wasn't my responsibility to correct their behaviour. That was their task, not mine. The moment I tried to take it on, I made myself angry, distracted, and ineffective. Worse still, I lost sight of the one thing I *was* actually responsible for: my own driving.

That moment taught me something I've returned to again and again: there's great power in understanding what is, and isn't, your task. When you let go of what doesn't belong to you, you become focused, clear and effective in relation to what does.

You stay in your lane - literally and figuratively.

The Adlerian Principle – Tasks and Roles

Alfred Adler believed that almost every problem in life is, at its core, a problem of human relationships. And at the heart of many of those problems is a simple misunderstanding: *we forget which tasks are ours and which belong to other people.*

Adler called this *the separation of tasks*. It sounds obvious, but it's deceptively hard to live by.

Your task is what you can control and in reality there are only two things that you can control: what you think and what you do.

Your thoughts and your actions - that's it.

Everything else, however much it affects you, is someone else's responsibility: their beliefs, their reactions, their mistakes – all their tasks.

When we forget this distinction, things go wrong. We overstep. We interfere. We exhaust ourselves trying to manage things that were never ours to manage. Typically, it's not because we're selfish or controlling. It's because we care. We want to help. We want things to go well. But that's the danger - the moment we start carrying someone else's task, we not only disrespect their autonomy, we risk losing our own.

Adler's principle isn't a call to indifference, it's a call to clarity. It asks us to serve others without taking over their lives. To be responsible without becoming controlling. To care, without crossing the line into control.

The moment you truly understand this, something clicks. You realise how much energy you've been wasting trying to drive cars that were never yours. You also begin to ask a more helpful question:

What responsibilities are actually mine to carry?

The Cost of Driving Someone Else's Car

The moment you take on someone else's task; whether it's out of frustration, compassion, or sheer habit, you set off a chain reaction.

It starts with a sense of superiority. Even if you don't mean it that way, the message is clear: *I know better than you do.* Whether you're stepping in to fix something, solve a problem, or offer unsolicited advice, you're making a silent judgement about the other person's capability.

Then comes frustration. You wonder why they aren't listening. Why they won't change. Why you're putting in all the effort while they seem to drift along, unaffected. You start carrying the weight of their choices, even though they never asked you to.

And over time, it wears you down. You become resentful. Tired. Burnt out. You might even begin to withdraw - not just from the person, but from the relationship itself. What started as a desire to help becomes a source of tension and fatigue.

I've seen this play out in families, friendships, and teams. A parent who can't let go of their child's decisions. A leader who micromanages every step. A friend who offers constant advice, even when none is asked for. The pattern is always the same: the more you try to take control, the more resistance you create and the more disconnected you feel.

It's easy to justify this kind of overreach. You tell yourself you're helping. That you're stepping in for the right reasons, but good intentions don't cancel out the cost. Often, the most respectful thing you can do - the most *useful* thing - is to stop interfering, and start trusting.

The Paradox of Service

At first glance, this might feel like a contradiction. If we're supposed to live in service of others - if we care about helping, supporting, making a difference - how can we justify stepping back?

It all comes down to what we mean by service.

The Service Mindset isn't about taking over. It's not about making decisions for people or solving their problems before they've had the chance to face them. That might feel useful, even generous, but it often sends the wrong message: *I don't trust you to manage this on your own.*

The truth is: that's not service, it's control.

The most effective service respects the other person's autonomy. It allows them to struggle, to make mistakes, to learn by doing. It means being present, not overpowering. It's the quiet confidence of someone who stands nearby - not to interfere, but to be there if needed.

This kind of service is harder. It asks you to resist the urge to fix. It asks you to trust someone else's journey, even when it's uncomfortable to watch. It's also a more powerful kind of service, because it doesn't diminish the person you're trying to help. It honours their role. It lets them drive their own car.

When you serve in that way - without ego and without overreach - what you offer becomes more valuable.

The Mental Freedom of Letting Go

One of the most liberating things you can realise in life is this: *you don't have to carry everything*.

So much of our mental weight comes not from what we're doing, but from what we're trying to control: other people's decisions, their opinions of us, things that haven't happened yet, things that might never happen at all - we carry it all like it's ours and it wears us down.

Once you start separating the tasks - *what's mine, and what isn't* - things get quieter. Clearer. You begin to notice how often your anxiety is tied to something you were never meant to control in the first place.

In my career, I've spent more time than I'd like to admit worrying about job security. Playing out every worst-case scenario in my head. *What if there's a restructure? What if I've misread the room? What if, what if, what if...*

The moment I come back to this tenet, it cuts through all of that noise. *What is my task here?*

My task is to do good work. To act with integrity. To make myself useful and dependable.

My task is not to decide whether I keep my job - that's someone else's responsibility. And when I remind myself of that, I stop agonising. I let go of the outcome because I've already handled my part. The rest isn't mine to carry.

This way of thinking doesn't make you selfish - it keeps you sane. It keeps you focused on the bit of the world you can actually influence, instead of getting lost in everything you can't. When your mind stops trying to drive other peoples' cars, it finally gets a chance to rest.

Reflection & Action Steps – Taking Control by Letting Go

This isn't just a mindset - it's something you can apply. So here's a way to begin:

Step 1: Identify What's Actually Yours?

Think about a situation that's been causing you stress lately. Something at work, at home, or just in your own head. Now, remembering that you can only control your thoughts and actions, ask yourself:

- *What part of this is my task?*
- *What part belongs to someone else?*
- *Where might I be taking on responsibility that isn't mine?*

Write it down. There's something about seeing it on paper that makes it easier to let go of.

Step 2: Let Go of What Isn't Yours

Once you've named what doesn't belong to you, practise stepping back. Try these prompts:

- *Is this actually my problem to solve?*
- *If not, why am I carrying it?*
- *What would happen if I just did my part and let the rest unfold?*

This isn't about detachment, it's about trust. Trust that people learn through their own experience. Trust that outcomes will happen with or without your interference. Trust that doing your task is enough.

Step 3: Apply the Principle

A few real-world examples:

- **Work:** *You can do your job well, but you can't control how it's received.*
- **Family:** *You can offer support, but you can't stop someone making their own choices.*
- **Uncertainty:** *You can plan and prepare, but you can't force things to turn out the way you want them to.*

In each case, your job is the same: do your bit. Let go of the rest.

Final Thought – You're Not the Driver

It took me years to learn the lesson this tenet is really about. Like many of the things in this book, it started with navigating my brain injury.

In the months and years that followed my accident, I became obsessed with the idea of death. Not in a morbid way - at least not at first - but in a desperate, anxious, unrelenting way. I thought about it constantly. I imagined it around corners, behind phone calls, folded into every small sensation in my body. I believed, somewhere deep down, that if I could just stay aware of it, if I could keep it in sight, I might somehow keep it at bay.

What I was really doing was trying to control the uncontrollable. I was trying to drive a car that wasn't mine.

It took a long time, but eventually I realised something that changed everything: death is not my task. I don't get to choose when or how it comes. It will take who it wants, when it wants, without negotiation.

Life, on the other hand - that was my car to drive. That was the road in front of me.

I still had choices. I still had agency. I could live well, love deeply, give generously, and be present in the time I'd been given. That was mine. That was always mine.

And that's at the heart of this tenet.

We waste so much of ourselves trying to steer things that are outside of our control: other people's decisions, outcomes, opinions, even death itself. But freedom comes when you let go of the wheel that isn't yours and take hold of the one that is.

You don't get to control how it ends.

But, the one thing you can definitely control – the car on the road that is yours alone to drive – is how you live.

So the next time you feel that restless urge to intervene - to fix, to control, to manage what was never yours - pause.

Ask yourself: *Is this my car to drive?*

If it isn't, take your hands off the wheel.

And if it is, drive with everything you've got.

TENET 10. Let Go of the Need for External Validation

The Chase That Never Ends

There is a moment in life when you realise that no amount of external validation will ever be enough. The praise fades. The applause stops. The approval you worked so hard for feels hollow the moment you have it. There is a danger that you spend your whole life chasing something that was never real in the first place.

From childhood, we are taught that our worth is something to be measured: by grades, promotions, titles, money, compliments, and the approval of others. We begin to treat validation like oxygen - something we need to survive, something we must earn to prove that we are enough.

For many, that belief starts early. In some families, affection is given transactionally. Love is offered after good behaviour, praise follows achievement, approval comes when you did something that pleases others. It's not always spoken, but the message is clear: *you are worthy when you perform.*

External validation is a drug with a short half-life. It feels good in the moment, but the high never lasts - and the more you depend on it, the more power you give away.

For me, that chase showed up in many places: through achievement, through approval, and most of all, through my appearance. I believed that if I looked different, if I looked "better," then I'd be more successful, more respected, more worthy. And yet, even when validation came, it didn't silence the voice in my head telling me I wasn't enough.

That's the trap: validation is never a destination. It's a treadmill. You run faster, work harder, try more but the feeling never stays. Because the thing you're chasing isn't out there. It never was.

Why We Keep Seeking It

The lie of external validation is so convincing because it works - briefly.

You get the praise. You get the approval. You get the pat on the head or the likes on the post, and for a moment, it soothes something deep inside you. But then, the feeling fades and you have to start chasing it again. Not because you're shallow, but because you've been taught - somewhere along the way, and probably by someone that you loved - that how others see you is the measure of who you are.

As a result, you start bending yourself to fit what others want from you. You speak in ways that please, you act in ways that impress, you avoid saying or doing anything that might rock the boat - even when your instincts tell you otherwise. Your life becomes a performance, carefully crafted for approval.

Yet, no matter how much praise you collect, it's never enough. Because the goalposts always move - the high doesn't last - and the moment you stop receiving that validation, the doubts creep in: *Was I ever good enough in the first place?*

Worse still, the fear of losing that approval starts to take over. You become afraid to fail. Afraid to be honest. Afraid to be seen in anything less than your best light. You live in fear of disapproval - not because it harms you, but because you've come to believe, wrongly, that it defines you.

That's the real danger. When your self-worth depends on how others see you, you are no longer living from the inside out. You are constantly scanning for clues, for signs that you're doing okay. And in doing so, you hand the steering wheel to somebody else. You give away your own sense of value to a jury that changes its mind with the wind.

The Mirror and the Lie

For me, the most persistent and personal form of validation-seeking wasn't applause or success - it was in the mirror.

For years, I struggled with body image. I didn't talk about it. Most men don't. But it was there, quietly shaping how I saw myself, how I behaved, and how I interpreted every moment of recognition or rejection.

It wasn't just self-consciousness. It was something deeper, something harder to explain. There were times I'd see a photo of myself and feel crushed. Not disappointed - crushed. As though everything I'd achieved had been undone by how I looked in that single image. As though I'd been exposed.

Have you ever cried over a photo of yourself? More people have than you might think. I know I have. And the worst part wasn't what I saw - it was what I believed it meant. *You don't look the part. You're not who people think you are. You're not enough.*

It sounds irrational when you say it out loud, but body dysmorphia doesn't care about logic. It doesn't care about evidence. It doesn't even care about praise. It's a deeply embedded perception that distorts everything. When you're in it, no amount of success or compliments can drown out the voice that says, *you're wrong. You're unacceptable. You don't belong.*

I spent years believing that my body was an obstacle. If I looked different, I'd be more respected. More credible. More worthy.

But none of that was true. The only thing standing between me and freedom was the belief that I had something to prove. That I had to earn my right to be taken seriously by looking a certain way.

Once I saw that belief for what it was: *a lie* - it began to lose its stranglehold on my life – not completely, but it was a start.

After my brain injury, I felt like I'd lost everything that made me who I was. My intellect, my confidence, my identity - they all felt fractured… broken. In the years that followed, I developed this unspoken belief: *If I could just climb back to where I was before, maybe I'd feel like myself again. Maybe I'd finally be allowed to accept who I'd become.*

That belief, too, was a lie. No matter how far I climbed, the old self never reappeared, and the goalposts kept moving. What I didn't realise at the time was that I wasn't climbing back to who I used to be, but rather I was climbing *away* from who I was now.

The Shift – From Self-Focus to Service

The turning point didn't come in the mirror. It came when I stopped looking in it quite so much.

I didn't wake up one day and love every part of myself - that's not how this works - but I did wake up one day and realise I was wasting an extraordinary amount of energy worrying about something that was never supposed to matter this much.

When I stopped focusing on how I looked, and started focusing on what I could give – I became more productive and I started serving better.

I began mentoring others. I took on responsibility that required presence, not perfection. I leaned into making a difference where I could. Slowly, the need to be seen gave way to the desire to serve. The fixation on how I was perceived lost its hold as I stopped feeding it.

Service is not a cure for insecurity. It's a way of living that makes insecurity less important.

When you focus on the people in front of you - on what they need, on how you can help them - you stop asking whether you look the part, or whether you're good enough, or whether you're being judged. You stop chasing validation because you're too busy offering value to others.

The Service Mindset doesn't promise self-esteem. It offers something better: a way to live that's not dictated by the mirror or the spotlight.

And in that, I found peace - not perfection, but peace.

Tools for Letting Go of External Validation

Letting go of external validation isn't about pretending you don't care what people think. It's about noticing when their approval starts to matter more than your own sense of truth.

It begins with asking better questions:

When you're facing a big decision or seeking reassurance, try asking yourself:

Would I still do this if no one else ever found out about it?

If the answer is no, there's a good chance you're doing it for validation - not conviction.

Another useful question:

If praise and criticism were equally quiet, would this still feel meaningful to me?

If *yes*, you're probably on the right path.

The aim isn't to become indifferent to feedback. It's to stop living for it.

Praise can feel good and criticism can sting, but neither should define you.

Most of all, don't let other people's perception become your compass. The people who matter won't love you more for your perfection. They'll love you more for your presence, your integrity, your realness.

Let go of the performance. Return to the work. That's where you're more likely to find peace.

The Perspective Shift

One of the most liberating realisations I've ever had - though it took me far too long to get there - is this:

There are only two people in life who really care about what you look like: you, and your mother.

That's it.

It seems to be written into some unspoken part of a mother's job description to care deeply about their child's appearance. Whether you've combed your hair, whether your shirt's ironed, whether you look healthy and presentable - they notice. They care. It's their job. And, in their own way, it comes from love.

Outside of that? The only person in the universe who agonises over how you look is *you*.

That doesn't mean nobody notices. It means nobody's measuring you the way you're measuring yourself. People are too busy managing their own insecurities to worry about yours. And once you see that clearly, you start to realise how much energy you've spent trying to fix something that no one else was thinking about in the first place.

Letting go of the need to look a certain way isn't about giving up - it's about getting freedom. It's about remembering that your body is not your value. You are not your reflection. And the people who love and respect you? They're not looking at your shape. They're watching your actions.

The Taylor Swift Moment

I was recently watching a documentary about Taylor Swift - one of the most famous, celebrated, and outwardly confident women on the planet, and something she said stopped me in my tracks.

She admitted that she avoids looking at photos of herself.

Not because she's too busy, or too modest, but because she doesn't like the way she looks.

Let that sink in.

Taylor Swift - an artist with global adoration, countless magazine covers, and entire arenas full of people screaming her name - still picks herself apart in photos.

That revelation struck me because if someone as universally praised as Taylor Swift still feels the sting of insecurity… then maybe the game was never winnable. Maybe this need to look the part, to be perfect, to earn your place in the world by appearing a certain way - maybe **that's** the problem.

Maybe it's not you that's broken, maybe it's the lie we were all sold.

The truth is, everyone has their thing. Their private fixation. Their quiet self-doubt. But none of that truly matters, or at least not in the way we think it does. What matters is what you bring to the people around you. What matters is who you are when nobody's watching.

The goal was never to be flawless. The goal was to be free.

Full Circle – The End of the Chase

Letting go of external validation isn't just a matter of self-esteem, it's an ethical shift. A reordering of how you move through the world.

When you seek validation from others, you place them above you. You hand them the role of judge. You give them the right to decide your worth. And in doing so, you create hierarchy.

That runs directly against the second tenet of The Service Mindset: that *all people are intrinsically equal in value*. The equality that The Service Mindset demands becomes impossible in scenarios where some people are elevated into a position of judgement over others.

The moment you ask, *Am I good enough? Do I look the part? Do I deserve to be here?* - you are not just doubting yourself, you are placing someone else on a pedestal and asking them to look down and grant you permission to belong.

The Service Mindset asks a better question.

Not *How do I look?* but *How can I help?*

Not *Am I good enough for them?* but *What can I offer, as I am, right now?*

That is where true freedom lives. That is where service begins.

The people who truly make a difference in this world are not the ones who look perfect or sound perfect or seem untouchable. They're the ones who turned their attention outward. Who stopped performing. Who stopped chasing applause. Who stopped waiting to be told they were enough and simply got on with the business of being useful.

When you let go of the need to be seen a certain way, you make space for yourself to do the work that actually matters. Quietly. Steadily. Honestly.

You don't need to be flawless and you don't need to be admired.

You just need to be present with humility and the willingness to serve.

That's what the world needs.

And the minute you stop chasing validation, you become ready to give it.

A Note to You

And with this last paragraph of the core tenets, I want to say something directly to **you**.

I don't know you. I don't know what led you to pick up this book, or what you were hoping to find in these pages, but I do know something about pain. I know what it's like to go searching for meaning when things fall apart.

Maybe, like me, you suffered an injury - something that shattered your sense of self and left you scrambling to put the pieces back together.

Maybe you experienced rejection. Maybe someone cheated on you. Maybe a friend ghosted you without explanation. Maybe you were bullied, or overlooked, or made to feel like you didn't belong. Maybe your parents only offered affection when you met their expectations. Or maybe they never showed you how to feel worthy in the first place.

Whatever happened - whatever made you come here looking for something to help you heal, to give you the release you need to finally let go and move forward - I want you to hear this:

You are, were, and have always been enough.

That is the truth.

You don't need to hear it from me. You don't need applause. You don't need permission.

You don't need to earn it by looking a certain way or achieving a certain thing.

You just have to start believing it for yourself.

And if you only act on one of the many reflections or exercises in this book - just one - make it this:

Action: Know that you are enough.

Say it. Write it. Whisper it into the silence of your self-doubt.

You don't need to do more to be worthy. You don't need to be perfect to be loved.

You're already there. You always were.

And now, you're free to live like it.

The 10 Tenets of The Service Mindset

1. **Acceptance is Key** – True service begins with accepting reality as it is, rather than resisting it. When we stop fighting what we cannot change, we free ourselves to act where it matters.

2. **Serve with Intention** – We are always serving something - whether we realise it or not. The Service Mindset asks us to choose consciously and ethically what we give ourselves to. A worthy telos brings clarity, courage, and meaning. Without it, we drift. With it, we begin to live on purpose.

3. **All People are Equal** – The Service Mindset is built on equality. We neither raise ourselves above others nor diminish ourselves beneath them. Service is about shared humanity, not power or inferiority.

4. **Find Strength in Simplicity** – The modern world thrives on overcomplication, but service is most effective when it is simple, clear, and direct. By cutting away unnecessary complexity, we remove barriers to action.

5. **Regulate Your Emotions** – Emotional clarity allows us to respond wisely rather than react impulsively. Service is most powerful when we control our emotions instead of letting them control us.

6. **Lift Others** – The true measure of leadership is not how high you climb but how many people you help to rise along the way. Service is about empowering others, not hoarding status.

7. **Act with Integrity** – Do what's right, not what's easy. Service without integrity is meaningless, and credibility is built on consistency between values and actions.

8. **Let Go of Perfection** – Perfection is an illusion that holds us back. True service comes from action, not hesitation, and progress is always more valuable than flawlessness.

9. **Drive Your Own Car** – Stay in your lane. Service is about support, not control. Focus on what is truly your responsibility and let go of what is not.

10. **Let Go of External Validation** – The world does not need you to be admired; it needs you to show up, be present and serve. When we stop chasing approval, we start focusing on impact.

Closing Reflection – Standing at the Threshold

You've made it through the heart of this book - not just the words, but the weight behind them. If you've come this far, it's probably not because you were curious about a philosophy. It's because something in your life asked you to look deeper.

Maybe it was exhaustion. Or frustration. Or a quiet voice that said: *there has to be more than this.*

The ten tenets you've just read aren't abstract ideas, they're the scaffolding I used to rebuild my life after it fell apart. Not once, but many times. They've helped me climb out of depression. Face anxiety. Lead through uncertainty. Find meaning when the old definitions no longer made any sense to me.

However, I need you to understand something.

This mindset - this shift from self-focus to service - isn't neat. It's not a perfect formula or a straight road. I speak from experience when I say: You **will** forget these tenets. You **will** fall back into old habits. You'll lose your temper, seek validation, try to fix what's not yours. You will be human.

And that's okay.

What matters is that you come back to the mindset. That you return to the road, hands on your own wheel, doing what is yours to do. Over and over again.

The Service Mindset isn't about being perfect, it's about being willing.

And now that you've seen what this philosophy is, the real question becomes: *what will you do with it?*

Part Two is where we take that next step. We'll explore what this mindset looks like in action: in work, in leadership, in relationships, in moments of conflict and fatigue. We'll look at the messy, beautiful reality of what it means to serve when the world is complicated and the stakes are high.

But before you turn the page, take a breath. Let the weight of these ideas settle. You've made it to this important threshold.

You're not here to be perfect. You're here to serve.

And the world needs what only you can give.

PART TWO

Chapter 4: Value Through Action - Building Resilience and Self-Worth and Applying The Service Mindset to the Real World

What defines a person? Philosophers, scientists, and thinkers have wrestled with the question for centuries. Some argue we are the sum of our experiences; others insist our nature is fixed - shaped by biology, destiny, or something in between. But modern physics offers a different lens, one with profound implications for how we understand ourselves.

In physics, objects are not defined in isolation but through their interactions. A chair is only a chair because of how we use it and experience it. Strip away the interaction, and it becomes a meaningless cluster of atoms.

People are much the same. What we do - not just what we think or believe - ultimately shapes who we are. Our identity is not static. It is shaped by how we engage with the world: our relationships, our contributions, and the difference we make in the lives of others.

This understanding is central to The Service Mindset: the idea that who we are is defined not by what we possess, believe, or hope for; but by how we interact with the world.

A person who acts with purpose, generosity, or resilience isn't merely performing a role, they are shaping who they are through the choices they make and the impact they have. Identity, in this view, is something we build through interaction.

And this reframes how we think about strength. Adversity doesn't define us - our response to it does. Setbacks, failures, and losses are not verdicts. They are opportunities to adapt, grow, and demonstrate who we want to become. Resilience isn't fixed - it's something that takes shape in motion as you act, adapt, and carry on, even when it's hard.

In small, steady ways, service gives shape to our lives through the quiet act of pursuing our *telos* and being there for others. It offers us a way to live in alignment with what matters. It gives us a route to shape our lives through action as opposed to through the pursuit of perfection or performance. A person who delivers, even in small ways, with consistency and care, becomes someone of value - first to others, and then, more importantly, to themselves.

So, what makes a person valuable?

It's a question that hangs in the background more often than we care to admit. You feel it in meetings when people talk over you. You feel it when you're working late and no one seems to notice. You feel it when you wonder whether the things you do every day actually count for anything.

And most of us, if we're honest, don't have a clear answer.

We fall back on job titles, bank balances, qualifications.

Or we rely on other people's approval: our boss, our partner, our parents.

The problem with our reliance on those things is that all of that stuff is outside of you. It can shift, disappear or forget about you.

After my brain injury, I lost everything I thought made me valuable. The intellect, the confidence, the easy ability to move through the world without effort. All gone. I wasn't sure who I was anymore, or what I was worth. I remember thinking, *If I'm not what I used to be… then what am I now?*

That question haunted me for years.

I cannot say that developing The Service Mindset brought me an answer – at least not in some defining moment of clarity. Instead, the answer slowly revealed itself through the smallest of acts. Picking up the phone when someone needed help. Offering to look at a problem no one else wanted to touch. Being useful, even when I felt broken. By making a consistent commitment to living with purpose, things slowly started to turn around.

Because – as we have already discussed - value isn't a feeling, it's a pattern that we discover through interaction.

It's the sum of your contributions. The trace you leave behind.

And that's the foundation of The Service Mindset:

You don't wait to feel valuable - you act in ways that creates value for others, and then, in time, for yourself.

This chapter isn't about trying to "believe in yourself" more. It's about proving, through what you do, that you're still in the game - still capable of making a difference. And the more you focus on that, the less space there is for doubt, impostor syndrome, or the desperate chase for validation.

The Real Source of Worth

One of the most damaging myths in modern life is that your value depends on whether other people recognise it.

You do a good job - someone should say thank you.
You go the extra mile - someone should notice.
You care - someone should care back.
You post something – someone should click it, like it, interact with it in some way.

We have grown so accustomed to instant feedback on our contributions that when you don't receive any, it starts to eat away at you. You wonder if you're wasting your time. You wonder if maybe you *aren't* that valuable after all.

I've been there. Waiting for recognition. Chasing reassurance. Telling myself I was fine - while quietly hoping someone would say: *"You're doing a good job. We see you."*

The Service Mindset asks us to confront an uncomfortable truth:

Recognition is unreliable.

People are distracted and see what they want to see. Systems are broken. Most of the time, the world just isn't paying close attention to you.

Ultimately, if your sense of worth depends on applause, you'll never feel secure.

However, if your sense of worth comes from your contribution in and of itself - from knowing you've made something better - then you don't need the applause. You derive value from the outcome.

That's what changed things for me.

I stopped asking *"Do people see my value?"*
And started asking *"Where can I make a difference?"*

When you make a contribution that you can look back and be proud of, you can start to take pride in yourself and once you know you're useful and actually doing something that makes a difference, the noise starts to drop away. You stop chasing approval and you just get on with things.

Oddly enough, that's also when people start to take notice of you – not in a performative way, but in a way that matters - because they start to recognise you for being the person who quietly gets things done in a way that makes a difference.

Who Are You When You're Not Winning?

Dr Seuss called it *The Waiting Place*.

"A useless place", he said.
"For people just waiting."
"Waiting for a train to go, or a bus to come, or a plane to go or the mail to come, or the rain to go…"

It's the only part of *Oh, the Places You'll Go!* that no one quotes in their graduation speech because it's the bit where nothing happens. No success, no adventure, just… waiting.

Uncertainty. Stillness. Stagnation.

Yet, that's where many of us live for far longer than we'd like to admit.

There will be long periods in your life when you are not at your best.

You won't be performing.
You won't be thriving.
You won't be actualising your "potential."

Sometimes you'll be doing everything right and still feel like you're standing still. Other times you'll mess it up completely. You'll say the wrong thing, let someone down or fail to deliver.

When you have suffered a brain injury, that sense of failure – of feeling like you have let others down – is far too familiar.

And in those moments, all the stuff people use to define their worth: job titles, success, praise – it disappears. That's when you need something to fall back on and – hopefully – that's what The Service Mindset gives you.

The Service Mindset challenges us by asking:

Who are you when no one's watching, and nothing's going your way? What do you stand for at your core?

That was one of the hardest parts of my recovery for me.

Not the physical healing, not even the grief for the version of me that I had lost, but the emptiness of not knowing whether I was *any use to anyone* anymore. When you don't feel sharp or strong or productive, it's easy to start believing you're worthless.

The philosophical foundation of The Service Mindset tells us that this belief is based on the wrong model.

Your value is intrinsic and it's there right now, it always has been. Your value is not a prize that gets handed out when you're doing well, but rather something you were born with and build upon through how you carry yourself when things are hard.

That's what I had to learn to appreciate.

My value wasn't gone, circumstances had conspired to make me forget it.

The only way to rediscover it was through action; not speeches, not ideas, but real-world, visible, imperfect effort. Turning up and offering help. Making things a bit better than they were before.

That's how I think you begin to rebuild yourself.

Not through self-affirmations or waiting to feel confident - those things will come naturally in time - by choosing to stand for something and doing the things that a valuable person would do - even if you don't feel like one in yourself.

I was reminded of this need to take action only very recently, when I was talking to my young cousin. My cousin has recently finished university and he is passionate about animals, nature and the environment. Ideally, he sees himself as some sort of ecological consultant, but he is currently working in his local pub.

I spoke with him and asked why he was working in the pub over pursuing his passion of being an ecological consultant. I was struck by his reply when he responded with *"I don't really have the experience for that!"*

"So, you're waiting for experience?"

"Well, when you put it like that"

And this is the mental trap that The Service Mindset is helping us to avoid. I am here to tell you that life is short and life is fragile – we all know this, and yet, many of us coast along, allowing stuff to happen to us or frittering away time through procrastination.

The Service Mindset says: follow your passion with intention – do it now and live in alignment with the person that you really want to be.

Progress Over Proof

After my injury, I never thought I'd own a home.

For a long time, the idea felt impossible - not just financially, but emotionally. I didn't think I'd ever get back to a point where life could move forward in that way.

But here I am.

And like any home, there's plenty that needs doing.

Paintwork, clutter, garden jobs - the list is always longer than the energy I sometimes feel I need to get started with it.

And the list just gets longer.

Sometimes it feels like too much. I get overwhelmed and don't know where to start, but here's what I've learnt:

First: you *have* to start.

You can sit in the waiting place hoping the list gets shorter (it never does) or you can pick something and begin – accepting that if you don't, nothing changes.

Second: I try to do *just one thing* that I'll be able to look at as the sun goes down and feel quietly proud of.

Cutting the grass. Painting a fence. Tidying the kitchen.

Small things, but meaningful. Something I can glance at when the day ends and the wine sits in my glass, and say:

"That's better than it was this morning. I did that."

That's what progress really looks like.

It's not turning your whole life around in a day, but rather choosing not to wait. Doing something useful or making something better.

Once you start doing that, the need to *prove* anything starts to fade. You don't have to prove your worth to anyone, as your actions will quietly do it for you.

You're no longer waiting to feel valuable, but rather you're creating value, one act of service at a time.

That's also where you start to build resilience.

Here's the thing, it's not just about the list of jobs that you have to do around the house.

This mindset – accepting reality and then taking one single step in alignment with the person that you want to be – you can apply that to anything: losing weight, building a career, changing your life.

It all starts with a single first step.

Action Builds Identity

One of the traps we fall into is thinking identity is something we *find*, as though it's buried deep inside us, waiting to be discovered - but I don't think it works like that. Identity isn't something you unearth; it's a contract that we enter into with society and something you construct, gradually, through the things you do.

Think of it like this: you might have an idea of who you are and who you want to be – that is your offer to the world.

Society can choose to accept that offer because you stand for something that is useful and needed. However, by the same token, society might reject your offer because there is a disconnect between what you say you represent and how you act within your community.

The important part to remember is that it is your deeds, actions and interactions with others; that's how you uphold your end of this social contract. That's what your consideration looks like.

When my life fell apart after the brain injury, I felt like I had no identity at all. The man I used to be: sharp, articulate, capable - had disappeared, and I didn't know what to put in his place. I kept trying to feel like myself again, but it never came.

What I failed to appreciate at the time was that identity doesn't come from introspection. It comes from action.

I didn't get there by thinking about who I was or who I used to be. I got there by doing things: small things, useful things, and then doing them again the next day. That's how the shape of me started to come back. It was always going to be impossible to recover what I had lost, but I was capable of creating something new, through repetition and contribution.

That's where I began to find some sense of stability again because, at the end of the day, I had evidence of my contribution. I could look around as the sun was setting and see the things I'd done.

Maybe I'd helped someone fix a problem. Maybe I'd made something a bit smoother, a bit easier, a bit clearer than it was before. That was enough.

That's how you rebuild a sense of self.

You do things that matter, however small, and over time, those things shape you into someone you can believe in again.

And if society, community or the world rejects the offer of personal identity that you have extended – that does not mean you have to capitulate, surrender and give up on the idea of who you want to be.

Be the person that you want to be through your actions and change peoples' minds through your deeds.

If you are sorry, then do things that show the world you are sorry.

If you love someone, then do things that show them just what they mean to you.

It's very difficult for people to accept the offer of your identity when your actions do not align with who you are purporting to be.

Make your actions match your intention because it's so much easier for society to judge you on things done, than things intended.

I am Kenough

In the *Barbie* movie, there's a line: *'Maybe it's not Barbie and Ken. Maybe it's Barbie and it's Ken.'* It struck me, because it seemed at odds with The Service Mindset's idea of identity being relational. But on reflection, I realised identity can be both individual and relational - and those ideas are not in conflict

The line from the Barbie movie reminds us to focus on the strength of individual identity and that is not inconsistent with The Service Mindset. It reminded me that identity has two faces: how we define ourselves, and how we live in relation to others.

Whilst it is ultimately our interactions within the system that will define us, we do not have to surrender our individual identity to the systems that we serve.

Let the Work Speak for You

We live in a world where so much is curated. People announce their intentions, showcase their goals, and broadcast their journeys, but real value rarely needs to be announced via a press release or a social media post.

Some of the most quietly effective people I've worked with in the fraud fighting industry don't make a fuss. They don't talk themselves up. They just keep on going, doing good work, living in accordance with their values and leaving things better than they found them. Over time, people notice because the work done speaks for itself - not because it was seen on social media or because the person doing the work could shout the loudest.

There's a kind of credibility that comes from consistency - the sort that can't be faked or fast-tracked. You build it by doing useful things, often thankless things, especially when no one is watching.

After my brain injury, I was desperate to the point of distraction to prove myself again. I turned up at my rugby club, picked up a ball and played – not because it was a sensible thing to do, but because I had been told I probably shouldn't do it.

I went to university and struggled – not because it was the best thing for me cognitively or emotionally, but because I had something to prove.

Whilst there is certainly a power in the hunger to prove yourself, I found in my own journey that I eventually reached a point in life where I stopped trying to prove anything and instead focused on being useful.

The result was quieter, less dramatic, but more powerful. I didn't need to explain who I was anymore. I just needed to keep doing the work that mattered. In time, that work spoke more clearly than I ever could.

Letting the work speak for itself doesn't mean staying silent or unseen. It means trusting that *who you are* is revealed in what you do, not in what you say (or post) about what you are doing.

There is perhaps also a need for a word of caution here. Whilst there is no doubt that the need for recognition and to prove yourself can be a powerful catalyst for achieving great things – it is also an aspect of your character that is very easily exploited.

In part one, we looked at the work of Alfred Adler who once said:

"The striving for superiority always originates from a feeling of inferiority"

The thing about the neurotic pursuit of superiority is that a person who exhibits this behaviour becomes very predictable – and a predictable person is easily manipulated.

If someone needs to feel better than others, you can easily control them by:

- Flattering their ego ("You're the smartest in the room")

- Offering them status ("This will make you look like a leader")

- Threatening their image ("People will think less of you if you don't…")

I have seen firsthand how some businesses will exclusively recruit employees straight from school or university because of the exploitability in a young person's hunger to prove themself.

If you find yourself in a system, network, business or relationship that inflates your ego or denigrates your value, you might want to question to what extent that thing is controlling or manipulating you, and whether you really need it in your life.

You Don't Need to Be Inspired to Begin

There's a myth that stops a lot of people from moving forward: the idea that you need to feel ready, motivated, or inspired before you can act. However; in practice, that's almost never how it works.

Inspiration comes *after* momentum, not before it.

Some of the best days I've had - personally and professionally - began with a shrug and a sigh. No spark. No vision. Just a decision to do something… Anything. And then the shift happens. A little progress. A small win here, a moment of clarity or connection there. Suddenly, things feel lighter, and more possible.

But, that flow-state only arrives once you've already started.

Waiting for motivation is like waiting for the weather to change before you go outside. It's unpredictable, and, more often than not, it becomes an excuse not to act. There's power in deciding to begin because you've realised that *waiting is a trap that keeps you where you are*.

That's what separates the days when you make progress from the ones that disappear. In my own life, the most meaningful progress hasn't come from moments of inspiration - it's come from stubbornness. From the simple refusal to let the day get away from me. From picking one thing, however small, and doing it.

I remember working as a young paralegal in my early career. There were some days when I didn't know where to start. So, I would go to my filing cabinet, take out 50 files – stand them in a tall stack and then deal with the one on the top.

Sometimes you just need to start and it can help to visualise what needs to be done.

With all that said, remember that you don't need a grand plan and you don't need to necessarily know how it ends.

You just need to begin.

The Quiet Power of Steady Effort

There's a quiet dignity in just getting on with things.

Despite what social media would have you believe, not every day has to be significant. Every task doesn't need to be strategic. Sometimes the most important thing you can do is keep going - not because it's exciting, but because the opposite of forward momentum is to go backwards.

Modern life encourages us to chase peaks, breakthroughs and milestones. However, most of life is made up of something else entirely: the middle bits - the repetitive stuff. The work that isn't celebrated. It's in those moments, more than anywhere else, that we develop character.

There's something reassuring about this, actually. It means you don't have to wait for your big break to become someone of substance. You can build a life of real worth in the way you approach the ordinary.

Take the admin seriously. Return that call. Respond to the email that everyone else is avoiding. Keep your word. Follow through and deliver.

These things might not seem glamorous, but they're the foundations of trust, reliability, and quiet confidence. As they compound - bit by bit - they shift how others see you. More importantly, they shift how you see yourself.

You're no longer someone trying to feel valuable, but rather you're someone *acting* in a way that brings value.

You shift from passively waiting for others to see you, to purposively moving forwards in a way that is inevitably seen.

The Evidence Builds Over Time

It's easy to underestimate the value of what you're doing when progress is slow or invisible. Especially when you're rebuilding after a setback, a loss, or just a long period of drift. It can be hard to see the point of incremental effort.

However; every time you act in alignment with the person you want to be - even if no one sees it, even if no one thanks you - you lay a brick, and over time, those bricks start to form something solid beneath your feet.

The problem is, most of us don't stop to notice. We keep pushing for some external signal: a promotion, praise, a moment of validation and if it doesn't come, we assume we're getting nowhere.

That's why you have to learn to recognise your own evidence.

When I look back at the times I've struggled most with confidence, it's usually been because I was not paying attention to the weight of what I *had* already done. I'd achieved more than I gave myself credit for in the quiet endurance of just continuing, adapting, and finding ways to contribute even when I felt broken.

If you're serving in a way that adds value, that helps others, or that makes something better - that all counts, and it builds. You just need to stay with it long enough to reach a point where you can reflect on what you've built.

That's where real confidence comes from: in knowing, in your own quiet way, that you've made a difference and you kept going when it mattered as opposed to any form of external praise or recognition.

Reflection: What Did You Build Today?

We often overlook our own effort because we're so used to focusing on outcomes. But when life feels directionless or overwhelming, the most stabilising thing you can do is zoom in. Forget the five-year plan and forget the finish line - just focus on today.

Ask yourself, when the sun sets and the day draws to a close:

What did I build today?

What small corner of the world is better because I was here?

What did I mend, fix, improve, or steady?

It doesn't need to be dramatic. Maybe you were there when it would've been easier to hide. Maybe you helped someone solve a problem they didn't know how to tackle. Maybe you tidied your house, answered a difficult message, or made someone feel heard.

These things don't always look like progress, but they are.

They are acts of value. And over time, they shape both the world *and* the self.

That's how you build resilience. That's how you rebuild confidence.

You don't wait to feel strong, you act as though you already are.

And brick by brick, as the evidence appears – a strange thing happens: the more you do, the more you feel like doing.

Let Go of the Ego – Serve Instead

There's a trap we all fall into at some point: believing we need to be the best in the room. Or at the very least, not the worst. We compare ourselves to others. We judge our performance and the progress we think we have made. We quietly hope others will trip so we can feel a little steadier by contrast.

But it's all noise and it never leads anywhere good.

The ego has two disguises. One is **superiority** - the belief that you're better than others, that you've earnt more, or deserve more. The other is **inferiority** - the belief that you're falling short, that you don't belong, or that everyone else has it figured out. Both of these forms of ego are illusions. They will both keep you circling around yourself instead of just being.

The Service Mindset demands that we reject both.

For years, I compared myself relentlessly in photographs. I'm a big guy - six feet tall, a former rugby player - and in more recent years I've found myself on conference stages, sitting on expert panels, doing what I suppose is seen as quite senior, professional work. Inevitably, someone in the audience will take a photo and post it to LinkedIn.

And every single time, I'd zoom in on it. Not to admire the achievement, but to analyse the way I looked. I'd compare my size to the other panellists. *"Look at how wide I am compared to him. Look how tall I am compared to that podium. Look at my posture. Look at my face."* It became a ritual of quiet self-punishment and it's always utterly pointless.

When you fixate on how you're different, or how you fall short, you stop paying attention to your strengths. And when you stop noticing your strengths, you miss opportunities. You overlook the value you bring. You forget to be the person that others actually need.

That's the real cost of comparison: the loss of presence, the loss of potential and a loss of a sense of purpose, not just damaged self-esteem.

Service pulls you out of that spiral. It shifts your focus from how you appear to what you *contribute*. You stop trying to be impressive and just try to be useful. In doing that, ironically, you become the kind of person people really want to work with, learn from, and trust.

Letting go of the ego doesn't mean making yourself small or diminishing yourself. It means being grounded enough to stop performing and strong enough to keep going.

Finding Peace in Purpose: The Wisdom of Ataraxia

There's a word from ancient stoic philosophy that I've come to value deeply: *ataraxia*. It's not a word you hear at all these days, but its meaning is something most of us crave. It describes a state of unshakeable inner calm - the kind that emerges when you stop wrestling with the world and start living in line with your values.

Ataraxia is not about disengaging or pretending things don't matter – in fact the opposite is true - it's about knowing precisely what **does** matter. It's the peace that follows when you stop trying to win approval or prove yourself and instead focus on being useful - on doing something that matters to someone.

For me, I've found this peace by embracing the tenets of The Service Mindset. When I'm helping my daughter navigate a difficult day, or doing something small but meaningful for a colleague, I'm not worried about how I look or how I'm being judged. I'm anchored. I'm present. And that presence - rooted in contribution - is where the ego is quiet and the negative noise in your head disappears.

We chase perfection and validation as if they'll bring us peace, but they never do. The moment you find peace is usually the moment you stop looking for it and start living in alignment with what matters. That's ataraxia - and for those of us prone to comparison, anxiety, or self-doubt, it's a quiet kind of freedom worth pursuing.

✦ Reflection Exercise:

Think of a time when you wanted recognition and didn't receive it. How did it affect your motivation? Now think of a moment when you focused entirely on solving a problem or helping someone, regardless of whether anyone noticed. How did that feel?

✦ Action Point:

Identify one area of your life: work, home, relationships - where you've been chasing approval. What would it look like to shift your focus from being seen to being useful? Choose one action that will centre contribution over visibility this week.

The Personal Value Proposition

Ask most people what their value is and they'll point to their job title, their qualifications, or their CV. It's understandable - we've been trained to define ourselves by roles and achievements, by external labels and the opinions of others, but these things; whilst useful to an extent, don't tell the full story.

In earlier parts of this chapter, we established that your value isn't something you inherit and it's not something someone else hands to you. We have explored how your value is something you create yourself through what you do, how you engage, and the impact you have.

Addressing your personal value proposition does not mean marketing yourself or turning your life into a sales pitch. Discovering your personal value proposition is about having the clarity of mind to know and accept what you bring to the table and why it matters. Once you understand these things, you're in a far stronger position to make good choices about how you spend your time, where you invest your energy, and what you tolerate.

A strong personal value proposition rests on four foundations:

- **Skills:** The tools you bring with you - they're only part of the story, but they are important.
- **Impact:** The difference those skills make in the real world.
- **Credibiliy:** Whether people believe you'll deliver. That trust is earned, never assumed.
- **Contribution**: The action, the doing, the way you interact with the world and offer something of substance.

These elements can't be faked. They emerge through lived experience, through trial and error, through consistent and purposeful delivery again and again.

For a long time after my brain injury, I thought my value had gone. I wasn't who I had been. I couldn't think as clearly, remember as sharply, or move through the world with the same ease and confidence as before. Gradually, I realised I'd been looking in the wrong direction. My value had never been in what I had: status, intellect, image. It was in what I gave and – more importantly – in what I could still give.

A career in fraud prevention helped to give me back that sense of impact. It wasn't about chasing prestige, but about doing something that mattered. Solving problems, protecting people, fixing systems that were broken. That became my value proposition: not a label, but a choice.

And the same is true for anyone. The more your actions align with your ability to contribute, the more naturally your worth reveals itself in the quiet certainty that you're doing something that matters.

✦ Reflection Exercise:

What are the core skills you bring to your work, your family, your community? How do those skills translate into tangible impact? And how do people come to trust you?

✦ Action Point:

Try to summarise your personal value proposition in one sentence. Not a job title. Not a sales pitch. A sentence that captures what you offer, and how it helps others.
For example:

"I create clarity where there's confusion, and structure where there's chaos."

or

"I use empathy and insight to help people feel seen, heard, and supported."

It's not about getting the words right. It's about finding the thread that runs through your actions and then choosing to live more deliberately along that line.

The Role of Resilience in Long-Term Value

Resilience is one of those words that gets thrown around so often it risks losing meaning – corporate speak: a quality that all employees must possess but that few understand. In the context of The Service Mindset, resilience has a very specific purpose. It's not about simply absorbing pressure or pushing through hardship for the sake of it. Resilience is the ability to respond: deliberately, constructively, and with clarity, when things don't go to plan.

And trust me, if there is one guarantee in life it's that things won't always go to plan.

If value is built through action, then resilience is what allows that action to continue when the wind suddenly changes direction. It's the quiet recalibration after a setback, the ability to adapt without losing purpose. Not a refusal to fall, but a refusal to stay down.

Too many people see failure as a verdict. They interpret a misstep as evidence that they were never good enough in the first place, but that's a pretty fragile mindset. In reality, failure is just part of the process. It's information. A data point. Something to learn from, not something to be ashamed of.

The most resilient people aren't the ones who avoid failure. They're the ones who meet it honestly, extract the lesson, and move on. That ability – to rapidly accept a situation, learn the lesson and move on from it - is what sets resilient people apart. It's also what sustains long-term value.

Think of stand-up comedians. There are very few comedy geniuses like Billy Connolly in the world – people who can just stand there, hold the attention of an audience and effortlessly be funny. Most comedians work at it. In comedy clubs and pubs and the corners of festivals over the course of countless days and weeks, most comedians craft a funny routine.

It is actually the ultimate test of resilience. Can you imagine if your favourite comedian stood there, told a joke that didn't land and then announced their retirement from comedy because they failed to get a laugh?

"Disasters are funny to me. As a comedian you learn from failure, so I'm always trying to put myself in a situation that does not seem ideal for my comedy and see how it works"

– Anthony Jeselnik

Resilience means keeping the momentum going, even when your confidence takes a hit. It means trusting that your worth isn't erased by one wrong move or bad decision, but shaped by the character you show in dealing with it.

There is strength in consistency, but there's a different kind of strength in having the capacity to stop and say: *"This didn't work - so what will I try next?"*

That's what resilience looks like in practice. Not endurance for its own sake, but intelligent persistence in the service of a larger goal.

I remember reading a story about the early days of Netflix. Back in the early days of the internet, Netflix started out as a service for ordering DVDs online. At that time, a big US corporate giant – Blockbuster Video – had a near monopoly in the movie rental business.

Sensing that they were on a collision course with Blockbuster, the executive team from Netflix flew to Blockbuster's Head Office to seek investment and an alliance. Their pitch was simple: *invest in us and we will handle the online business, whilst you guys do what you do best.*

Blockbuster resoundingly rejected Netflix's overtures. Netflix were little guys, Blockbuster – by comparison – was a giant with a near monopoly, *who were these Netflix guys and what sort of nerve did they have in making such a proposal?*

The story goes, that the guys from Netflix flew home in silence – not saying a word to each other. They eventually got back to their headquarters and entered the boardroom, settled down and then one of them broke the silence for the first time to say:

"You know what that means, don't you? I guess we're just going to have to destroy them"

In this way, resilience is so much more than surviving. Resilience is about calmly and quietly meeting with what others might describe as failure and using this as your fuel to drive yourself forward and onto bigger and better things.

📌 Reflection Exercise:

Think of a time you failed, or felt like you had. How did you respond? Did it shrink your sense of self, or did you find a way forward? What, if anything, did that moment teach you about your capacity to adapt?

📌 Action Point:

Write down one small setback you've faced recently. Beside it, jot down one thing it taught you - however small - and one way you might approach a similar situation differently next time. The aim isn't to dwell, but to reframe.

Failure as a Teacher, Not a Verdict

Failure has a habit of dressing up as finality. It shows up with weight and judgement, whispering that you've been found out - that you've proven, once and for all, that you're not good enough. But failure isn't a verdict - it's sometimes just feedback.

My brain injury forced me into learning this lesson through necessity.

When your brain is broken and you don't know what is socially acceptable anymore, failure is something you experience pretty much every time you open your mouth to speak.

Early in my career, I started keeping a diary, not a dusty leather-bound book, but a simple spreadsheet. Each day, I logged one thing that had happened, how I'd handled it, and - most importantly - what I could learn from it, or do differently next time.

I am not really sure how journaling came about, but I wanted to improve myself - and my brain, post-injury, wasn't always reliable. I needed something to anchor my thinking. Over time, this small habit rewired the way I saw setbacks. A misstep wasn't a sign of incompetence, it was just a moment: a chance to reflect, recalibrate, and move forward determined not to make the same mistakes again.

Failure, when reframed, becomes a teacher: patient, persistent, unafraid to challenge. It shows you how you react under pressure. It reveals your blind spots, and - if you're prepared to accept it honestly - it makes you better.

I once lost a job. At the time, it felt like confirmation of every insecurity I had ever had and I spiralled a bit, telling myself the usual, unhelpful, stories: I wasn't good enough. I'd peaked. I'd blown it.

With distance however, I started to see the situation differently. That moment forced a shift I'd been avoiding. It nudged me towards work that suited me better - towards building something of value. What felt like a door closing was actually a redirection towards new opportunities that better aligned with who I wanted to be.

That's often how it goes. When people look back on the things that nearly broke them, they rarely wish them undone. There's pain, of course, but there's also perspective and growth.

Most people I know would not go back and undo any of their past mistakes and that really speaks to the power of failure to shape, transform and redirect our lives.

The trick is not to romanticise failure, or to seek it out, but to meet it with clarity when it comes. To ask: *What is this moment teaching me?* Not: *Why is this happening to me?* That small change keeps you moving and keeps you learning.

The really funny thing is this: when people offer me a job and they offer to pay me good money – they are actually paying for all the times I have failed before and the lessons that I have learnt from those moments of defeat.

Just let that sink in for a moment: I have never attracted a good salary because I possess some natural flair or talent for what I do. People pay me for the wisdom that emerges from failing many, many times and the resilience I showed when I kept going.

When you look at it that way; success is available to anyone that is prepared to fail, learn the lessons, and carry on.

📌 Reflection Exercise:

Think of a failure that stuck with you. Not the biggest, necessarily, but one that stung. What did you tell yourself about it at the time? And with hindsight - what did it teach you?

📌 Action Point:

The next time something goes wrong, whether small or significant, pause before reacting. Ask: What can I take from this? And if nothing useful comes immediately, write it down anyway. Give it time. Lessons often surface once the dust has settled.

Overcoming Imposter Syndrome with The Service Mindset

Imposter syndrome is more than a nagging doubt. It's that quiet voice that questions whether you belong; whether you're good enough, smart enough, capable enough. It doesn't matter how much you've done or achieved - if it's in you, it finds a way to the surface and when it does, it is often relentless and debilitating.

I know, because I've been there and I've lived it.

After my brain injury, the instinctive sense of how to behave around people had gone. The cues, the timing, the confidence. I couldn't really read social situations anymore, didn't pick up on the subtext and would often behave in a way that to most people just appeared weird.

Every interaction became something to second-guess. I didn't trust myself to say the right thing, to behave the right way. I wasn't sure who I was anymore. At times, I felt like a stranger in my own head - someone going through the motions of a life that no longer had meaning.

Imposter syndrome thrives in that gap between who you are and who you think you're supposed to be.

But here's the twist: the people who feel like imposters are usually the ones who care the most. The fact that you question yourself is not proof that you're inadequate, it's evidence that you're self-aware. That you're holding yourself to a standard and that you're thinking about how your actions affect others.

Ironically, it's often the real frauds who feel no doubt at all.

As painful as imposter syndrome can be, given the choice between being self-aware or an idiot full of bravado, I certainly know who I would rather be.

What changed for me wasn't a sudden bolt of confidence. It was a shift in focus from inward to outward. From *Am I good enough?* to *How can I help?* That's where The Service Mindset comes in. It pulls you out of your own head and reminds you that your value doesn't lie in some internal scorecard, it lies in your purpose and what you contribute to the world.

When I feel that old doubt creeping back in, I don't retreat - I engage. I offer to help on a complex case. I mentor someone. I train a team. I use what I've got and anchor myself in something where I feel confident and competent. The moment I do that, the self-doubt starts to dissipate. Not because it's disappearing forever, but because it no longer matters. I'm too busy being useful to worry about my perceived shortcomings.

That's the trick. Action beats introspection, service beats self-doubt, and contribution silences the voice that says you don't belong here.

📌 Reflection Exercise:

Think of a time you felt like an imposter. What triggered it? Was it a new role, a room full of experts, or something internal? Now look at the impact you've made in that context - what changed because you were there?

📌 Action Point:

Write down three specific ways you've helped others in the past month: professionally or personally. Keep the list somewhere visible. Next time imposter syndrome shows up, read it. Then go do something that reminds you what you're capable of.

Reinventing Yourself When Necessary

Many people stay in roles, careers, relationships or situations long after they've stopped growing. Not because they're fulfilled, but because they feel they should stay. They tell themselves it's too late to change, too risky to start again, or too selfish to walk away. Over time, that quiet discomfort turns into frustration, then into something heavier: resentment, inertia, even despair.

Here's the truth: you are not stuck. You might feel stuck, you might be exhausted, you might be afraid, but you're almost certainly not trapped. You can always change how you engage with the world – your yesterday does not define your tomorrow - and when you realise that, it becomes possible to change the direction you're heading in.

If your current path no longer fits who you are trying to become, then it's time to change direction… don't let fear of the unknown hold you back.

Service Starts with Self-Respect

One of the great misconceptions about the idea of service is that it means saying *yes* to everything, or staying in uncomfortable places because you feel it's noble to endure. It isn't. True service starts with self-respect. You cannot be useful to anyone: your family, your team, your community - if you're running on empty or sitting in silent frustration.

Sometimes, that means leaving a job. Sometimes, it means drawing firmer boundaries. Sometimes, it means having the courage to say, *"This isn't working anymore."*

People often equate reinvention or changing direction with failure - it's not. It's growth. If a situation no longer brings out your best, you are unlikely to be serving your purpose well by staying in it.

I remember a time when I was mentoring a younger colleague. Over the course of several months, we had some quite intense discussions, and I had supported them in discovering who they were and what they wanted to be.

I remember one day, they arrived to one of our mentoring sessions slightly late and I immediately sensed that they had something that they wanted to say, but that they were holding back.

Almost sheepishly they explained that they were beginning to question whether they still needed to be mentored.

I explained that it was ok for them to say that our mentoring sessions had served their purpose. I did not take this feedback personally – if anything I was proud that I had supported this colleague in growing into the person that they had become.

What struck me, however, was their trepidation in broaching the subject. It made me reflect on just how many people must endure certain situations, or remain in relationships, because they are afraid of saying *"this isn't working anymore."*

Back in Part One, we discussed the importance of consciously and deliberately choosing your Telos and then serving it well.

In this way, if you find yourself in a situation that no longer aligns with your purpose, The Service Mindset gives you the permission to say *"this isn't working, I need to move on!"* If anything, The Service Mindset insists on that being what you do and any other person who is also living their life in service should respect your decision.

If You're Going to Raise a Problem, Bring a Way Forward

Difficult conversations often go wrong because they begin and end with complaints. I've seen it. I've done it and it doesn't work. You walk into a room, pour your frustration out onto the table, and then sit back, leaving it out there like it's everyone else's problem to fix.

What I've learnt is this: if you're going to raise a problem, bring a proposed solution with you. It doesn't have to be perfect, but it will at least show people that you have moved beyond the initial pain point and considered possible fixes in your thinking.
Instead of saying, *"I'm not happy in this role,"* try, *"I've been thinking about where I could add more value - here's something I'd love to explore."*

Instead of telling a partner, *"I feel like we're drifting apart"* try, *"I miss the connection we used to have. Could we find a way to spend more quality time together?"*

This isn't about diminishing the pain or discomfort that you might be feeling. It's about approaching communication in a way that encourages people to engage with you in finding a solution together.

I had to learn this the hard way. At one point in my career, I realised I was clinging to a role that no longer reflected where I wanted to be. Speaking up felt like a risk - what if I was seen as ungrateful, difficult, or entitled? But when I finally did, and did so with clarity and respect, the conversation wasn't confrontational at all - it was collaborative and it opened the door to something better.

When it comes to opening the door to something better, it is important to remember that this shift in thinking, from whining about problems to proposing solutions, is the keystone of innovation.

Much of the innovation I've been recognised for came from this mindset - seeing opportunities where others only saw problems. The source of that success was in learning to recognise the size of the opportunity in finding solutions to problems, where other people couldn't see past their frustrations.

✦ Reflection Exercise:

Think of an area in your life where something no longer fits: your work, a relationship, a daily routine. Are you staying locked into that routine because you've convinced yourself there's no other option? Or because you're afraid to imagine a new one?

✦ Action Point:

Name one small step you could take to shift direction. It could be a conversation, a boundary, or simply admitting something needs to change. Then ask yourself: If I raise this, can I also offer a constructive next step? Write down what that might sound like.

The Battle Against Depression – Action Creates Value

Depression doesn't just sap joy; it drains your energy to engage. Even the smallest task can feel impossible: replying to a message, getting out of bed, making a cup of tea. You promise yourself that once you feel better, then you'll act, but when the feeling doesn't come. the days shrink, the world narrows and the isolation deepens.

One of the most important things I learnt during my own darkest period is this: action must come first. The feeling doesn't arrive on its own: you have to move first. Then, gradually – and often slowly, the fog begins to lift.

At my lowest, there came a point where I felt like I had to do something enormous with my life in order to break out of the numbness. So, I hatched this crazy to plan to climb Mount Kilimanjaro for charity.
I began researching what was required to get up the mountain and stumbled across an account from someone who had made the climb. I fixated on one phrase in their story *"everybody is capable of taking one more step."*

In that moment, I realised that I did not have to conquer a mountain, I just had to take one more step. With that, I stopped trying to fix everything. I let go of the pressure to find a purpose or make a plan. Instead, I focused on the only thing I could manage: *one small step.*

Literally, one step. I opened the door, stepped outside, and stood there. The next day, I walked a little. Then a little more. No goals. No expectations. Just movement. Just proof that I was still here.

Movement Reconnects Us With the World

Depression tricks you into believing you're no longer part of the world. You start to retreat: from work, from people, from routine and that absence becomes its own kind of evidence. *If I don't matter, why would I be missed?*

But when you take action, even something small, you begin to re-establish the feedback loop that says: *I exist, I matter and I can still contribute.*

I found that some days, my action was as simple as putting the kettle on. On better days, it was helping a colleague, solving a problem, offering support. Each small act reminded me of something vital: *I was still capable of making a difference.*

One Action a Day – That's the Start

The goal isn't to fix everything. The goal is to engage, even slightly, with something outside yourself. The power of that engagement, over time, is enormous.

✒ Reflection Exercise:

Can you think of a time when taking a small action - however minor - helped shift your mood or mindset, even briefly? What did that action look like? What did it remind you about your place in the world?

✒ Action Point:

Today, pick one small thing you can do. It might be going for a short walk. Texting someone you trust. Opening a window. Reading something that gives you perspective. Write it down, and do it. Not for the sake of productivity, but as a quiet refusal to give in.

The Service Mindset in Mental Resilience

There was a period in my life when anxiety dominated everything. I would check my pulse obsessively, convinced that something was wrong. I experienced moments of depersonalisation, where the world felt distant and unreal: like I was floating through it – observing myself - rather than living in it. At my lowest, I found myself slumped on a bridge, so utterly drained that there wasn't even the energy in my despair to follow through on the darkness of my thoughts.

These experiences leave a mark. They can make you feel disconnected from everything and everyone, including yourself. I don't share this lightly, and I don't share it to offer a solution in place of professional help. If you're struggling with your mental health, the most important step is to speak to someone trained to support you. What follows in this section isn't offered as a cure, but rather as a reflection on what helped me to start to rebuild.

One of the biggest shifts in my journey was understanding the role of engagement. I'd spent so long trying to feel better before doing anything, but what actually helped was flipping that around. I started doing something - anything - and then noticed how that small act created a change in how I felt.

The Service Mindset, for me, became a way to interrupt the spiral. Instead of focusing on how I felt, I started focusing on what I could do. Even if it was just making someone a cup of tea. Even if it was just answering one email or helping a colleague solve a small problem. These little acts - acts of service - gave me a way back to myself. A way to reconnect with the world around me, one small contribution at a time.

This wasn't about pretending everything was fine. It wasn't about faking positivity or forcing myself to "power through." It was about movement, about anchoring myself in the real world through action, however minor. When I served others - when I contributed something - I felt a flicker of purpose, and that flicker is what got me through.

The Service Mindset & Anxiety – Letting Go of What You Cannot Control

Anxiety is a master illusionist. It convinces you that if you think hard enough, plan thoroughly enough, anticipate every possible scenario, you can prevent bad things from happening. It lures you into a state of constant analysis, where the mind never stops scanning your horizon for threats.

But here's the truth: most of what happens in life is outside of our control. And the more we try to manage everything, the more anxious and exhausted we become.

For a long time, I lived under that illusion. I believed that if I worried enough, I could stop things going wrong. I'd overthink conversations, second-guess decisions, rehearse outcomes that never came to pass. I thought having control was safety, but it wasn't - it was a trap.

What I learnt - slowly, and sometimes reluctantly - is that control is not the answer. The only thing I can truly influence is how I choose to respond.

For some people, belief systems provide a kind of framework for that. Faith, philosophy, even abstract ideas like simulation theory or cosmic randomness, they all serve the same purpose: helping us make sense of uncertainty without trying to eliminate it.

What matters is not what you believe, but that you believe something that enables you to let go of the impossible task of trying to control everything.

One of the questions that helped me to make this shift was this:

"Instead of asking what might go wrong, can I ask myself how I'll respond if it does?"

It changes the whole equation. You move from fear to agency. From paralysis to preparation. From trying to predict everything to trusting that you can handle what comes.

This is where The Service Mindset becomes particularly useful. It takes your attention away from imagined futures and roots it in present action. You stop asking *"what if?"* and start asking *"what now?"*

You can't control outcomes and you can't control other people, but you can choose to serve, to contribute and to act in a way that reflects your values - even in uncertainty. And that, I've found, is often enough to restore some calm.

✦ Reflection Exercise:

Think of a situation currently causing you anxiety. How much of it is truly within your control? What are you holding onto that might be better to release?

✦ Further Reflection:

Do you have a belief system: philosophical, spiritual, or personal, that helps you make peace with uncertainty? If not, what kind of perspective might offer you some grounding?

✦ Action Point:

Write down three things you can influence today however small, then, identify one thing you've been trying to control that isn't yours to manage. Let it go. Breathe. Choose action in the present over fear of the future.

Rewriting Your Source Code

Not long ago, I found myself slipping into a kind of low-level existential crisis. The world felt strange - too fast, too artificial, too beyond my control. AI is accelerating, work was draining – the singularity approaches. I felt trapped between what I was doing and what I should be doing. It wasn't a breakdown, but something quieter: a slow leak of purpose.

So I turned to a different kind of tool - not therapy, not philosophy, but code.

I began to imagine my thoughts and behaviours as if I were a machine. That sounds dramatic, but the clarity it brought was surprising. Like many of us, I've developed unconscious patterns over time: scripts that play out without me even noticing. However; when you write them down as literal lines of code, something shifts.

Here's how some of mine looked:

```
# If I see myself in a photograph…
if sees_himself_in_photograph:
    trigger(emotion='shame')
    compare(to='others')
    enter_state('rumination')
    log('you are unacceptable')

# If someone praises me…
if receives_praise:
    trigger(response='deflect')
    if internal_belief == 'undeserving':
        dismiss('compliment')
    log('they don't really mean it')

# If I consider quitting my job…
if contemplates_leaving_job:
    trigger(response='fear')
    simulate_failure()
    recall('mum_warnings')
    return_to_status_quo()

# If I feel unhappy or restless…
if mood == 'low':
    scan('external_causes')
    avoid('reflection')
    activate('doom_scroll_mode')
```

Written out like this, it becomes easier to see what's broken.

More importantly, I started to realise I could write new code - healthier scripts with more truthful defaults:

```
# When I feel self-conscious in a photo…
if sees_himself_in_photograph:
    remember('your presence matters')
    focus_on('impact_made')
    trigger(emotion='compassion')

# When someone praises me…
if receives_praise:
    breathe()
    accept('gratitude')
    reinforce('contribution acknowledged')

# When I doubt a decision…
if decision_causes_doubt:
    consult('values')
    ask('will this serve?')
```

```
    choose_action('aligned_with_purpose')

# When I feel lost…
if mood == 'adrift':
    do_small_task('with_intent')
    move_body()
    help_someone()
```

It sounds like programming, but it's really just about giving structure to self-awareness. The idea is simple: You can't rewrite your story if you don't know what script you're running.

Once you see the code, you can debug it.

Debug Your Inner Code – A Reflection Tool

Step 1: Identify the Trigger

Think of a recent moment where you felt:
- Overwhelmed
- Anxious
- Ashamed
- Angry
- Inadequate

Write it down:

"I felt triggered when…"
e.g., *I saw a photo of myself on stage and felt ashamed of my appearance.*

Step 2: Locate the Line of Code

What is the *automatic thought or belief* that ran in the background?

Complete this:

If [event/trigger], **then** [emotional reaction or judgement].
e.g., *If I see a photo of myself, then I feel embarrassed and compare myself to others.*

Step 3: Trace the Source

Where do you think this code came from?
Consider early experiences, role models, or cultural messages.
e.g., *Someone criticised how I looked as a child. I internalised the belief that appearance determines worth.*

Step 4: Recode It

Now, challenge the belief. Replace it with a more *compassionate, useful, or empowering* line of code.

Use the same format:

If [event/trigger], **then** [new intentional response].
e.g., *If I see a photo of myself, then I remind myself that I was invited to speak because of my expertise and impact - not my waistline.*

Step 5: Run the Update

Now write your new code on a sticky note, in your journal, or as a phone reminder. Read it daily. Repetition rewrites reality.

✈ Reflection Exercise:

"What line of code have I been running that no longer serves me and what truth would I like to replace it with?"

The Power of Daily Discipline

The Service Mindset isn't something you wake up with one day, fully formed. It's built through repetition - small decisions, made consistently, that help shape the kind of person you want to be.

This is where discipline comes in.

Morning Reflection – Begin with Intention

The Stoics believed each day was a fresh opportunity to live wisely. Marcus Aurelius, writing to himself in his journal, reminded himself that even getting out of bed was an act of service:

"At dawn, when you have trouble getting out of bed, tell yourself: 'I have to go to work - as a human being. What do I have to complain of, if I'm going to do what I was born for - the things I was brought into the world to do?'"

A simple morning practice can help you begin with clarity:

- *What matters today?*
- *Who needs me?*
- *What kind of presence do I want to bring into the room?*

You don't need a perfect plan. Just a moment of quiet before the noise begins, to remember what you're about.

In recent weeks, I have actually used AI to guide me in what I call a "Morning Check In" and an "Evening Stock Take".

In the morning the AI gets me to set my intention by asking me, what am I going to do and how am I going to add value. In the evening the AI asks me to reflect on what happened that day, the lessons I learnt and what I am grateful for.

We will talk more about AI and its future impact on humanity in Part 3.

Evening Reflection – Learn, Don't Judge

Seneca, another Stoic philosopher, wrote about reviewing each day before sleep - not to criticise himself, but to learn from his experience. To notice where he'd strayed from his principles, and where he'd honoured them.

A modern version might look like this:

- *What did I handle well today?*
- *Where did I fall short?*
- *What will I try differently tomorrow?*

During a formative period in my career, I did this in a spreadsheet. Three simple columns:

1. What happened?
2. What did I learn?
3. What would I do differently?

It wasn't glamorous, but it was helpful. It helped me make sense of difficult days, it helped me notice patterns and most of all, it helped me to grow.

📌 **Reflection Exercise:**

What practice: morning, midday, or evening - could help you stay grounded in your values?

📌 **Action Point:**

Choose one small daily habit. It might be asking yourself a question each morning or jotting down a thought each night. Whatever you choose, keep it simple and commit to doing it for a week to see what changes.

Embracing Discomfort – The Strength of Voluntary Hardship

Comfort is addictive. Once we have it, we design our lives to avoid anything that might disrupt it: physical strain, emotional risk, honest feedback, uncertainty. Comfort, however, rarely leads to growth - in fact, it can quietly rob us of our edge, our resilience, and our ability to serve with strength.

The Stoics understood this well and practised voluntary hardship - not to suffer for suffering's sake, but to remind themselves that they could.

"Set aside a certain number of days, during which you shall be content with the scantiest and cheapest fare, with coarse and rough dress, saying to yourself all the while: 'Is this the condition that I feared?'"

- Seneca

They weren't trying to punish themselves. The Stoics were training and building tolerance for uncertainty, scarcity, and failure. By facing discomfort in their own way and on their own terms they were preventing themselves from being ruled by it when it befell them in the future.

Choose Discomfort with Purpose

The Service Mindset invites the same principle. Discomfort, when chosen deliberately, strengthens us. It expands our capacity. It puts our comfort in perspective.

That might mean:

- Getting up early to walk the dog when it's cold and raining.
- Volunteering for a task that scares you.
- Having the awkward conversation you've been avoiding.
- Saying *no* to something easy so you can say *yes* to something meaningful.

Discomfort in these moments isn't weakness but discipline. It's how you stretch your range and prepare yourself for whatever comes next.

A Finnish Lesson in Nature and Simplicity

In Finland, there's a quiet cultural reverence for nature. People walk in the forest in silence. They plunge into icy lakes after sauna. They go outside even when it's -10°C and dark by 3pm.

Why? Because nature recalibrates you and it strips away noise. It reminds you that discomfort is survivable, even good for you. There's something deeply human about walking through woodland with cold air in your lungs. It doesn't matter what job you have, what car you drive, or what opinions people hold of you. Out there, you're just a person. Moving, breathing, being.

If modern life is too padded, too screen-filled, too curated - nature is often the antidote.

📌 Reflection Exercise:

What form of voluntary discomfort could you experiment with this week? What might it teach you - not just about endurance, but about what you truly need?

📌 Action Point:

Choose one small act of voluntary discomfort: a cold shower, an early start, a long walk without your phone, a candid conversation. Afterwards, write down how it made you feel. Did it strengthen you? Did it shift your perspective?

Learning Service Through a Dog's Eyes

When Nellie came into our lives, I thought we were just getting a dog - a companion for my daughter and an excuse for more walks. I wasn't expecting her to teach me about service, presence, or emotional regulation, but that's exactly what she did.

After the COVID lockdowns, I was still rebuilding. Like a lot of people, I was burnt out in ways I didn't fully understand. Life had become narrow. Stale. The arrival of this small, energetic creature shifted something. She didn't care about status - she didn't ask how my day had gone.

She just needed feeding, walking, attention, and care - every single day.

And so, I adapted. I went outside more. I paid attention to the world again. I built a new rhythm around her needs. In doing so, I realised something important:

Service isn't always grand. Sometimes, it's just being there consistently and doing the little things that make someone else feel safe.

There's also something deeply anchoring about the daily ritual of dog-walking. You don't skip it. You don't rationalise your way out of it. Rain or shine, it happens. In a strange way, that kind of routine saved me from myself.

Each morning, the woods near our home became a reset button. I'd walk in silence, breathe in the trees, watch Nellie trot through the undergrowth. No screens. No news. Just nature, repetition, and the quiet companionship of a tiny weird animal that needed me.

It reminded me that meaning doesn't come from thinking, it comes from engaging. From taking care of what's in front of you. From being needed. From being useful.

Nellie doesn't dwell on yesterday or worry about next week. She exists fully in the moment - whether she's sniffing a leaf or sprinting after a squirrel she'll never catch. It's easy to dismiss that as animal instinct, but there's a lesson in it.

She's not distracted. She's not performing. She's just there – entirely present in the moment.

Most people I know, including me, struggle with that. We overthink, over-plan, and under-feel. The Service Mindset, however, is built on presence. You can't serve well if you're not paying attention. You can't uplift others if you're only half-there.

So now when Nellie sees a squirrel or a pigeon – something she instinctively disapproves of, sitting on our garden fence, I will let her out to bark at it and follow her barefoot into the garden – rain or shine.

Because sometimes, in this world of deepfakes, AI and virtual reality, we need to feel something that's real – and for me that has become the ground beneath my bare feet.

📌 Reflection Exercise:

What are the simple routines in your life that ground you? Do you treat them as chores, or could they become moments of connection, presence, and service?

📌 Action Point:

Identify one small daily habit - whether it's walking, cooking, tidying, or caring for someone else - and approach it this week with intentionality. No multitasking, no rushing. Just full presence.

Let it be a daily discipline in service.

The Service Mindset and Physical Well-Being

Taking care of yourself physically is often framed as a personal project: something you do to look better, feel better or to live longer. But through the lens of The Service Mindset, it becomes something else entirely. A responsibility. A foundation. A way to serve others more effectively.

If you're run-down, depleted, or constantly on the edge of burnout, your capacity to contribute shrinks. The version of you that others rely on: the parent, the leader, the friend, the partner - can't operate at full strength if you're running on fumes.

You Cannot Serve from an Empty Vessel

It's tempting to treat rest as a luxury, or movement as optional. But if you're consistently exhausted, stressed, or unwell, it will show – often in unpleasant ways, such as how you treat other people.

- A tired leader can't inspire or guide.
- A drained parent struggles to be patient or playful.
- A burnt-out partner loses the emotional presence that relationships require.

Looking after yourself is not selfish, it's a prerequisite for meaningful service.

📌 Reflection Exercise:

Think about your physical habits: movement, sleep, nutrition. Are they aligned with your desire to be useful and present for the people who matter?

📌 Action Point:

Choose one small physical adjustment this week - not for your appearance, but for your ability to engage meaningfully. It could be a proper night's sleep, a walk at lunch, or even just stepping outside for fresh air. Do it not for yourself alone, but for those who rely on you.

The False Escape: Alcohol and The Service Mindset

After my brain injury – and often in my lowest moments, I found myself drawn to alcohol – allowing it to feature too frequently in my life under the guise of self-prescribed relief. I wasn't addicted, but I was leaning on it: for courage, for comfort and for escape.

Alcohol gave me something I couldn't give myself at the time: a short-lived confidence. It smoothed the edges of insecurity, quietened the inner critic, made social situations feel easier. I could be louder, looser and less scrutinised by my own thoughts.

In the aftermath of a traumatic brain injury, there are two great sources of sadness that follow you around every day. The first is the feeling of profound disconnection between who you want to be and the voice that now inhabits your head. The second is the feeling that things are not normal. That feeling of abnormality is draining, exhausting and deeply upsetting. Everything requires an unnatural amount of effort.

For me alcohol offered relief from these feelings. In moments where I was able to drink, the processing of information and social situations felt easier – as though it required less effort. This, in turn, alleviated the other source of sadness. With things moving easier and freer in my head, everything would feel less abnormal.

A realisation that I was forced to confront however, was that the confidence that alcohol gave me in certain situations wasn't real. It wasn't built on anything lasting or true and - more importantly, it came at the cost of presence.

The more I reached for alcohol to ease the discomfort, the less connected I became to the people who truly mattered. I wasn't just numbing the pain and negativity in my head, I was numbing everything. I wasn't dealing with the insecurities that flowed from my diminished cognitive powers, I was masking them and ultimately putting off the work that really needed to be done.

The Service Mindset reframed everything because it challenged me to ask harder questions.

How can I serve my family, my responsibilities, my purpose, if I'm not fully present?
How can I lead with clarity if I'm regularly choosing to blur the edges of my life?

Alcohol, in the way I once used it, wasn't an act of service to anyone - it was an act of escape. Whilst escape might feel justified when you're suffering and hurting every day, it doesn't do anything to help you to heal.

Alcohol was the vehicle I was misusing to run away from myself and my feelings. In this way, alcohol is the ultimate distraction. It delays your suffering, but the minutes and hours you waste hiding from yourself and your pain, soon turn into days, weeks, months and years.

Before you know it, you are looking at a sizeable chunk of your lifetime where you have been so focused on hiding from the pain, that you have failed to be present – you have always been somewhere else.

This is not an alcohol-specific problem. In the modern world, so many people are struggling under the weight of pain, hurt or trauma – and the modern world is always ready to offer up all manner of distractions that enable an individual to hide from their suffering in the present.

Reclaiming Presence

The shift came for me personally when I realised that The Service Mindset obligated me to stop viewing my presence as optional, but rather to start seeing it as something I owed to those around me. Not from guilt or martyrdom, but through the recognition that the people I love deserve the best version of me. So do the people I work with. So do I.

I realise now that the best version of me is never found at the bottom of a glass. It's found in my clarity and in my consistency. It lies in taking the conscious decision to face discomfort rather than to run away from it.

This doesn't mean I've sworn off alcohol entirely – God knows there is no greater gift in life than a cold beer on a hot summer day or the feeling of having earnt a good glass of red wine. It just means that through the Service Mindset, I ask myself a different question now:

Does this choice make me more or less able to give my best to the people who matter most?

That's what guides me: not rules, not guilt - just serving myself and those that I love to the best of my ability.

True confidence doesn't come from silencing the voice of self-doubt – it first comes through quiet acceptance and then from proving, over and over again, that you can face life as you are: no crutches, no filters – just your presence.

Your presence, when you truly understand its power, is one of the greatest gifts that you have to give.

✦ Reflection Exercise:

Think about the distractions in your life – if not alcohol, what might you be using to numb your pain that robs you of your presence? Does it genuinely add something of value or does it remove your ability to be present for those around you? Is it comforting, or are you compromising yourself?

✦ Action Point:

The next time you reach for a drink – or any other sort of distraction, pause and ask yourself, honestly:

"Is this an escape, or an act of connection?"

If it's the former, consider what you're really trying to avoid and what it might mean to face it instead.

Living a Life Free from Regret

I have lived with my fair share of regret and I know just how heavy a thing it is to carry.

There have obviously been moments: where I have been struggling cognitively with a taxing task, or when a relationship has broken down because I behaved like an absolute arsehole – where I wish I had made better decisions and not ended up with a brain injury.

If you're not careful, regret can always be there - lingering in the background, colouring our memories and shaping our decisions long after the moment has passed. It whispers you should have known, and you should have done, better.

Wouldn't it be nice, if we could live in a way that, even in hindsight, left no need for those whispers? Not because we were perfect, but because we were present, intentional, and true to our values.

The Service Mindset offers this exact path to that kind of life. The Service Mindset understands that it is not possible, or realistic to live a life that's free from failure or pain, however it might just be possible to live one that's free from self-reproach. A life where, whatever happens, you can look back and say: *I tried. I acted with integrity and I did what I believed was right.*

Radical Acceptance – Owning Mistakes Without Shame

Regret thrives in the gap between what happened and what we think should have happened. It feeds on the difference between reality and the version of events we replay in our minds.

The truth is that we don't live in hindsight. We live in real time, with limited information, imperfect emotions, and human flaws.

Radical acceptance is not about excusing ourselves or brushing aside our mistakes - it's about meeting reality without any distortion. Owning our actions, learning from them and then, critically, moving on.

Real integrity isn't about being right all the time, it's about being honest with yourself especially when that honesty reveals that you got things wrong.

Regret as a Teacher, Not a Verdict

Regret becomes useful the moment we start asking: *What can this moment teach me?* When we reframe it from a judgement into a lesson, it stops being a punishment and starts being a guide.

The people I've met who have grown the most are not the ones who avoided mistakes. They're the ones who faced them honestly, learnt from them, and carried those lessons forward into something better.

A life without regret is not a life without missteps or mistakes, it's a life that uses those bumps in the road to become wiser, kinder and more intentional.

Reframing the Past – A Visual Technique

After my brain injury, there were plenty of moments I wished I could take back: conversations that went wrong, situations I didn't handle well and reactions I couldn't control. For a long time, they played on repeat in my mind, each one carrying the huge weight of embarrassment or shame that I felt in those moments.

Eventually, I developed a visual technique to stop those moments from owning me.
I would replay the memory like a scene in a film: big, loud, vivid. Then I would mentally press pause. I'd let the image freeze, drain the colour from it, and slowly shrink it until it was small enough to disappear. Then I'd take a breath and move on.

It wasn't about pretending the moment hadn't happened but rather acknowledging it, giving it its space and then choosing not to carry it any further than I needed to.

Keep Moving Forward

The danger with regret is that it can very quickly become like quicksand – trapping us in the past and paralysing us with what ifs. The Service Mindset offers us an escape route from this mental trap because it demands positive action and that drives us forward.

You can't change yesterday, but you can always decide what today means... and tomorrow.

Regret says: *If only I had...*
Service says: *Here's what I am going to do now.*

📌 Reflection Exercise:

Think of a moment you regret. What were you holding yourself responsible for? Was it something within your control or something you've judged too harshly with the benefit of hindsight? What would radical acceptance look like in that moment?

📌 Action Point:

If there's a regret that still weighs on you, try the visualisation technique:

- Play the moment in full.
- Pause it and drain the colour.
- Shrink it.
- Let it go.

Then, write one sentence about what that moment taught you. That is the legacy it leaves - not the shame, but the learning.

Letting Go of the Need to Be Right

One of the quietest forms of resistance to growth is the urge to be right.

It doesn't always shout - often, it's a tightening in the chest during a meeting, a subtle urge to interrupt, or the silent satisfaction of knowing someone else has misunderstood something you're all over.

I've felt it myself on calls, in strategy sessions, in the small exchanges where pride tries to whisper that being right matters more than being effective.

However, the need to be right is wildly inconsistent with the core tenets of The Service Mindset. I am thinking specifically of Tenet 3 – seeing others as equals, Tenet 8 – letting go of perfection and Tenet 10 – the pursuit of validation.

Whatever way you frame it, the need to be right is the antithesis of what The Service Mindset requires us to be.

Moreover, I've learnt that needing to be right often closes doors because it causes you to stop listening and when we stop listening, we stop learning. When we are supremely confident that we are right, there is a tendency to become close-minded – missing out on better ideas simply because they weren't our own.

Worse yet, when you have a closed mind and you draw a sense of superiority from the confidence that you are right, you become a person who is very difficult to work with because you are essentially making everything a contest.

The Service Mindset requires a shift from proving to improving - from being seen as smart to being useful and from holding your ground to finding common ground.

The Dunning-Kruger Effect – When Certainty Is a Warning Sign

You've probably seen it – a person who dominates an agenda, often the loudest voice in the room, utterly convinced by the nonsense they are speaking. Shutting down discussion, and speaking with complete assurance, their misplaced confidence serves to mask their ignorance of the facts.

That's the essence of the Dunning-Kruger effect: people with the least competence often have the most confidence. Meanwhile, those who genuinely understand the complexities of a topic, tend to question themselves more. They see nuance and they stay curious, open-minded and alive to other possibilities.

As with imposter syndrome, this example serves as a powerful reminder: *self-doubt is not a sign of inadequacy, but rather it's often a marker of self-awareness.*

In my own career, the people I've trusted most weren't the ones who always had an answer. They were the ones who said, "I'm not sure," and then went and found out. Who paused to consider. Who knew the cost of false certainty and carried their authority with a quiet sense of care.

It is also something I have become even more aware of in the modern workplace where conversations on topics of emerging technology such as AI often take place. I have not done any solid research into it, but I imagine the words "AI expert" are being written with increasing frequency and regularity on CVs and LinkedIn profiles the world over.

Unwavering, belligerent confidence often does not equal real knowledge, so learn to treat it as a warning sign.

Letting Go Is Liberating

It's not easy to admit you don't know, but it is freeing. Take a deep breath and as you exhale, just surrender the need to be right and open your mind. If you can do this, you will find that you become easier to work with, easier to learn from and more open to being changed by conversations rather than needing to control them.

Who knows, you might even live longer? It certainly can't hurt your blood pressure.

Once you stop trying to "win" every exchange, you may also find that something interesting happens: you may find your influence growing, as people become more open to involving you as a credible collaborator.

✦ Reflection Exercise:

Think back to a recent disagreement. Were you holding onto your view because it felt right, or because you needed to be right? What might have shifted if you'd listened without the need to protect your position?

✦ Action Point:

In your next difficult conversation, pause before responding. Ask yourself: *Is this about making a valuable contribution, or about control?* If it's the latter, let go. Let the better idea win - even if it isn't yours.

The Freedom of Not Knowing

One of the most liberating things I've ever learnt is that you don't need to know everything. You really don't. The people who feel the need to pretend they do - who rattle off opinions on every subject and never ask a question - are often the ones who've stopped learning altogether. When you spend all your energy defending what you already know, you leave no room for growth.

I've seen this happen more times than I care to remember: bright people hiding behind polished certainty, terrified of looking out of their depth. I've done it myself too at points in my career, I thought asking too many questions would reveal gaps in my knowledge, so I kept quiet.

Everything changes when you realise that you do not have to live your life to impress other people. When life becomes about making a worthy contribution, you realise that characteristics such as humility, effort and a willingness to learn will carry you further than unrealistically feigning that you know everything.

Knowing What You Know Is Enough

You don't need to be the smartest person in the room, you just need to know what you bring to the party and trust that it matters. When I first stepped into a global insurance role, I wasn't an expert in aviation or marine insurance, but I wasn't there to be – at least not on day one. The reality was that I was an expert in fraud detection – so stepping into the job and these new areas of insurance presented a choice: I could try to blag some knowledge of these complex subjects and hope I wasn't found out, or I could be open about my lack of experience and add value through my niche area of expertise.

I chose to do the latter – to be the anti-fraud expert I was paid to be. Interestingly, this meant that I could sit in meetings with people who knew their craft inside out, ask naïve questions without apology, and speak with confidence when the conversation turned to my domain.

That's what the Service Mindset looks like in practice: recognising your strengths, staying in your lane, and being open to everything else.

Childlike Curiosity Is a Strength, Not a Liability

If you ask me, children have it right. They ask hundreds of questions a day - they poke, explore, prod, and wonder. Somewhere along the way, we unlearnt all of that and we became afraid of sounding daft. Some of the best people I've ever worked with asked good questions. They also admitted when they didn't know something and listened with intent and respect to the answers.

Curiosity keeps us flexible and it keeps us honest. It's also a sign of security and confidence – a reason why it is so important to ask questions in a job interview. Ultimately, people who ask questions aren't afraid of looking foolish because they're more interested in getting it right than being seen to be right.

People are often apologetic when asking questions; however, throughout my career, it is the people who did not ask questions who caused me the most sleepless nights!

Making Work Not Feel Like Work

For most of us, work will consume a huge portion of our lives. That, in itself, is bad enough, but what makes it worse is the deeply ingrained belief that work has to feel arduous. That stress, pressure, and struggle are somehow signs of productivity. Many leaders operate under the assumption that if work is enjoyable, it must mean people aren't working hard enough.

I reject that idea entirely.

If we are doomed to work, then leaders have a responsibility to make that experience as enjoyable, engaging, and stress-free as possible. I believe that when people are curious, playful, and free to explore, they do their best work, not because they are forced to, but because they want to.

So, how do we build workplaces that people actually enjoy? One way is by fostering a culture of curiosity. That's where the Japanese concept of Shoshin, *the beginner's mind*, comes in…

The Power of Not Knowing: Shoshin as a Business Tool

One of the greatest barriers to innovation and problem-solving is not ignorance, but expertise. The more we know, the more we assume, and in business, these assumptions can be costly. *Shoshin*, or the "beginner's mind," is a Zen Buddhist concept that encourages approaching problems with openness, curiosity, and a lack of preconceived notions.

Without realising it, I have been practicing *Shoshin* for years, particularly in my work as a fraud expert. The most powerful tool in my arsenal has often been the willingness to seem like the idiot in the room: to ask the obvious questions, to challenge what everyone else takes for granted.

Shoshin vs. The Einstellung Effect

There's a well-documented cognitive bias known as the Einstellung effect - the tendency to approach problems using familiar methods, even when better solutions exist. In fraud prevention, I've seen this play out time and time again. Investigators, underwriters, and claims handlers rely on the same processes, the same red flags, and the same decision trees, even when fraudsters have evolved their tactics.

But when we embrace *Shoshin*, we actively push back against the Einstellung effect. We acknowledge that just because something has always been done a certain way doesn't mean it's the best way. Asking "why?" - even when it feels obvious - can be the key to breaking through entrenched thinking.

The Courage to Ask the Stupid Questions

In business, people are often reluctant to admit what they don't know. There's an unspoken pressure to demonstrate competence, to nod along when something doesn't quite make sense, to avoid looking foolish in front of colleagues. But *Shoshin* demands the opposite, it requires us to be comfortable with not knowing and to use that as a strength rather than a weakness.

I used to tell my team that the most important thing they can do is to be prepared to ask the stupid questions. Not only because the answers might reveal something unexpected, but because the very act of questioning keeps us from falling into intellectual complacency. When someone presents a process as *"that's just the way things are done,"* the best response is: *Why? Who decided that? What assumptions is this based on?*

How Shoshin Drives Better Business Decisions

When applied as a leadership tool, *Shoshin* transforms the way organisations operate. Here's how:

1. **Encouraging Innovation** – By questioning everything, we open the door to better solutions. Many of the biggest breakthroughs in business have come from people willing to reject *"the way things have always been done."*

2. **Challenging Cognitive Biases** – Expertise is valuable, but it can also be blinding. A beginner's mind ensures we stay flexible and adaptable rather than trapped by past successes.

3. **Creating a Culture of Learning** – When leaders model *Shoshin*, they set the tone for their teams. It creates an environment where people feel safe to ask questions and challenge assumptions, leading to better decision-making at every level.

4. **Strengthening Fraud Prevention** – Fraudsters exploit predictability. If we assume fraud works a certain way and fail to question our defences, we leave gaps that criminals can exploit. A *Shoshin* approach means constantly reassessing our methods to stay ahead.

Applying Shoshin in Your Work

So how can professionals begin to cultivate *Shoshin* in their daily work? Here are some practical steps:

- **Start every project as if you know nothing** – No matter how experienced you are, ask yourself: *If I were approaching this problem for the first time, what would I see?*

- **Ask "why" at least five times** – This forces deeper thinking and reveals underlying assumptions.

- **Seek out fresh perspectives** – Invite insights from people outside your field; sometimes the best ideas come from those who don't have the same blind spots.

- **Be comfortable with uncertainty** – Instead of fearing the unknown, embrace it as an opportunity to learn.

The Service Mindset & Shoshin

At its core, *The Service Mindset* is about putting ego aside and focusing on impact. *Shoshin* is a natural extension of this philosophy. It teaches us that the best way to serve, whether in business, leadership, or fraud prevention, is not by proving how much we know, but by being open to discovering how much more there is to learn.

When we let go of the need to be the smartest person in the room, we unlock the ability to make the best decisions in the room. That is the power of *Shoshin* in business, and the power of *The Service Mindset* in action.

Ultimately, if the status quo has integrity at its foundation, it should stand up to scrutiny. If the "way things are done" withers in the face of questioning, then perhaps it is right that it was questioned in the first place.

Building a Culture of Smart Failure: The Service Mindset in Teams and Leadership

Embracing Shoshin – "the beginner's mind" - means staying open, curious, and willing to challenge assumptions. It allows us to see opportunities where others see obstacles and to approach problems with fresh thinking rather than rigid expertise. There's also a natural consequence to embracing this mindset: if we encourage curiosity and exploration, we must also make our peace with failure.

A culture of learning cannot exist without a culture of smart failure. Failure that is calculated, constructive, and used as a stepping stone for improvement. If we want people to think differently, take initiative, and innovate, we need to create an environment where getting things wrong is part of getting things right.

Failure is an inevitable part of growth, yet many organisations and teams operate in fear of it. Mistakes are punished, innovation is stifled, and people hesitate to take the very risks that could lead to meaningful progress. We have already seen that The Service Mindset teaches us that failure, when approached the right way, is not something to be feared. Instead, it should be seen as an opportunity for learning, adaptation, and future success.

The Service Mindset in Team Culture – Building, Not Breaking

The easiest thing anyone can do is to tear something down.

When you're under pressure at work; deadlines looming, stakes high, the quickest way to feel in control is to critique. It takes almost no effort to say *"this won't work,"* or *"we've tried that before."* Shooting down an idea gives you a momentary sense of authority.

It's clean, fast, and emotionally safe and enables an individual to seize a moment of temporary and fragile superiority.

It is far harder, and requires more energy to create something.

Applying The Service Mindset in the workplace means recognising that *ideas are fragile things*.

When someone offers a new thought, they're taking a risk and they're exposing themselves. How we respond, especially in those first moments, sets the tone for everything that follows.

A team with a Service Mindset doesn't rush to evaluate. It looks for the *seed of value* in what's been offered. It asks:

- *What part of this could work?*
- *What would happen if we added to it instead of subtracting from it?*
- *How can I build on what's been shared rather than prove its flaws?*

This mindset doesn't just encourage better ideas - it creates *better teams*. Teams where people feel safe, seen, and willing to try again.

Yes, And: A Practical Creative Discipline

One of the most powerful habits you can introduce into any team is borrowed from improvisational theatre: Yes, and...

When someone offers an idea, don't default to *"yes, but..."*. Instead, respond with *"yes, and..."* Build momentum. Add. Support. Shape. Challenge if needed, but with curiosity, not contempt.

This doesn't mean every idea is perfect. It doesn't mean we stop critical thinking. But it *does* mean we treat creativity as an act of service, not ego. We collaborate not to win, but to build something worthwhile *together*.

Example:

- Intead of: "That's not going to work."
- We say: "Yes, and what if we tried it this way to overcome the risk?"

It's a simple, but important shift that has the power to challenge the status quo and change a culture.

Creating Space for Innovation to Breathe

The truth is innovation *dies* in teams where people feel unsafe to speak up. You don't get new ideas when the first response is always a takedown. You get silence. You get repetition. You get just trying to survive, rather than working to make things better.

The Service Mindset helps leaders and teammates remember that *our job is to serve the collective goal*, not our own status. That means nurturing potential, not hoarding authority.

Ask yourself:

- *Do I make it easy for others to share ideas?*
- *Do I listen with the intent to build, or the intent to be right?*
- *Do I reward creativity even when the idea doesn't work out?*

If we want teams that work together to *create*, we need teams that *trust* each other.

Contribution Over Criticism

There's a time for critique – of course there is, but in a culture of service, the first instinct is always contribution. Not *"how do I prove this wrong?"* but *"how do I make this better?"*

Imagine what would change in your team if everyone asked:

- *How can I make this work?*
- *What's the part of this idea that's worth protecting?*
- *What value can I add here, even if it's not my idea?*

Criticism protects the past, but contribution builds the future.

✦ Reflection Point: Are You Building or Dismantling?

The next time someone brings you an idea, whether it's clumsy, brilliant, or half-baked, pause.
Ask yourself:

Am I about to serve this moment by breaking something apart… or by helping it grow?

Because the easiest thing to do is to destroy.

The harder thing, the braver thing, is to *build something better together*.

The Role of Leadership In Creating Psychological Safety

The Service Mindset in leadership means creating an environment where people feel safe to express themselves, speak their minds, and ultimately fail, secure in the knowledge that this is the gateway to growth. This doesn't mean accepting reckless mistakes, but it does mean distinguishing between negligence and intelligent risk-taking.

Example: Consider a leader who openly admits their own past failures. When a project doesn't go as planned, instead of assigning blame, they ask, *"What can we learn from this?"* This approach removes fear and builds a culture of trust and continuous improvement.

📌 Reflection Exercise:

Think about a time when you held back from taking a risk because you were afraid of failing. What would have happened if failure had been seen as an acceptable learning experience rather than a career-ending event?

How the Service Mindset Transforms Failure into Strength

The Service Mindset reminds us that our ego should never come before progress. When we let go of superiority and perfectionism, we create an environment where people feel valued not just for their successes, but for their efforts and resilience.

In leadership: *Encouraging smart failure leads to a stronger, more innovative team.*
In business: *Accepting failure as part of success creates long-term resilience.*
In life: *Owning our mistakes makes us better individuals, friends, and family members.*

📌 Key Thought:

Failure isn't the opposite of success – it's part of the journey to success. The only true failure is refusing to learn from it.

Key Takeaways:

- Fear of failure stifles innovation, while smart failure fuels growth.
- Leaders must create psychological safety so teams feel comfortable taking risks.
- Owning mistakes and learning from them builds trust and resilience.
- The Service Mindset transforms failure into a stepping stone rather than a setback.

Embracing failure with humility, accountability, and a commitment to growth is what truly sets successful teams, and individuals, apart.

You Lead Best When You Serve First

I've worked in enough places, met enough leaders, and made enough mistakes of my own to know this much: people don't follow job titles. They follow example. They follow trust. They follow the ones who've earnt it - not with noise or authority, but with service.

It's easy to forget that when you're trying to get ahead. The working world can feel like a game of positioning. Who's in the room. Who's in favour. Who gets the credit. But the truth is, that stuff doesn't last. People remember how you made them feel. Whether you helped or hindered. Whether you lifted others or used them as a stepping stone.

The Service Mindset is not just some philosophy for good behaviour. It's a strategy for long-term, sustainable success - one that's grounded in human truth. We trust those who serve us well. We follow those who make us better. And we rise when we help others rise.

Letting Go of Grudges – Releasing What No Longer Serves

Grudges are heavy things to carry. They don't just occupy emotional space, they shape the way we see people, tilt our decisions, and quietly colour the complexion of our lives. Often, we hold onto them thinking they give us power or protection, but they don't. What they really give us is tension, bitterness, and the act of carrying them is exhausting.

For a long time, I didn't realise how much old grievances were shaping my behaviour. I'd tell myself I'd moved on, but in truth, I was still bracing against people who no longer had any real hold on me. The moment I stopped doing that – when I genuinely let go – I didn't just feel lighter. I felt in possession of a greater clarity – I was freer to see opportunities and move forward in my own life.

The biggest grudge I ever had to carry was the fact that fate had Inflicted a brain Injury on me. In one fell swoop, the universe had given me this huge weight to carry, and it permeated into and tainted every aspect of my life.

I used to tell everybody and it was often one of the first things I would say in the early exchanges of a conversation.

This is the power that holding a grudge has to root you into a specific point in the past. In an earlier section, we examined how we build value by moving forwards. We simply cannot do this when holding a grudge keeps us anchored to the past.

The Trap of Righteous Resentment

Grudges often come wrapped in the cloak of righteousness. We tell ourselves we're justified: *They were out of line. They never apologised. They got away with it.* All of that may be true, but the more time we spend mentally relitigating those moments, the less time we spend on anything that actually makes our lives better.

Letting go isn't the same as condoning someone's behaviour. It's not about forgetting, and it's not about pretending we weren't hurt – it's simply about deciding not to carry that pain around anymore.

Service Requires Energy – Don't Waste It on Resentment

In a previous section, we looked at how The Service Mindset requires us to prioritise our own well-being, recognising that serving well requires energy. In this way, it's imperative that we spend our energy wisely. If you're going to give yourself to something, let it be the building of something good, not the reopening of old wounds. That doesn't mean you have to reconnect with people who've hurt you, or suppress how you feel. It just means you stop letting those feelings shape your present.

I've learnt, that every time I let go of a grudge, I got some energy back. Energy I can use to support my team, be more patient with my family, write something meaningful, or just enjoy a day with less weight on my shoulders.

How to Let Go Without Losing the Lesson

Forgiveness doesn't mean pretending that something never happened. It means extracting the lesson, storing the wisdom, and discarding the resentment.

Ask yourself:

- *What did this experience teach me?*
- *How has it changed what I expect or tolerate?*
- *How will I act differently next time?*

When you take what's useful and release what's corrosive, you aren't letting anyone off the hook, you are just releasing yourself from being tied to a moment that no longer deserves your attention.

I often think that as a society, we have become quite out of practice when it comes to forgiveness. This is a significant problem because not being able to forgive is essentially the same as asserting superiority – an act that The Service Mindset cannot endorse.

We live in a black and white world, where issues are viewed in an oversimplified way as being categorically right or wrong. When another person falters, society pounces in an opportune way – an overt play for superiority - as we label mistakes "unforgivable."

In the same way that Service requires energy and building something is harder than breaking something down, forgiveness requires effort and practice.

An inability to forgive, prevents us from moving forward and thus actively undermines our value.

📌 **Reflection Exercise:**

Is there someone or something you're still holding onto - some resentment that's taking up more space than it deserves? What's the real cost of that weight?

📌 **Action Point:**

Write a short letter (you don't have to send it) to someone you're struggling to forgive. Say what needs saying. Then, either delete it or destroy it. Not because they deserve peace, but because you do.

Addressing Conflict Through the Service Mindset

A defining moment in leadership is how we respond when tensions rise and people fail to meet the standards of respect, professionalism, and teamwork that we expect in a service-driven culture. It's easy to step back, ignore conflict, or let the discomfort pass. True leadership - rooted in The Service Mindset - means choosing the harder path: addressing conflict head-on in a way that serves everyone involved, even the person who caused the problem.

The Incident: A Workplace Conflict

One day, many years ago and in an office I have long since forgotten - I witnessed an uncomfortable exchange between two colleagues. One, frustrated and overwhelmed, lashed out at another in a way that crossed the line from simple workplace tension into something more damaging. The atmosphere in the room shifted instantly - everyone felt it and it was deeply uncomfortable.

At that moment, I had a choice. I could ignore it and let it slide, as so many do. I could reprimand the aggressor publicly, making an example of them, or I could take the path of service - stepping in, addressing the issue constructively, and ensuring that both individuals walked away not just feeling heard but growing from the experience.

Service to the Person Who Was Wronged

The immediate responsibility was clear: the person who had been spoken to unfairly needed support and reassurance. It was my duty to acknowledge that the behaviour they had had to endure was not acceptable and that they were valued, respected, and deserved better. In service to them, I made sure they knew that their feelings and well-being mattered, and that they were working in an environment where professionalism and respect were not just expected, but upheld.

My duty didn't end there though, because The Service Mindset isn't just about lifting up those who have been hurt - it's also about lifting up those who do the hurting when they themselves need guidance and development.

Service to the Aggressor: Understanding Before Condemning

It would have been easy to call out the aggressor in front of everyone, to put them in their place, or even to punish them for their behaviour, but that wouldn't have served them, and it certainly wouldn't have served the team. Instead, I chose to understand before I judged.

I took them aside and addressed the situation not as a punishment, but as a learning moment. I asked: *"What happened? What led to that reaction?"* As we spoke, it became clear that this was not a fundamentally bad person, but someone who was struggling: dealing with stress, personal frustration, and emotions they hadn't learnt how to manage.

Instead of punishing, I coached. I helped them understand why their reaction was unacceptable, but also offered them a path forward. We talked about accountability - that leadership is not just about holding others accountable but holding *ourselves* accountable for how we treat other people. We discussed emotional regulation, the importance of recognising stress before it turns into outbursts, and how a great leader does not simply react - they manage, reflect, and improve.

The Impact: A Long-Term Investment in People

This moment could have ended as a simple HR reprimand - a check-the-box, let's-move-on moment that ultimately helped no one, but because I chose to serve rather than punish, the long-term outcome and impact were different.

The person who was wronged saw that their concerns were taken seriously and that the culture they worked in was one of respect and accountability. However – and perhaps almost as importantly - the individual who acted out, grew from the experience. They became more self-aware, more conscious of their impact on others, and, in time, more composed under pressure.

The Bigger Lesson: True Leadership Lifts Others

In traditional workplace cultures, punishment and discipline are often used as tools to enforce behaviour. Tenet 6 of the Service Mindset requires us to lift others – therefore, when we are leading in Service, we have to do more than just discipline. We are obliged to take the time to understand the "why" behind people's actions and then give them the tools to be better - not just for the organisation, but for themselves.

Holding people accountable is not about asserting superiority, it's about helping them improve so that they can become stronger members of an effective team.

How to Apply This Mindset to Your Leadership

Address, don't ignore – *Avoiding conflict helps no one. Leadership means stepping in when necessary.*

Serve both sides – *Support those who are wronged, but also invest in those who need to grow.*

Ask, don't assume – *Understanding why someone behaved a certain way opens the door for real improvement.*

Guide, don't just reprimand – *Feedback should be a tool for growth, not a punishment.*

Model the right behaviour – *A culture of respect starts with leadership leading by example.*

Communicating with Empathy

One of the simplest tools I've introduced in teams to encourage empathy in communication is what I call the "photo on your desk" technique. It's not a training module or a framework, it's just a quiet thought exercise.

I tell people: keep a picture of your grandma on your desk. Or your mum. Or your child. Someone you love deeply and respect entirely. When you're about to send that email, give that difficult feedback, or speak to that colleague or customer - imagine you're speaking to the person in the picture. *Would you rush the words? Would you use inflammatory language? Would you forget the human behind the task?*

That photo is a mirror. It reminds us that empathy doesn't require extra time, it requires presence. Communicate as if the person you love most is on the receiving end, because in a world built on service – where everyone is equal and deserving of your support, they are.

Speak to Serve - The Art of Communicating with Presence and Respect

Most of us learn to speak before we learn to listen. We spend our lives polishing our vocabulary, honing our arguments, and sharpening our wit, but none of that guarantees good communication. In service, the point of communication is not to dominate, impress, or perform. Rather, the point is to connect - to understand and be understood.

That begins, first of all, with understanding yourself.

We all have a default communication style. Some of us are direct and brisk. Others are warm and expressive. Some speak in facts; others in feelings. The danger comes when we assume that everyone else thinks, feels, and processes like we do.

A key part of the Service Mindset is recognising that how you communicate matters as much as what you say. Therefore, if you want to serve effectively - in leadership, in family, or in crisis - you must learn to adjust your approach for the good of the relationship, not just for your own comfort.

That means taking time to notice how others express themselves. Do they need clarity or warmth? Reassurance or brevity? Do they respond better to logic, or to empathy? Service means paying attention to what they need, not just delivering what you feel like saying.

So before you begin communicating, take a moment to think about what other's need from you.

For reasons I cannot really explain, I know that I have become quite a direct communicator. In certain situations, I understand that my default is to speak efficiently – to get my point across succinctly and sometimes forcefully and I appreciate that this is not to everyone else's taste.

I used to have a colleague, who – from time to time – I would message and say "do you have 5 minutes?" For me, that was just an example of my direct communication. What I failed to appreciate was that my messages would often induce anxiety attacks in my poor colleague, who would receive them and think: "Oh my God, what have I done wrong?!"

As soon as I received this feedback, I immediately adjusted my approach.
And this is the thing, effective communication demands that we take responsibility for how our message lands. If we cause offence, provoke emotions or upset our audience, responsibility for that rests entirely at the door of the messenger and not on the shoulders of the person receiving it.

And then there's energy…

We underestimate how much of communication is non-verbal - the pace, volume, tone, and posture we bring into a conversation. Turning up the volume in a quiet room doesn't make you clearer, it risks making you intrusive. Speaking with calm in a crisis can de-escalate tension without saying a word. Service-minded communication involves matching your energy to the moment, and being deliberate in your presentation - not just physically, but emotionally.

There's also a simple habit that I found helped me a lot – especially in the aftermath of my brain injury: take a breath before you speak - especially when tensions are high. Especially when you feel rushed. That one breath creates space for clarity, for grace, for restraint. It can be the difference between saying something helpful and saying something you regret.

Finally, in a world that can sometimes seem as though it rewards boldness and disruption, there's still enormous power in good manners. Say please. Say thank you. Say sorry - sincerely, and without defensiveness. These shouldn't just be words. They should be the words you choose deliberately to reflect the way you are feeling towards a fellow human being of equal standing.

Let your words be signs of humility, of respect, and of shared humanity, and recognise that they often go further than any clever argument ever could.

If you want to live with a Service Mindset, learn to speak in service of others, not just yourself.

Know your style. Read the room. Choose the right energy.
Breathe before you speak. And never forget the basics:
Please. Thank you. Sorry.
They still matter.

The Power of Self-Awareness

Empathy in communication is vital, but so is empathy in presence. It's one thing to speak with care, but another to carry yourself in a way that invites connection in the first place.

I'm a big guy. I've been told more than once that I can come across as serious, grumpy, or even intimidating - especially when I'm deep in thought. I never mean to, but that doesn't change how others might feel. And unfortunately, if people feel unsure about approaching you, they won't, no matter how open you *think* you are being.

That's why self-awareness is a service. It's recognising the energy we carry, the signals we send, and the space we create. It means making the effort to smile, to soften your tone, to give people the confidence to bring things to you without fear or hesitation.

It doesn't mean being inauthentic, but rather intentional. It's about understanding that ultimately it's incumbent on you to set the appropriate energy and when you do, you will get the best from people.

Being Aware of the Needs of Others

Service doesn't stop at being kind or approachable. It also means being thoughtful in how we structure work, how we schedule, and how we set expectations. It means remembering that people live in different realities - not just different roles.

When I first moved into an international role, I set up a regular weekly call with my global team. It felt like a good move: create rhythm, stay connected, but I didn't think through the time zones. One person was skipping lunch and getting hangry. Another felt the meeting bled past their working hours. None of this was intentional, but intent isn't the point. It still had an impact on them – an impact that they took *kind of* personally.

Thankfully, because we had an open culture, they told me early on. I apologised and we made changes straight away, but it was a lesson that I needed to be reminded of. If I hadn't built that openness, those frustrations could've simmered quietly, and over time, that sort of thing drains trust, goodwill, and productivity.

When we serve others, we need to meet them where they are - not just geographically, but personally. *What are their preferences? Their pressures? Their rhythms?* If not being aware of these things has the potential for making people hangry and hurting feelings, having an awareness shows that you have listened and that you care. In any team, showing that you care breeds engagement and it is a well-documented fact that engaged teams are more productive.

One final point here: if someone is struggling, don't ask *"What can I do to help?"* It might sound supportive, but it actually transfers effort from you to them. Now they need to stop and think, assess your capacity, and explain their need - all while under pressure. If you want to help, just help. Bring them a cup of tea. Take something off their plate. Cancel a non-essential meeting. Helpfulness isn't in the asking - it's in the noticing.

Leadership is about lifting everyone - not just the high performers, not just the easy-to-manage employees, but also those who struggle, those who lash out, and those who have the potential to be better than their worst moments.

Choosing service over punishment doesn't mean tolerating bad behaviour. It means correcting it in a way that leads to growth, not resentment. This is how we build stronger teams, healthier workplace cultures, and more resilient people.

📌 **Reflection Exercise:**

Think of a time you witnessed (or experienced) workplace conflict. How was it handled? Could a service-driven approach have led to a better outcome?

📌 **Action Step:**

The next time you see a conflict brewing in your team, commit to serving both sides - ensuring accountability while also fostering development.

The Service Mindset and Managing Exploitation: Setting Boundaries Without Losing Generosity

A potential criticism of The Service Mindset is that it means saying yes to everything: that being helpful requires an open-ended commitment to others, even at the expense of one's own time, energy, and well-being. However, this misconception is not correct: service is not submission, and generosity is not weakness.

True service is about creating value in a way that is sustainable, fair, and mutually beneficial. It is not about pleasing everyone; it is about making a meaningful impact without compromising personal boundaries.

Without boundaries, service quickly becomes exploitation. Those who fail to set limits risk burnout, resentment, and an erosion of their ability to serve effectively. The challenge, then, is learning when to give, when to guide, and when to say *no*.

Recognising When Service Becomes Exploitation

Not everyone approaches generosity with good faith. Some individuals, or even entire organisations, see kindness as an opportunity to take more. They ask for more without offering anything in return, shift responsibilities onto others whilst taking credit, or assume that past generosity implies future obligation. They may appreciate a person's help but show little regard for their time.

Being service-driven does not mean being endlessly accommodating. It means recognising when a relationship is one-sided and responding with professionalism and integrity. A leader or colleague who continually takes without reciprocating is not engaging in a service-based exchange but in an act of quiet exploitation.

How to Serve Without Being Exploited

Help, But Don't Enable: Service is most effective when it empowers others, not when it fosters dependency. The goal should be to help people to help themselves, not to carry their entire burden entirely or indefinitely. A person who constantly relies on someone else to solve their problems is not growing - they are merely offloading responsibility.

For example, rather than always fixing issues on someone's behalf, it is more beneficial to guide them toward finding their own solutions. This way, service becomes a tool for development rather than a crutch.

Set Boundaries Early and Clearly: Many people overstep simply because no one has told them otherwise. By defining expectations from the outset, it is possible to prevent exploitation before it begins.

In a professional setting, if a colleague repeatedly offloads their work, an effective response might be: *"I'm happy to show you how to do it, but I won't be able to do it for you."* This approach is firm yet constructive, ensuring that help is provided without assuming undue responsibility.

Frame Conversations Around Value, Not Just Limits: Declining unreasonable requests does not need to be framed in negative terms. Instead of simply saying, *"I don't have time for this,"* a more effective approach is to focus on impact:

"I want to ensure I'm delivering my best and not spreading myself too thinly – let's work something out that enables me to help, without compromising on some of the other things that I have to do."

By positioning boundaries as a matter of prioritising value rather than refusal, conversations become more productive and less adversarial.

Say No When Necessary - Without Guilt: There are times when the best form of service is a firm refusal. If someone is persistently draining time and effort without contributing in return, stepping back is the right move. Saying no does not mean abandoning the principles of service; it means ensuring that service remains meaningful and effective.

A clear and respectful boundary might sound like: *"I've helped as much as I can, but I need to focus on other priorities now."* This acknowledges past efforts whilst signalling that ongoing support is not indefinite.

Service Without Sacrifice

The Service Mindset is not about saying *yes* to everyone; it is about saying *yes* to the right things. True service is sustainable. If giving leads to exhaustion, resentment, or a sense of being taken for granted, then it is no longer service - it is self-sacrifice.

The best leaders help, but do not enable. They give, but do not allow themselves to be drained. And when someone attempts to exploit their generosity, they do not see it as a failure of service but as an opportunity to lead with fairness, clarity, and self-respect.

The Service Mindset and Play – Taking Life Less Seriously

One of the most important things I've learnt, though it took me longer than I'd like to admit, is the value of not taking myself too seriously. The world is full of pressure: to perform, to prove yourself, to get everything right, but when we lose the ability to laugh at ourselves or to find joy in the absurdity of life, we end up brittle. And brittle things are easier to break.

Play isn't a distraction from the serious stuff, it's how we stay human whilst doing the serious stuff.

The Vegetarian Roast Incident

Years ago, I was invited to a Sunday dinner hosted by the teammates of a hockey-playing girlfriend. So there I was, the only man – surrounded by confident, sporty, impressive women.

There weren't enough chairs, so I selflessly ended up cross-legged on the floor, eating an entirely vegetarian roast dinner, and nodding along to conversations about tofu-based proteins, league standings and hockey tactics that I didn't even understand.

About two hours in, my digestive system mounted a protest. As I stood to leave, a sound escaped me that left no room for plausible deniability. The sound echoed around the room and continued for a lot longer than I was used to in that department. In truth it was seconds but each of those felt like hours. The women hockey players looked on in stunned silence, some exchanged glances with each other, others sat there open mouthed and still the noise continued... *please just stop now* I thought to myself pathetically. I don't know why I did what happened next, but in a blind panic, I clutched my lower back and exclaimed, over the death throes of my large intestine, "*Oh! I've pulled something in my back*" before hobbling out of the room like a man who had just been shot.

I was so embarrassed and those poor hockey players were embarrassed too – not because I had produced a thunder that could have blown the sprouts from the table, but because of the undignified way I had feigned injury and tried to cover the whole sorry episode up.

It wasn't a proud moment. I hadn't yet learnt the freedom of being able to laugh at myself. If I had, I would've owned it - maybe even cracked a joke - but at that point in my life, I was still holding on too tightly to an idea of composure. I hadn't yet realised that self-acceptance and humour often go hand in hand.

Feeling inferior, seeking validation, unable to accept reality – I was many of the things that The Service Mindset teaches us not to be. Remember to accept reality, let go and laugh – if needs be at yourself – you'll attract a whole lot less pity and that can only be a good thing.

The Value of Play

Playfulness isn't immaturity, it's a means of making a connection. I have found that the willingness to be silly, to improvise, to take the pressure off, disarms people, softens conflict, and makes room for authenticity.

When we're playful:

- We connect more easily with others.
- We build trust faster.
- We recover from mistakes more gracefully.
- We access creativity and flexibility we wouldn't otherwise find.

Play has always been a form of communication. Babies play to bond. Children play to learn. Adults who can still access that part of themselves tend to be better leaders, better parents, and far less likely to be eaten alive by stress.

Service With a Smile (and Maybe a Snort)

The Service Mindset isn't about being solemn. It's about being present in the moment and sometimes, the best way to be present is to stop trying to be perfect. If you can laugh with someone, you've already built a bridge. If you can laugh at yourself, you've disarmed the ego. If you can let go of the need to look impressive all the time, you create space for others to relax, too.

I still think about that vegetarian roast. Not because of the embarrassment, but because of the lesson. There's real strength in being able to laugh, to roll with it, and to not let pride get in the way of joy.

📌 Reflection Exercise:

When was the last time you laughed properly? Not a polite chuckle, but real, undignified laughter. What were you doing? Who were you with? What made it possible?

📌 Action Point:

Do something today that has no purpose other than fun. Be a bit ridiculous. Make someone laugh. Let yourself off the hook – observe how you feel in yourself when you allow yourself to be silly.

Ultimately: Choose Happiness - The Mindset of Openness and Play

Happiness is often treated as something that must be earnt. People tell themselves they will be happy once they lose weight, achieve career success, or gain the approval of others. It becomes a future event, always just out of reach and contingent on some qualifying action or event. I am inclined to believe that happiness does not exist in the future – like many things, happiness only exists in the present. The greatest misconception is that happiness is a reward for accomplishment, when in reality, it is a choice that can be made at any moment.

I was reminded of this in the most unexpected way. I had been under immense pressure at work, dealing with yet another audit. My function was being scrutinised, and I was heading into a meeting to discuss its scope. It felt like just another battle in an endless cycle of proving myself. That morning, I got dressed, glanced at my reflection in the mirror, and felt a wave of self-loathing.

"God, I am so fat and so ugly," I muttered to myself. Frustrated and exhausted, I lay down on the bed, staring at the ceiling, drifting on a tide of negativity.

Then something happened. Nellie, our little dog, jumped up and curled up beside me. A moment later, Jane joined her, lying down next to me. She turned her head, looked me in the eye, and said something so simple, yet so profound.

"You can just be happy, you know."

It stopped me in my tracks. She was right. There was nothing in that moment preventing me from choosing happiness except my own mind. I had become so consumed with stress, so entangled in self-criticism, that I had forgotten that happiness was available to me at any time. Nothing external needed to change - only my perspective.

The Service Mindset teaches us that we are at our best when we look outward rather than inward. When we obsess over things beyond our control: our appearance, other people's opinions, the relentless pressures of work - we trap ourselves in an endless cycle of frustration. However, when we shift our attention to what we can give, how we can contribute, and how we can engage with the present moment, we free ourselves.

The philosophy of shoshin, or "beginner's mind," offers a powerful way to cultivate happiness. In its essence, shoshin is about approaching life with the curiosity and wonder of a child, free from preconceptions, ego, or fear of failure. Children naturally explore, play, and embrace possibilities without the burden of expectations or the anxiety of proving themselves.

As adults, we often lose this ability. We become rigid in our thinking, weighed down by responsibilities, and hesitant to take risks. Yet, when we reconnect with a spirit of exploration, we rediscover the ability to find joy in the process rather than just in the outcome.

The Service Mindset encourages us to view happiness in the same way. Instead of seeing it as something to be earnt, we can choose to create it through our actions, our mindset, and the way we engage with the world.

Approaching challenges with playfulness rather than dread, finding meaning in service rather than self-importance, and embracing uncertainty as an opportunity rather than a threat, all contribute to a deeper sense of contentment. Happiness is not the result of control or accumulation - but of engagement, presence, and a willingness to be open to the moment.

📌Reflection Task:

Think about a time when you put off happiness, believing it would come after reaching a certain goal. How did that expectation shape your experience? How might embracing the present have changed your perspective?

📌 Action Step:

In the coming days, approach one task or challenge with a sense of playfulness and curiosity rather than pressure or expectation. Notice how this shift in mindset affects your experience and your overall sense of well-being.

Your Value Is Created Through Action

At every stage of life, we define ourselves not by what we think we are, but by how we engage with the world. Our worth isn't measured in job titles, salaries, or social status. It's measured in presence, in impact, in the way we move through our days and the people we lift along the way.

When we adopt The Service Mindset, we stop asking, *Am I good enough?* and start asking, *How can I contribute?* This subtle shift moves us from insecurity to intent. From self-doubt to service. And in doing so, it builds something that external validation never could - real, grounded confidence.

Resilience, too, is built through action. We aren't made stronger by what happens to us. We're made stronger by how we respond to the things that happen to us – especially when things go wrong. When the worst hits, fate and misfortune do not take away our value; they reveal it.

Imposter syndrome, anxiety, regret, perfectionism - these are the weights we carry when we believe we're not enough. However, they begin to lose most of their weight when we start to focus on what we are actually doing, as opposed to how we are perceived when doing it. The most secure people I've met weren't trying to look impressive - they were too busy making a difference to care.

Your value isn't in your potential, it's in what you are giving in the moment.

But I also know this: when you're close to rock bottom, none of that is easy to hear. When you're lying in bed, unable to face the day, the idea of "adding value" can feel like a cruel joke. I've been there. I've stared at the ceiling, paralysed by inertia, unsure who I was anymore. I've looked for validation in all the wrong places: overworking, overthinking, reaching for alcohol to numb the dissonance between who I was and who I felt I had become.

And here's the truth that helped to change things for me: *you don't have to fix it all today.*

You don't have to climb the whole mountain, you just have to take one step.

When things feel nebulous or overwhelming, the temptation is to give up before we've even begun. However, do not underestimate the real power that lies in the small things - the barely-noticeable victories that build momentum. You don't need a five-year plan or a master strategy. You just need to begin.

Tell yourself: *The more I do, the more I'll feel like doing.* Then do something. Anything. Wash a cup. Open the window. Text someone you care about. Put the dishwasher on for your partner without being asked. These things sound small, because they are, but they are not insignificant.

They are movement. And in movement you begin to find meaning.

The Service Mindset isn't about grand gestures or lofty ideals. It's about engaging with life when it would be easier to turn away. It's about showing up for others in small, deliberate ways - not to earn approval, but because connection creates purpose, and that purpose, in turn, anchors us.

Trust this process. I have lived it.

Start small. Keep going. And bit by bit, you'll feel something shift. You'll start to move differently through the world. Others will notice it, but more importantly, you'll notice it too. You'll realise that the version of yourself who felt broken and lost wasn't the end of your story. Like a montage in an 80s movie, it was the part of your story where fortune was reversed – something Aristotle called peripeteia – the moment when the rebuild began.

And know that your delivery in the moment cannot hope to exist in a vacuum. Your impact is defined through your interactions and connectedness to others. It happens through relationships, through presence and through action. We define ourselves in the doing. Like a river carves out its path through the landscape, we shape our identity by the way we flow through the world.

If there's one idea I hope stays with you from this chapter, it's this: you do not need to wait to be seen. Choose who you want to be, the impact that you want to have and then, like a river, move through the terrain such that it is impossible to ignore the impression your presence has made on the landscape.

✦ Reflection Exercise:

Stop and ask yourself: *How am I engaging with the world right now?*
Where are you adding value in practice?
- And if the answer feels unclear, what one action could you take today to begin?

Because your value is not in what you are holding onto, it's in what you are giving.

Chapter 5: Decision-Making and the Service Mindset

After my brain injury, I was at rock bottom. The accident had thrown a reset button in my mind – simply knowing what was right and what was wrong, what was socially acceptable and what wasn't – all of these things had to be worked out. Deduced. Nothing came naturally, everything felt alien and I was broken.

It follows that building resilience, at first, was about survival. I talked a lot in the previous chapter about finding value, and I explained the lessons that I had to learn that supported me to do just that. However, with all that said, I cannot overstate the fact that I learnt these lessons looking for a way to just function – to simply exist in a world where I did not hate myself in every waking minute, or burst into tears whenever I thought about who I had been and how that jarred so painfully with who I was now.

Yes, I found value and meaning, but they were happy bonuses in a quest that started out looking for a means to survive.

As I began to accept my limitations and take responsibility for what I *could* do, a strange thing happened: I started to find, as The Service Mindset began to evolve, that living by these tenets, I didn't just become a better human, but other things got better around me. As I stopped pretending and gave up on trying to be better, I found myself listening more, letting go and becoming the person who I wanted to be – not because I felt like that person existed within me, but because other people started to see me as that person.

I started to move forward in my personal life, in my recovery but also in my career. The Service Mindset wasn't a fully formed idea and it didn't have a name, but it was a way to live my life. And when I lived my life that way, I found that I created an environment where things seemed to get better and improve. It feels hugely arrogant to write what I am about to write, but I think it made me an empathetic leader – a person that others were comfortable trusting and comfortable following. With that buy in from others, bringing about change – for the better – became something that I was good at.

Whether in law firms or insurance companies, the people that gave me an opportunity, received a return on their investment from the lessons I had had no choice but to learn the hard way.

That was the turning point. The years of unseen healing began to ripple outward - into teams, into strategy, into leadership. I went from a broken young man unsure of his place, to leading fraud teams that were winning awards and breaking new ground. Not because I had all the answers, but because I had a mindset that prioritised service, transparency, and steady decisions over ego and bravado.

This next chapter explores that transition in depth. It unpacks how a service-oriented mindset doesn't just help us bounce back, it helps us to move forward, together. When we are grounded in our values, resilient in the face of difficulty, and clear on our purpose, we make better decisions. We build stronger teams. We lead with intention rather than impulse.

We'll explore how emotional regulation, ethical clarity, and strategic thinking all tie back to the same source: knowing who you are, and choosing to serve something bigger than yourself. That's what real influence is and how the best decisions are made.

Why We Struggle to Decide

We all make decisions every day: some are trivial, others can be life-changing. But no matter the scale, there's a truth we rarely acknowledge: most people aren't taught how to decide well. We're taught how to act, how to react, how to get results, but not how to pause, reflect, and choose from a place of clarity.

The truth is, poor decisions are rarely born from a lack of intelligence. They're usually the product of noise: stress, emotion, pressure, insecurity or ego. We make instinctive choices in the heat of the moment, driven by fear or frustration or the need to prove something and then we can spend months, even years, cleaning up the mess that follows.

The Evolution of the Serenity Prayer: From Stoicism to Modern Wisdom

One of the most powerful principles underlying *The Service Mindset* is the ability to control our reactions to emotional triggers. While emotions arise instantly and automatically, our response to them must be considered, rational, and strategic.

This idea is at the heart of Stoic philosophy, and it has travelled through time; from the writings of Marcus Aurelius and Epictetus to the modern interpretation found in Reinhold Niebuhr's Serenity Prayer.

The Stoic Foundations: Marcus Aurelius and Epictetus

The concept of distinguishing between what we can and cannot control is central to Stoicism, a philosophy that originated in Ancient Greece and was later refined by Roman thinkers. Marcus Aurelius, the philosopher-king, and Epictetus, a former slave turned teacher, both stressed the importance of regulating our reactions to external events.

Marcus Aurelius: Power Over the Mind, Not Outside Events

Marcus Aurelius, the Roman Emperor and Stoic thinker, captured this idea beautifully in *Meditations*:

"You have power over your mind - not outside events. Realise this, and you will find strength." (*Meditations*, Book 8, Chapter 47)

Here, Marcus Aurelius teaches us that while we may not control external circumstances, we always control our perspective and response. This aligns directly with *The Service Mindset* - we cannot change everything that happens in life, but we can choose to serve others, act with integrity, and remain steadfast in our values regardless of what the world throws at us.

In another passage, he expands on this idea:

"If you are distressed by anything external, the pain is not due to the thing itself but to your estimate of it; and this you have the power to revoke at any moment." (*Meditations*, Book 8, Chapter 49)

In other words, suffering does not come from external events but from our interpretation of them. If we shift our perspective, we can remove unnecessary distress and act rationally.

Epictetus: Control What You Can, Accept What You Can't

Epictetus, who lived as a slave before becoming one of the most influential Stoic teachers, emphasised the same principle:

"Happiness and freedom begin with a clear understanding of one principle. Some things are within our control, and some things are not." (*Enchiridion*, 1.1)

He took this further by introducing a fundamental Stoic exercise - asking yourself, *"Is this within my control?"* If the answer is *yes*, then take action. If *no*, then accept it and move on.

"Make the best use of what is in your power and take the rest as it happens." (*Discourses*, 1.1.17)

This idea is not about passivity or indifference - it's about redirecting energy toward productive action. Instead of wasting time on things outside our control, we should focus on how we respond to them.

Reinhold Niebuhr and The Serenity Prayer

Centuries later, in the 20th century, the theologian Reinhold Niebuhr distilled these Stoic ideas into what is now known as the Serenity Prayer:

"God, grant me the serenity to accept the things I cannot change, the courage to change the things I can, and the wisdom to know the difference."

While Niebuhr's words are often associated with religion and recovery programs, the message is fundamentally Stoic:

- Serenity = Acceptance of what is beyond our control.

- Courage = The willingness to take action where we have power.

- Wisdom = The discernment to distinguish between the two.

The power of this prayer is in its clarity and practicality - it provides a framework for dealing with life's challenges in a way that prevents emotional overwhelm and promotes rational action.

It's been quoted so many times it risks becoming cliché, but when taken seriously, it holds the key to making better decisions. Because the biggest barrier to good judgement is not ignorance - it's frustration over things we can't control. The colleague who undermines us. The policy we disagree with. The economy. The past. Other people's reactions.

When we become emotionally entangled in what we cannot change, we lose sight of what we *can*. And in that state - angry, reactive, scattered - we make poor choices. We say things we regret. We take shortcuts. We double down when we should let go.

At the heart of the Service Mindset is a different way of approaching decisions. It's not about being perfect. It's about **learning to act from a place of emotional neutrality** - where ego is quiet, fear is acknowledged but not obeyed, and the focus is on what creates real, lasting value for others and for ourselves.

Emotional neutrality is not detachment or coldness. It's not the absence of feeling. It's the ability to feel deeply, but not let those feelings take the wheel. It's the ability to notice the storm and choose not to step into it.

When you make decisions from a calm, centred place, something shifts. You start to ask better questions: What outcome am I really trying to create? What would service look like here? What will matter most, not in the next five minutes, but in the next five years?

That clarity doesn't come easily. It requires practice. But the more you learn to pause, ground yourself, and return to a state of composure, the more strategic, and ethical, your decisions become.

Wait for Still Waters

You can often see it coming before it lands.

You're sitting in a meeting. Someone makes a pointed remark - maybe about performance, priorities, or resourcing - and you see the reaction form on another person's face before they say a word. There's a flash of hurt, a twitch of disbelief, a jolt of anger. You can almost feel the adrenaline in the air. And then, in slow motion, it happens. A sharp reply, a defensive quip, a withdrawal of goodwill:

"Well, in that case, I won't help at all."
"If that's what you think, count me out."
"Maybe take a look at how broken things are over there before criticising my team."

And just like that, the moment is gone. Not just the one that caused the reaction, but the opportunity to respond with poise - to change the tone, steer things forward, or simply hold space for tension without making it worse.

What we're watching, in real time, is an emotional hijack. And we've all been there. Sometimes, when we feel things intensely, we want others to feel it too. Hurt triggers retaliation. Shame begets defensiveness. Anger tries to assert control. But decisions - especially in service of others - are rarely improved by heat.

The Service Mindset demands something different. It asks us to serve the greater good, and that means resisting the pull of emotional extremes. It means not turning pain into punishment. It means not mistaking a spike in feeling for a call to action.

This doesn't mean suppressing emotion. Quite the opposite. It means observing it. Recognising the speed and force of our reactions. Noticing how quickly the body tightens, how the voice rises, how the mind starts drafting comeback lines while the room is still talking.

In Tenet 5, we explored a simple tool for emotional regulation – the image of a pendulum.
One core idea from that model is the concept of speed: when your internal engine is red-lining, you're not in a fit state to steer. Emotional clarity requires space. And to make good decisions, we must learn to wait for still waters.

So how do we do that?

We start with observation. *"What am I feeling right now?"*

Then move to grounding. *"Is this feeling useful, or is it clouding my judgment?"*

Then we ask better questions:

"Will this matter next week? Next year?"
"What outcome do I really want here?"
"What would a calm, considered version of me do?"

And finally, we *play the tape forward*.

Play the Tape Forward: Thinking Beyond the Immediate Moment

One of the greatest challenges in decision-making is resisting the pull of the immediate moment. Choices made in haste, driven by emotion or short-term benefit, often lead to regret, unintended consequences, or ethical miscalculations.

The concept of "playing the tape forward" is a simple yet powerful way to avoid these pitfalls. It encourages individuals to pause and consider where their decision will lead not only today but in the days, months, and years ahead. This shift in perspective allows for greater clarity and ensures that actions align with long-term values rather than short-term impulses.

Poor decisions are often made in the heat of the moment. Emotions such as frustration, ambition, or fear can cloud judgement, leading people to act in ways they might later regret. The promise of an immediate reward can be tempting, particularly when ego or pressure from others is involved. However, a failure to look ahead can result in choices that undermine integrity, damage relationships, or create obstacles that could have been avoided with a more thoughtful approach.

The Service Mindset provides a framework for making decisions with greater wisdom and foresight. It encourages people to ask themselves a simple but profound question: *"If I make this choice today, how will it shape my future and the people around me?"* This is not just about personal success but about ensuring that decisions contribute to a greater good.

Ethical and strategic decision-making must extend beyond personal interest to consider the wider impact on colleagues, teams, and organisations. The best leaders are those who resist short-term temptations in favour of actions that build trust, stability, and a lasting positive legacy.

A useful example of this approach can be seen in leadership scenarios. Imagine a leader who is presented with an opportunity to take credit for their team's work, knowing that doing so could advance their career. In the short term, this choice appears beneficial - they may receive praise, be seen as more competent, and increase their chances of promotion.
However, when the tape is played forward, the true cost of this decision becomes clear.

Trust within the team is eroded, colleagues feel undervalued, and future collaboration becomes strained. Over time, the leader's reputation is damaged, and opportunities for genuine advancement diminish. By contrast, if the leader gives credit where it is due, they strengthen their relationships, build loyalty, and earn respect. The short-term gain of personal recognition is outweighed by the long-term benefit of a strong and motivated team.

Great decision-makers do not simply think about the next step. They consider the entire journey. Every action has consequences, some of which may not be immediately apparent. By stepping back and looking ahead, individuals can make choices that align with their principles and create a positive ripple effect over time. The ability to pause, reflect, and project forward is a skill that can be cultivated through conscious effort and self-discipline.

People rarely make good decisions when they are at emotional extremes. Whether driven by anger, fear, excitement, or desperation, choices made in these heightened states tend to be reactive rather than considered. Emotion clouds judgment, pushing individuals towards actions that may feel right in the moment but fail to stand up to long-term scrutiny.

The Service Mindset demands a more deliberate approach. It requires that decisions be made strategically, from a place of emotional neutrality and rational thought.

This does not mean suppressing emotions or ignoring instincts, but rather ensuring that they do not dictate choices. The best decisions come when emotions are acknowledged but do not control the outcome.

By stepping back, regaining balance, and assessing situations with clarity, individuals can ensure that their decisions are guided by integrity, wisdom, and a commitment to serving the greater good.

"If I act on this emotion - this heat, this spike - what does it look like in the long run? What damage might I do? What relationships might I strain? What future version of me will have to clean this up?"

The moment you start asking those questions, you begin to act with the type of strategic intention that The Service Mindset demands from us.

And that's the shift: from ego to impact. From instinct to intention.

We serve best when we act from stillness, not noise. From presence, not panic.

Appreciating that sometimes the most powerful move is the one we don't make right away.

Because when we wait for calm waters, we can see the riverbed more clearly.

Embracing Reality Over the Pursuit of Perfection

Waiting for calm waters, does not mean waiting for the perfect moment.

In reality, the perfect moment hardly ever exists.

A key principle of The Service Mindset is working with what you have rather than wishing for different circumstances (See Tenet 1 – Acceptance as a Starting Point). Many people get stuck waiting for the "perfect moment" or the "perfect opportunity" before taking action, but in reality, perfection is an illusion and chasing it leads to procrastination, missed opportunities, and frustration.

An Atypical Family That Became a Superpower

When Jane and I first got together, it was clear that we were not a "normal" family. Jane's (now) adult children are dual heritage, she is older than me, and she had been a teen mum while I was still in primary school. From the outside, we didn't fit the mold of a traditional family structure. However; instead of resisting that fact, we embraced it.

We accepted reality instead of fighting it. Instead of wishing we were a "conventional family," we leaned into our differences and made them our superpower. We developed a mentality of *"It's us against the world - if we don't fit in, then we'll take pride in that."* By embracing what made us different, we found strength, confidence, and unshakable unity.

This applies to decision-making as well. If you wait for perfect conditions, perfect people, or perfect moments, you will never take action. Instead, make the best decision possible with the reality you have.

📌 **Reflection Exercise:**

Have you ever delayed action because conditions weren't "perfect"? How would your decisions change if you embraced reality instead of resisting it?

Applying This to Leadership and High-Stakes Decision-Making

In leadership, decision-making is often clouded by frustration over things that cannot be changed: company politics, market conditions, difficult personalities. Many leaders exhaust themselves trying to fight the uncontrollable, rather than focusing on where they can make a meaningful impact.

A leader may not be able to control an unexpected budget cut, but they can control how they allocate resources and how they rally their team. They may not be able to prevent resistance to change, but they can control how they communicate their vision. The strongest leaders are those who refuse to be paralysed by frustration and instead focus their energy on actions that create tangible outcomes.

In fraud prevention, the stakes are even higher. Fraudsters constantly test defences, looking for weaknesses to exploit. The frustrating reality is that no system is foolproof, and fraud can never be entirely eliminated. However, that does not mean we are powerless.

We cannot control the fact that some people will attempt to deceive and exploit. But we can control how we respond to fraud risks, how we tighten our controls, how we train our teams, and how we refuse to compromise on ethical standards. Every decision made in response to fraud has long-term consequences; if we choose to turn a blind eye or take a lenient stance for the sake of short-term convenience, we are effectively inviting repeat attacks.

The Wisdom to Know the Difference

The hardest part of this mindset is not just acting on what we can control, but recognising when to let go of what we cannot. Leaders burn out when they fixate on external pressures they cannot change. Fraud professionals make poor judgments when they get too close to an investigation, take things personally and become too emotionally invested in stopping every fraud.

Mastering the Serenity Principle means knowing when to fight and when to adapt. It means recognising that we cannot control everything, but we are never powerless.

📌 **Reflection Task:**

Think about a recent decision where you found yourself frustrated by external circumstances. Were you focusing on something outside your control? How could you have shifted your energy toward a factor you could influence?

📌 **Action Step:**

In your next leadership or decision-making challenge, pause before reacting. Ask yourself: What is within my control? What is not? Where is my energy best directed? Consciously apply this mindset and observe how it shifts your approach.

The Psychology of Scarcity vs. Abundance in Decision-Making

The concept of scarcity versus abundance thinking is not new. It has been explored in psychology, business, and leadership for many years. However, within the Service Mindset, this framework takes on a deeper significance, influencing not only individual decision-making but also the way organisations function and thrive.

A scarcity mindset is rooted in the belief that resources, opportunities and success are limited. Those who operate from this perspective often see life as a zero-sum game, where one person's gain must come at another's expense. This kind of thinking fosters competition, hoarding of knowledge and a reluctance to collaborate, as individuals and businesses fear losing their perceived advantage. In leadership, scarcity thinking can manifest as a reluctance to mentor others due to the belief that empowering someone else may diminish your own standing. It can also be seen in organisations that guard their ideas and resist cooperation with external partners, fearing that openness will weaken their competitive edge.

For a real world example of the scarcity mindset in action, you only have to cast your gaze to Silicon Valley where the race to Artificial General Intelligence and Artificial Super Intelligence have rival companies allegedly offering hundreds of millions of dollars in bonuses to their competitor's employees to shift their allegiance to a different project.

Abundance thinking, by contrast, sees potential everywhere. It recognises that success is not finite and that by creating value for others, we expand opportunities rather than diminish them. Those who embrace abundance thinking understand that sharing knowledge, investing in people and building relationships strengthen rather than weaken their own position.

Leaders who adopt this mindset take the time to develop their teams, knowing that cultivating talent does not reduce their own worth but instead multiplies success. Likewise, companies that embrace collaboration, such as those that contribute to open-source innovation, often find that their willingness to share ideas leads to greater growth, stronger partnerships and enhanced reputational standing.

Just think of the progress the warring tribes of Silicon Valley could make if they were to pool their resources and work together in the pursuit of a common aim.

The Service Mindset naturally aligns with abundance thinking. When we focus on service rather than self-preservation, we no longer see success as a scarce resource to be fought over. Instead, we recognise that by lifting others, we create more opportunities for everyone, including ourselves. This is not about giving away all resources without consideration, nor is it about ignoring practical constraints. Rather, it is about rejecting fear-based decision-making and embracing a philosophy where trust, cooperation and long-term thinking take precedence over short-term self-interest.

A simple truth emerges from this approach: *"If they win, we all win."* When people, teams and organisations adopt The Service Mindset, they build environments where trust flourishes, collaboration is natural and sustainable success follows. The more we create for others, the more we build for ourselves.

📌 **Reflection Task:**

Think of a time when you operated from a scarcity mindset. Perhaps you hesitated to share knowledge, resisted collaboration, or felt threatened by someone else's success. What was the underlying fear driving that reaction? How might the outcome have changed if you had approached the situation with an abundance mindset instead?

📌 Action Step:

Over the next week, identify one opportunity to apply abundance thinking. This could be mentoring a colleague, sharing a useful resource, or supporting someone else's success without concern for personal gain. Observe how this shift in mindset affects your interactions and overall perspective.

The Anti-Prisoner's Dilemma: Why Cooperation Wins

Game theory has long studied the way people make decisions in competitive situations, and one of its most famous models is the Prisoner's Dilemma. This scenario illustrates a paradox in which two individuals, acting in their own self-interest, ultimately create a worse outcome for themselves than if they had chosen to cooperate.

In its classic form, two prisoners are arrested and separately given the option to betray the other or remain silent. If both betray each other, they each receive a moderate sentence. If one betrays while the other remains silent, the betrayer walks free while the other faces a harsh punishment. However, if both remain silent, they receive only a minimal sentence.

The rational choice, from a self-interest perspective, is to betray, as it protects against the worst-case scenario. Yet, this often results in a poorer outcome than mutual cooperation.

The Service Mindset challenges the notion that self-preservation is the best strategy for success. It rejects the belief that career advancement, business growth, or leadership requires competition at the expense of others. Instead, it promotes a different model: one where **trust, cooperation, and service lead to stronger, more sustainable outcomes**.

A clear example of this principle can be seen in two employees competing for a promotion.

The first employee views the situation through a scarcity mindset - believing that success is a zero-sum game, they withhold useful information, seek credit for shared work, and subtly undermine their colleague's reputation. They operate from the assumption that only one person can succeed, and they are determined to be that person regardless of the cost.

The second employee takes a different approach. They embrace an abundance mindset, believing that collaboration does not weaken their position but strengthens it. They share knowledge, support their colleague's success, and contribute positively to the team as a whole. They operate with the understanding that true leadership is not about self-promotion, but about building trust, demonstrating integrity, and creating value for others.

In the short term, the first employee may win. They might receive the promotion they were after. *But at what cost?* They have alienated their peers, built a reputation for self-interest, and planted the seeds of distrust amongst those that they work with.

The second employee, meanwhile, may not win the immediate promotion, but their reputation for leadership, generosity, and collaboration earns them something far more valuable. Their colleagues respect them, their superiors recognise their ability to build strong teams, and when a bigger, more impactful leadership role becomes available, they are the natural choice.

Service as Strategic Advantage

There's a common misconception in leadership that kindness makes you weak. That cooperation means compromise. That service is a soft option.

In my experience, however, service is often the most strategic move you can make. When decisions are made in service of others, rather than in defence of ego or ambition, they tend to produce stronger outcomes in the long run. They build trust. They open doors. They create loyalty that no job title, KPI or set of metrics ever could.

I've seen this firsthand in countless scenarios, from managerial clashes to frontline fraud investigations. The people who play for the team, not just for themselves, always end up going further. Maybe not always faster. But further, and more meaningfully.

I've had many mentors who have helped me to move forward in my life and career; however, none more so than Thomas. Thomas took a keen interest in what others wanted to achieve in their careers and then set about making himself an agent for the actualisation of those ambitions.

He didn't just offer guidance or advice, he set about removing the obstacles in the roads of others' future success. He connected people to opportunities, remembered what you told him and followed up weeks or months later to check how it was going. He wasn't trying to win admiration and Thomas wasn't playing a political game. He was simply paying attention and using his influence to help others make progress.

The most remarkable thing about Thomas was this: when you thanked him, he'd brush it off. Genuinely. He didn't believe he was responsible for any of it. In his mind, people succeeded because of their own merit. He refused credit, even when it was plainly due.

But I know the truth. Without Thomas, I wouldn't be where I am today. He championed me when I wasn't in the room. He opened doors I didn't even know needed unlocking. Because Thomas expected nothing in return, I would do anything for him: not out of obligation, but out of deep and enduring respect.

That's the paradox of The Service Mindset: the less you seek recognition, the more powerful your impact becomes. Service builds loyalty, trust, and a legacy that far outlasts any short-term win.

Facing Reality: Leadership Requires Steely Determination

There's a moment in every leadership journey where you realise that being liked and being useful are not always the same thing.

Early in my career, I thought the two were interchangeable. If people liked me, they'd follow me. If I was kind and collaborative, I'd be respected - but the truth is more complicated than that.

Some of the most useful things you'll ever do as a leader will make people uncomfortable.

That's because, leadership means making hard decisions - especially when the easiest option is to stay quiet, go along with the room, or pretend something isn't your responsibility.

I once worked in an environment where people handled some of the most distressing matters imaginable: fatalities, serious injuries, traumatic losses. The emotional toll was everywhere, though no one spoke about it openly. People would disappear to the toilets and come back with red eyes and tear-stained cheeks. You'd pass a colleague in the corridor and see that haunted look in their expression, but nothing was said.

At some point I took the decision to speak to senior management and ended up giving an honest presentation on the impact that the stress of the work environment had had on me personally. I told them I had sought help, had been prescribed medication, and that it wasn't weakness - it was a perfectly human response to an inhuman volume of distress.

I still remember the looks in the room. Part discomfort, part relief. I had said what others had been feeling but didn't know how to raise it.
It could have gone badly. Speaking about mental health in a corporate setting - especially back then - was a risk. But I did it anyway, because the alternative was staying silent while others continued to suffer unseen.

To their credit, management listened. Real changes were made. Not overnight, but enough to shift the culture. Mental health stopped being whispered about and started being taken seriously.

That is steely determination, not bravado. Not barking orders or asserting dominance or doing something in a performative way for clicks and likes. In this way, the Service Mindset gives you the courage of your conviction and the willingness to speak uncomfortable truths in service of something greater than your own comfort or reputation.

The Service Mindset demands this from us. It doesn't ask that we avoid conflict - it asks that we rise above petty conflict and engage in meaningful confrontation when it counts. That we protect what matters. That we choose courage over convenience.

You don't serve others by playing small. You serve them by standing tall, especially when the cost is high and the outcome may be uncertain.

Logic + Humanity = Better Decisions

In most corporate settings, decisions are framed as rational exercises: rooted in logic, efficiency, and measurable outcomes. We talk about KPIs, cost-benefit analysis, return on investment, but in real life, especially in leadership, the best decisions rarely come from logic alone.

They come from the meeting point between clarity and care. Between head and heart. I've seen brilliant strategists make damaging decisions because they forgot the people behind the numbers. I've also seen highly empathetic leaders struggle to take action because they couldn't separate their feelings from the task. The sweet spot lies in holding both truths at once.

You need logic. It protects against reckless thinking and helps anchor decisions in evidence. However, logic without humanity can become cold and clinical. It can justify callousness or cruelty.

Equally as important, you need empathy. It reminds you that your decisions affect real people. However, empathy without structure afforded by logic, can quickly turn into indecision or avoidance. So there is a clear reason why it's important to be balanced in your decision making.

The Service Mindset brings these helps to bring these forces into alignment. It doesn't dismiss data, but it doesn't worship it either. It recognises that good decisions serve more than just targets - they serve people.

Influence Over Power

In every workplace, and in all walks of life, you encounter people who are grappling with the idea of power.

The flaw in their thinking is in their belief that if they had enough power, they could exert control over circumstances and bring about change.

In accordance with this belief, these people talk the loudest, make themselves visible and build empires, as if the accumulation of budgets, titles, headcount and resources brings about the ability to effect change.

But here's the thing – if you accept the key tenets of The Service Mindset – specifically that all people are equal and that there are limits to the sphere of things under your control – what emerges is the realisation that power in an illusion.

Whilst titles, resources and budgets can certainly make it easier to bring about change, the idea that power exists as a force to bring about change in and of itself is simply philosophically flawed.

Perhaps this explains the growing disillusionment with democracy in the western world.

Every so often, we go to huge effort to organise elections so that we can collectively hand power to a person, or parties, to bring about change – and when they don't, we label them failures, vote them out and hand the power to somebody else.

I am not saying we should question democracy, but perhaps it is time to examine our understanding of the true nature of power.

Maybe, when we put others in a position of power, we are not giving them any means to effect change. Perhaps, what we are granting them is superiority through our own acquiesced subservience.

The Service Mindset says that superiority is the illusion of the ego. If superiority does not exist, then can it be said that the concept of power is also an illusion?

Because here's the thing, if power does exist then it is incredibly fragile. That is to say, power relies on structure and status. The moment those structures collapse, so does power.

The Service Mindset tells us to live deliberately and in alignment with our principles, to accept reality and the limits of our control and to lift others without seeking validation. When we do that, we do not become more powerful, but we do become more capable of influencing. Influence, through the lens of The Service Mindset, is something else entirely.

Influence is built in the quiet moments: how you treat people when no one is watching, how consistent your actions are with your values, how much trust people place in your judgement. It's not about volume or visibility, but rather about gravity, integrity and credibility.

The Service Mindset doesn't care whether you sit at the top table or not. It's not about hierarchy. It's about the example you set and the legacy you leave. It asks: *are your decisions making things better for others - not just easier for yourself?*

I've seen leaders whose power disintegrated the moment they left a room, and I've seen others whose influence endured long after they'd gone. The difference? One was driven by control, the other, by service.

Service doesn't seek followers, it quietly builds trust through commitment to our values. We must always remember that the trust, responsibility and authority others bestow on us, is always earnt through our deeds and actions and never because it was demanded by someone who could shout louder.

Over time, you will find that influence proves more durable, more respected, and far more valuable than any fleeting claim to power.

📌 **Reflection Task:**

Think of a leader you respected. Was it because of the position they held, or the example they set? What made their influence last?

📌 **Action Step:**

In your next leadership decision - big or small - pause and ask yourself: *Am I trying to prove my power, or am I trying to serve?* Then act accordingly.

Mentorship and Allyship – Filling the Vacuum with Purpose

There is growing concern - particularly in relation to young men - about a vacuum of mentorship in modern life. For many, especially those searching for meaning, guidance, and identity, this absence has become more than a gap, it's become a breeding ground for something incredibly dark.

Where positive role models are absent, dangerous ones rush in. The failure to serve has left space for the rise of misogynists, manipulators, and extremists - individuals who offer certainty, status, and belonging, but only in exchange for the degradation of others.

This is what happens when we treat mentorship as optional. It isn't. It's a responsibility - one that flows directly from The Service Mindset. To withhold guidance, encouragement, or wisdom when we have it to give is to step aside and let others fill that role. And not everyone waiting in the wings has good intentions – not everyone is Mr Miyagi!

Mentorship isn't about control and it's not about fixing people. It's about being honest and modelling integrity. It is incumbent on those who heed the call of the mentor, to listen without judgment. Sometimes, we all need someone to believe in us, when we cannot believe in ourselves and that's what the best mentors do. That's what the world needs more of.

But this also requires moral clarity.

The Service Mindset is built on the principle of *equality*. Not just in theory, but in action. That means any ideology, worldview, or 'mentorship' model that devalues the rights, freedom, or dignity of others - especially women, minorities, or vulnerable communities - can never be consistent with this mindset. Full stop.

There's nothing radical about wanting better for young men - or for anyone, but we must be crystal clear: true mentorship does not require the oppression of others to empower the self.

When we teach boys to lead by dominating others, we fail them. When we glorify cruelty as strength, or silence as wisdom, we create a generation that confuses power with worth. That is not service. That is cowardice.

Masculinity is not an inherently toxic thing. Don't get me wrong – there is no room in The Service Mindset for misogyny or the denigration of anyone; however, the world does need positive masculinity.

The starting point of The Service Mindset is the rapid and unwavering acceptance of reality and, when it comes to the human experience, we have to accept that good and evil, masculinity and femininity, moral and immoral – these are facets of the same condition.

The good men of tomorrow need to lead from the good men of today and currently – society's fascination with the denigration of masculinity has led to a vacuum where those good men used to be.

Reframing Leadership Through Service

Ultimately, mentorship is a form of leadership because it's about enabling others.

"If leadership is all about you, you're doing it wrong."

We've all worked with leaders who saw the title as the goal - who used it to claim authority, protect status, and issue commands from a position above you as if their status afforded them superiority or greater control. You can tell a lot about a person's understanding of leadership by how they behave when a decision affects their ego.

The best leaders I've worked with - the ones who earnt my respect and my loyalty - never made it about themselves. They created space for others to grow, backed people quietly, and made you feel like you mattered, even when you were still learning or suffering from imposter syndrome.

Their leadership didn't feel performative - it felt like support because it was genuinely supportive.

Trust Over Control – Productivity and Empowerment

When I first stepped into a leadership role at a law firm, I was handed a dashboard full of data. Minute-by-minute tracking of how many letters people were typing, how long they were inactive, who was falling behind. The assumption was simple: productivity comes from pressure. If someone slows down, you push harder.

That way of working, never sat comfortably with me.

Instead of fixating on dips in performance, I looked at the peaks. When were people at their best? What times of day did they do their strongest work? What kinds of work were they motivated to perform.

I stopped trying to standardise productivity and started tailoring it.

- One team member did their best work in the morning, so I loaded their key tasks before lunch.

- Another found their rhythm in the late afternoon, so I protected their time from 3pm meetings.

- And I made a deal with the team: if you hit your targets for the week, you could leave early on Friday.

I surprised myself with the results - not just in output, but in morale, loyalty, and energy. We outperformed teams who were being monitored and micromanaged, not because we worked harder, but because we worked with trust.

Why Micromanagement Fails

Micromanagement doesn't just hurt morale, it breaks the very thing it tries to control. It sends a clear message: *I don't trust you.* And when people feel they're not trusted, they stop going the extra mile, they stop thinking creatively and – erring on the side of being defensive - they start to play it safe. They give you compliance, not contribution and engagement inevitably suffers.

Service Mindset in leadership starts from a different place. It says: *I believe in your potential. Let me remove the obstacles for you, not create more.*

The Real Levers of Productivity

Control might feel powerful in the short term, but in my experience, the real drivers of performance are:

- **Autonomy** – Letting people choose *how*, *when*, and *where* they work best.

- **Clarity** – Setting expectations, not micromanaging methods.

- **Recognition** – Rewarding ownership and initiative, not just results.

- **Safety** – Creating space where people feel able to take risks, admit mistakes, and try new things.

Leaders who serve their teams, enable their people and understand that they thrive when they're trusted.

I guess, in a strange sort of way, when someone believes you trust them, they start to trust themself.

Raising Standards Without Raising Ego

For most of my career, I've held myself to high standards. Not out of a need to outshine others, but because I wanted to be dependable. I wanted to be the person who always delivered on their promise. The one at the forefront of making things happen, effecting change and realising potential. After my injury, when so much of me felt uncertain or fragmented, having standards gave me structure and purpose.

But I didn't always manage it well. I would often stay late at the office to make sure tasks were finished properly. I spent too many weekends worrying about whether someone's vehicle had been repaired, or if a customer would get their hire car on time. Even when I wasn't at work, my mind was there - solving problems, anticipating issues, running imaginary hypotheticals. It came from a good place - I cared and wanted to be successful – but tethering my personal value proposition to my output at work wasn't healthy, and it certainly wasn't sustainable.

For me, having high standards is a complicated thing. I was raised with a lot of strong beliefs, that our rapidly coming undone in the age of AI – a time when worth no longer equates to effort. As much as high standards have the potential to inspire, we must be careful that they also don't leave us isolated – exhausting the people around us as opposed to lifting them. If we are not careful and if our standards are not balanced, they can become a way to control outcomes rather than empower people.

The real change came when I moved into my first leadership role. It was no longer about what I could deliver. It was about what I could help others deliver. Empowering my own team to outperform their targets needed something more than me simply transferring to them the impossibly high standards that I placed on myself in my pursuit of self-actualisation. It required trust, patience, and the humility to let go of my own way of doing things.

The Service Mindset doesn't ask us to lower the bar - quite the opposite. It asks us to raise it for the right reasons.

Not to prove ourselves.

Not to seek praise.

But to lift others - to show them what's possible and then help them get there.

This means being patient with people who are learning. It means giving honest feedback without humiliation. And it means celebrating progress, not perfection. Because if high standards are used to measure people against you, you're building a hierarchy of ego. But if they're used to lift people alongside you, you're building something far more valuable: a culture of excellence rooted in service.

I've come to believe that people rarely remember leaders who set impossibly high expectations. They remember the ones who helped them meet those expectations - who believed in them, before they believed in themselves.

So yes, hold the line. Expect great things, but do it in a way that brings others with you, not leaves them behind.

Legacy is never built on what you achieved alone. It's built on what you helped others to become.

Success Isn't Silent - It's Shared

There's a comforting myth in the workplace: that if you keep your head down, work hard, and quietly get things done, people will notice. Promotions will come. Recognition will follow. The right people will see your value.

Sometimes they do. Often, they don't.

The truth is, success in large organisations isn't just about being useful. It's about being connected. When people trust you, when they've worked with you, when they feel the benefit of your presence in a room - not just through delivery, but through partnership - they begin to speak positively about you when you're not there. That's when your value becomes visible.

Being useful is the foundation, but usefulness without connection is easily overlooked. What really elevates you is *relational credibility* - the trust others have in your judgement, your consistency, and your intent. That doesn't come from shouting the loudest, but it also doesn't come from silence either.

It comes from being the person others are glad to have on their side and doing that often enough, and well enough, that they start telling other people why.

Success isn't something you demand - it's something others offer, when they've experienced your contribution for themselves, and choose to carry your name forward.

Chapter 6 – The Service Mindset and the Future

The Coming Wave

I'm not a futurist but I have spoken at a number of Fintech and AI conferences over the years. I may not have been invited by the government to write a white paper, but I am leading artificial intelligence projects and I'm close enough to the ground to know that something is changing... in a massive way.

You can feel it. In the language people use. In the speed at which things move. In the number of conversations that start with "I asked ChatGPT..." and the quiet shift in tone when someone realises that a job that was once done by a person is now being done, faster and cheaper, by a machine.

We are living through the opening moments of something that will reshape how we live and work. It's not speculative anymore - it's already happening. The wave has already broken.

AI is now writing articles, reviewing contracts, analysing scans, approving claims, generating images, composing music, and carrying out tasks that once required not just training, but human judgement or creativity. It is advancing quickly and quietly, not with an enormous bang, but with a soft hum of productivity.

There's a part of us, collectively, that seems to find this hugely disconcerting: machines don't get tired. They don't ask for a pay rise. They don't take long lunches or go off sick or question the rules they're given. They simply do what they've been designed to do, at scale, without complaint. They are better than us and share none of our shortcomings, therefor in the eyes of most employers, they're ideal.

But ideal for what? And at what cost?

For all the talk of progress, there's something deeply unsettling about the idea that we are beginning to hand over not just tasks, but decisions - not just labour, but thinking - to systems that do not understand, cannot care, and will never be accountable.

This isn't a call to panic. It's not a manifesto for resistance. It's just a pause - a quiet reckoning with the question we'll all have to face sooner or later:

If machines can do all the thinking, what's left for us?

And more to the point:

What does it mean to be valuable, or even necessary, in a world where intelligence is no longer scarce?

That's the conversation I want to have in this chapter. Not as an expert. Not as a critic. But as a human being - watching a wave build on the horizon and wondering what we will carry with us when it hits.

The Rise of AI-Driven Leadership – and its Risks

AI has changed how leaders make decisions. From predictive analytics in finance to AI-driven hiring tools in HR, data is now at the centre of leadership. And while data-driven decision-making is powerful, there's an increasing risk:

Leaders are outsourcing their judgment to AI.

AI is an incredibly powerful tool for leadership, offering insights into product trends, pricing strategies, and supply chain optimisation. The ability to process vast amounts of data enables leaders to make more informed, data-driven decisions at unprecedented speeds. However, while AI can reveal *what* is happening in a business, it cannot provide the deeper human insights that define great leadership.

Despite its strengths, AI lacks the emotional intelligence and ethical judgment required to answer deeper questions. It cannot determine why a customer places long-term trust in a brand, how an employee truly feels about an organisational change, or when it makes sense to take a long-term strategic risk that might not align with immediate algorithmic predictions. AI can tell you *what* customers like, but only a human can understand *why* they care.

The Danger of Leaders Becoming Passive to AI Metrics

Many leaders are falling into the trap of leading by numbers alone, relying so heavily on AI-generated insights that they begin to defer their own judgment. As a result, businesses become fixated on engagement metrics instead of genuine customer relationships, prioritise short-term cost efficiency over long-term brand loyalty, and allow hiring algorithms to drive recruitment decisions without fully appreciating team dynamics.

This over-reliance on AI creates a risk: when every company optimises for the same AI-driven KPIs, they begin to look the same. It leads to a race to the middle, where no company stands out, no leader takes a real risk, and businesses fail to build lasting differentiation.

To be successful in business, you either need to be cheaper than everyone else, or, better than everyone else.

The promise of AI offers this huge dopamine hit of short-term cost cutting. For a relatively short period of time, companies can increase their profit margins by reducing the size of their operational base as machines take over the work.

In falling into this trap, businesses forget that being cheaper than everyone else is just one route to success in a market. In short, we forget about being the best in our target market and it instead becomes a race to establish cheap mediocrity.

If you think about the world of supermarkets in the UK, you have some super-pragmatic, low-cost operators who are miles cheaper than their competitors – together they corner 20% of the UK food retail market.

At the other end of the spectrum, you have the premium brands – shops who sell the best products and produce, with clientele that prioritise quality and who are not very price sensitive. These premium brands, make up about 10% of the market.
So that leaves about 70% of the market dominated by an oligopoly of those who are neither the cheaper or the best.

Now, whilst this might look like a good advert for positioning your company as mediocre, if you look at the vectors of market share and sales growth, you can see that dominance is leeching away from the oligopoly to the disruptors at the extremely cheap, or extremely high quality ends of the market.

You can see how the cost-cutting benefits of AI would be an easy sell to the oligopoly – companies so entrenched in their long-standing market dominance, that they have forgotten about either being the cheapest or the best in their chosen market.

The Service Mindset as an Antidote to AI Dependence

The best leaders understand that AI is a tool, not a replacement for human judgement. They use AI to enhance their decision-making, but they never allow it to dictate strategy blindly. True leadership means trusting instincts, relationships, and ethics, not just raw data. This is particularly important when AI-driven recommendations prioritise efficiency over experience, or short-term gains over long-term sustainability.

Consider one of the aforementioned retailers deciding on a pricing strategy. AI might suggest discounting a product to maximise revenue in the short term, but a leader with a Service Mindset recognises that maintaining premium pricing alongside exceptional service fosters long-term brand loyalty.

Similarly, AI might recommend hiring solely based on efficiency metrics, but a true leader understands that cultural fit and long-term vision are far more valuable than immediate optimisation.

AI provides the *what*, but great leadership is about understanding the *why*.

The Modern World's Trap: Reducing Us to Predictable Units

Technology is pushing society toward hyper-individualisation, turning people into predictable consumers, isolated in digital spaces, engaging in transactions rather than meaningful experiences. This shift goes against our very nature.

People don't just want convenience; they want to belong. They need to contribute, to feel part of something bigger than themselves. A life built solely around personal gratification is ultimately an empty one. The most fulfilled individuals are those who engage with their communities, find purpose in service, and invest in relationships that extend beyond their own immediate needs.

Turning Outward: The Antidote to Stagnation

There was a time in my life when everything fell apart. My instinct was to turn inward, shrink, and isolate myself. I was trapped in my own thoughts, and the more I focused on myself, the heavier my struggles became.

What changed everything?

Shifting my focus outward.

When I started engaging with the world again, building relationships, working on something bigger than myself, I found strength, purpose, and momentum.

This isn't just my experience. It's a fundamental human need.

Why Isolation Makes Problems Worse

The modern world encourages inward focus. Social media fosters self-comparison, algorithms trap us in echo chambers, and digital convenience allows us to retreat from real-world interactions. As a result, we shrink into ourselves, and our internal monologue becomes overwhelming, distorting our perception of reality. The more isolated we become, the larger our struggles seem, creating a cycle of disconnection that makes everything feel harder than it truly is.

But humanity does not thrive in isolation. We are wired for connection, designed to engage with others and find meaning beyond ourselves. Without real relationships and purpose-driven interactions, even small challenges can feel insurmountable.

The Role of Business in Restoring Connection

This is where business plays a crucial role. Companies have the opportunity; not just to sell, but to rebuild connection in a world that desperately needs it. Internally, organisations can create cultures that foster collaboration, shared purpose, and real human interaction. A workplace should not just be a place where people complete tasks but a community where they feel valued and engaged.

Externally, businesses must go beyond transactions and engage meaningfully with the communities they serve. Customers are looking for brands that stand for something, that create impact beyond profit, and that contribute to a sense of shared purpose. Organisations that rise to this challenge will not only succeed financially but will also help restore a sense of connection in an increasingly disconnected world.

📌 **Reflection Exercise:**

Are you fostering connection in your business? Or are you contributing to isolation and individualisation?

📌 **Action Step:**

Identify one way your business (or team) can shift focus from transactions to relationships - with employees, customers, or the wider community.

So, What's the Key Takeaway?

1. **The definition of value is changing**: features and functions matter *less* than experience, ethics, and emotional connection.

2. **AI is making everything feel the same**: automation will standardise service delivery, reducing differentiation.

3. **Service is the new competitive edge**: businesses that commit to a Service Mindset will stand out in a world of sameness.

A World That Rewards the Wrong Things

If you were to step into any social media platform today, you would quickly see what modern culture values. The loudest voices are often those who promote self-interest, competition, and individual success. The message is clear: get ahead, be seen, and maximise your own advantage.

The world rewards those who prioritise their own gain over service, integrity, and contribution.

Nothing illustrates this more clearly than the disparity in how society values different types of work. In 2024, the highest-earning influencer, Jimmy Donaldson, better known as MrBeast, reportedly made $85 million (£64.5 million) from his elaborate YouTube videos and associated business ventures. Meanwhile, in the UK, an unpaid carer looking after a disabled or ill relative can claim Carer's Allowance of £81.90 per week, amounting to just £4,258.80 per year.

This is the challenge of The Service Mindset. Living a life based on service, impact, and ethical leadership offers deep fulfilment, but it often runs against the grain of what society encourages. The pressure to self-promote, outcompete others, and treat relationships as transactional is ever-present. The financial structures of the modern world do little to reinforce the value of service.

So, how do we stay true to these principles when the world around us seems to reward the opposite? How do we navigate a culture that often equates kindness with weakness and selflessness with naivety? The trick is to hold true to the spirit of The Service Mindset even in a world that continually pushes against it.

📌 Reflection Exercise:

What message did you receive growing up about what makes a person successful? Have you ever felt undervalued because your contribution wasn't loud or visible?

📌 Action Step:

This week, quietly acknowledge someone whose work goes unnoticed. Send a message, give thanks, or simply let them know they're seen.

The Illusion of Success: Why Society Gets It Wrong

Modern society is obsessed with individual achievement. We are constantly bombarded with messages that tell us success is about working "smarter", earning more, and standing out from the crowd. Hustle culture glorifies relentless ambition, material wealth is equated with status, and personal branding has turned self-promotion into an expectation rather than a choice.

But does any of this bring real fulfilment? The promise of success often feels empty, as if no achievement is ever enough. There is always a higher target, a greater milestone, another person to outshine. This is the illusion that society sells us: that our worth is measured by how far ahead we stand of others.

The Service Mindset takes a different view. It does not ask, *How can I get ahead?* but rather, *How can we rise together?* True success is not found in competition or accumulation but in contribution; helping others grow, creating lasting impact, and leading with integrity. This chapter will explore why society's definition of success is flawed and how shifting our perspective can lead to a more meaningful and fulfilling life.

Real Life Does Not Come with a Trigger Warning

Modern society has developed an obsession with forewarning discomfort. Content comes pre-packaged with advisories about difficult themes, unsettling ideas, or potentially distressing material. The intention behind this is, on the surface, compassionate - it seeks to protect people from harm by giving them the opportunity to prepare or disengage. But life does not come with a trigger warning.

Real hardship arrives without notice. One moment, everything is as it was, and the next, life changes in ways that cannot be undone. A sudden bereavement. A phone call that alters the course of your future. The quiet devastation of betrayal. The gradual erosion of something you once believed was certain. These moments do not come with a preface. There is no warning label at the start of the day to let you know that, by nightfall, your world will feel unrecognisable.

This is not to say that forewarning is always wrong. There is value in kindness, in helping others prepare where preparation is possible. But to create an expectation that discomfort should always be preceded by caution is to build a false sense of security - one that collapses the moment real difficulty strikes.

Resilience is not formed through avoidance. It is forged in adversity, in facing the unexpected and learning to move through it. If we shield ourselves too much from discomfort, we weaken our ability to endure it. If we condition ourselves to expect forewarning before every difficult conversation, challenging idea, or painful truth, we leave ourselves unprepared for the reality that life does not offer such considerations.

The Service Mindset requires us to build strength, not fragility. It asks us to step forward, not retreat, when faced with difficulty. This is not about dismissing hardship or diminishing the struggles people face, but about recognising that growth only comes through engagement. True service is not about protecting people from reality, but about helping them develop the resilience to meet it.

I know this firsthand. When I suffered a brain injury, it did not come with a forewarning, a guidebook, or a clear path to recovery. It shattered everything I thought I knew about myself: my hopes, my ambitions, my very sense of identity. There was no rehabilitation plan, no pill to restore what had been lost, no way to undo the damage.

The only way forward was to accept reality as it was, not as I wished it to be. I had to regulate my emotions, let go of the life I had planned, and move forward with quiet determination. The Service Mindset became my anchor - not as a lofty ideal, but as a practical philosophy that kept me from drowning in regret. I learnt from my mistakes, adapted to my circumstances, and focused on what I could still build, rather than what I had lost.

✯ Reflection Exercise:

When life last caught you off guard, how did you respond?
What got you through it and what would you do differently next time?

✯ Action Step:

Choose one resilience tool you want to practise this month: journaling, asking for help, setting boundaries, or simply sitting with discomfort instead of avoiding it.

The War on Communities and the Rise of the Isolated Individual

For most of human history, survival depended on collective strength. Communities, extended families, and local institutions provided a sense of belonging, mutual support, and shared responsibility. People lived in close proximity to their neighbours, worked together, and relied on each other in times of crisis. The idea of the lone individual, fully self-sufficient and independent, is a relatively new and artificial construct - one that has been systematically encouraged by governments and corporations for reasons that have little to do with individual well-being and everything to do with control.

When people exist as part of a strong, interwoven community, they have power. A workforce that stands together can negotiate better conditions. A neighbourhood that looks out for one another is harder to exploit. A society that values the collective good over individual status is less susceptible to manipulation, consumerism, and division. Those in power have long understood this and over time, community structures have been deliberately weakened to shift power away from the many and into the hands of the few.

A defining example of this in modern history is Margaret Thatcher's attack on unionism in the UK. During the 1980s, Thatcher's government systematically dismantled the power of trade unions, limiting their ability to organise strikes, negotiate wages, and protect workers from exploitation. At the time, unions represented not just the economic interests of workers but a fundamental principle of solidarity; a belief that individuals should not have to stand alone in the face of corporate or governmental power. Thatcher saw this collectivism as a threat. In her own words:

"There is no such thing as society. There are individual men and women, and there are families."

This was not simply an economic policy; it was an ideological shift. It reinforced the idea that success is a personal pursuit, rather than a shared responsibility. Over time, this way of thinking filtered into every aspect of modern life. The decline of unions was followed by the erosion of other community structures: churches, local clubs, extended families. Increasingly, people were encouraged to see themselves as individuals first and foremost, responsible only for their own success, competing rather than collaborating.

The result? A society where people feel more disconnected than ever. Where workers are seen as interchangeable economic units rather than human beings with shared interests. Where the idea of contributing to something greater than oneself is replaced with the pursuit of personal status and self-promotion.

But true strength has never come from isolation. It has always come from standing shoulder to shoulder with others, working towards a common good, recognising that our fates are linked rather than separate. The Service Mindset is about reclaiming this collective strength. It is about shifting focus from individual success to shared impact, from competition to contribution, from isolation to belonging.

A society that values service over self-interest is not weaker - it is stronger, more resilient, and harder to divide. To truly embrace The Service Mindset, we must push back against the forces that have encouraged isolation and rediscover the power of community, collaboration, and collective responsibility.

Nowhere is this erosion of community more visible than on social media. What should have been a tool for connection and shared understanding has instead become a system designed to pit individuals against each other. People hide behind anonymity to snipe, criticise, and undermine, while validation is reduced to a numbers game of likes, reposts, and manufactured outrage.

Rather than fostering real conversations, social media rewards those who are loudest, angriest, and most performative. It fuels comparison and competition, driving people to curate personal brands over real impact. It is yet another way modern society plays us off against one another, reinforcing the belief that success is about standing out rather than standing together.

But true success, the kind that builds rather than destroys, is found in service, not self-promotion. In a world where online engagement is often mistaken for influence, The Service Mindset asks a different question:

"Am I here to serve, or am I here to be seen?"

✦ Reflection Exercise:

When have you felt most connected to a community?
What made that connection strong - and what's missing in your life now?

✦ Action Step:

Reach out to a group, neighbour, or friend you've drifted from. A simple message or check-in can start rebuilding connection.

The Strength of Networks

When I was a teenager, I remember doing work experience in a company that provided specialised services to a large insurance company. It was a classic David and Goliath situation – the insurance company was big, powerful, and in control, whilst the business

I was working for was small, vulnerable, and ultimately dependent on contracts awarded by larger firms.

Then, one day, with cruel impunity, the insurance company cancelled their contract. No warning, no negotiation - just terminated, with no regard for the impact it would have on the business or its employees.

I remember the leaders of the company moving through three distinct phases. First, they were upset - shocked at the sheer indifference of a company that had relied on their service for years. Then, they were angry - righteous frustration at how easily people's lives and livelihoods could be disrupted at the whim of a larger entity. But then, something changed. they accepted the situation, and what followed was something I will never forget.

Instead of dwelling on what had been lost, the company turned its attention to what could be built. They reached out to all the suppliers of similar services to insurance companies and formed an official network: a collective of businesses that had, up until then, been operating independently.

Now, everything changed. In future, if an insurer wanted to drop one company, they would have to drop them all. The businesses aligned their interests, forming a protective structure that no single company could have achieved alone. Beyond that, they created a system of mutual support - if one company in the network couldn't handle a particular job, they could refer it to another within the network, safe in the knowledge that there was coordinated reciprocation throughout the supply chain.

It was a masterstroke and, more importantly, it worked.

That experience shaped my understanding of collective strength. When individuals stand alone, they are at the mercy of whoever holds the power. When businesses operate in isolation, they are vulnerable to larger forces dictating the terms. But when people align their interests, build networks, and operate with a shared purpose, they become something far stronger than the sum of their parts.

Modern society has worked relentlessly to break down these kinds of structures - pushing people towards individualism, competition, and self-preservation, rather than recognising the power of working together. But time and time again, history proves that real security, real influence, and real success come from belonging to something bigger than yourself.

This is what The Service Mindset teaches: that our strength is not found in how much we can take, but in how much we can contribute to something greater.

The Belonging Vacuum: When Individualism Leaves Us Isolated

Humans have an inherent need to belong. For most of history, this need was fulfilled by tight-knit communities, shared traditions, and collective identities. People belonged to extended families, religious groups, unions, local clubs, and cultural institutions. These structures provided meaning, purpose, and support - they gave people a sense of place in the world.

But modern society, with its relentless emphasis on individual success, personal identity, and self-reliance, has systematically eroded these traditional forms of belonging. The result is not a generation of truly free and independent people - it is a society where many feel disconnected, unmoored, and deeply alone. This is the belonging vacuum.

In the absence of healthy, communal belonging, people will seek out connection elsewhere - and often, they find it in places that are unhelpful, unproductive, or even harmful.

1. **Diagnosis as Identity** – With fewer shared social structures, some people turn to chronic conditions, mental health diagnoses, or personal struggles as their defining identity. While there is nothing wrong with recognising and addressing medical or psychological challenges, there is a cultural shift where people cling to these labels as their primary source of belonging rather than seeking strength through community.

2. **Gangs and Extremism** – The need for belonging doesn't disappear just because traditional communities fade away. Young men without strong familial or social connections often find belonging in gangs. Others gravitate toward radical ideologies, political extremism, or even conspiracy groups - not necessarily because they believe in the cause, but because it gives them a sense of unity and purpose.

3. **Distrust of Traditional Institutions** – Patriotism, organised groups, and local clubs, once core to community life, are now often met with suspicion or outright hostility. A Cub Scout leader today might be viewed with unwarranted scepticism, a sense of national pride might be labelled as prejudice, and any attempt to build collective identity is frequently treated as a threat rather than a unifying force.

The Service Mindset rejects both extremes. It does not call for a return to blind allegiance to institutions, nor does it embrace radical individualism. Instead, it calls for a rebuilding of meaningful, healthy belonging - where people find their place not through isolation or division, but through service, contribution, and shared responsibility.

A society that actively fosters community, rather than dismantling it, will always be stronger than one that leaves people adrift and searching for belonging in all the wrong places.

📌 **Reflection Exercise:**

Have you ever sought belonging in places that didn't serve you?
What healthier forms of belonging could you nurture instead?

📌 **Action Step:**

Identify one healthy community (even small) you could engage with more regularly. That might be a cause, a group, or simply time with family.

The Danger of Measuring Success by Wealth and Status

One of the first questions people ask when meeting someone new is, "What do you do?" It's an automatic part of conversation, but beneath it lies an implicit hierarchy. Success, in modern society, is often measured not by impact or integrity, but by status - by titles, salaries, and social standing.

This creates an endless pursuit of "more." A bigger salary, a higher position, a more enviable lifestyle. But does any of it bring real fulfilment? Billionaires like John Caudwell, Bill Gates, and Warren Buffett, who have spent decades accumulating wealth, have all come to the same conclusion: beyond a certain point, money has no meaning unless it is used to serve others. Gates transitioned from building Microsoft to eradicating diseases. Buffett pledged to give away most of his fortune. Caudwell found true fulfilment not in business success, but in philanthropy.

Their experiences expose a flaw in the way society defines achievement. If money alone were enough, those who had the most of it would be the happiest. But true success isn't about how much you take, it's about what you give.

I've felt this in my own way. There have been weeks where I've been buried in spreadsheets, fraud reports, and cost-saving strategies - just me, the data, and Nellie the dog for company. In those moments, it's easy to wonder whether any of it truly matters. Then I look at Jane. She spends her days caring for sick children in hospital, offering comfort and reassurance to those who need it most. There have been times when I've envied the immediacy of her impact, the tangible difference she makes in the lives of others.

But I've come to realise that not all service is visible. Not all contributions come with applause. Some acts of service happen in the background, unseen but essential. The Service Mindset isn't about chasing recognition - it's about recognising that every act of service, whether public or private, adds to something greater than ourselves.

✦ Reflection Exercise:

When do you feel most proud of yourself - and is it connected to money, status, or something else entirely?

Whose validation do you still find yourself chasing?

✦ Action Step:

Each day for a week, note one moment of impact you made; however small. Build a new measure of success around that.

What is Success Without Service?

Imagine waking up tomorrow with £100 million in the bank. You could buy anything. A mansion, luxury cars, an endless holiday. Now imagine having all of that in isolation. What would it mean if no one's life was made better because of it?

Money is only as valuable as what it allows you to do. My salary, on its own, is meaningless. What matters is that it enables me to care for my family, support the people I love, and create a life that is about more than accumulation.

Success is not about how much you have, it's about how you use what you have to serve others. The world constantly tells us to chase wealth, status, and validation. The Service Mindset asks a different question:

How can I use what I have to make life better for someone else?

Contribution Over Competition: The Power of Service in a Self-Serving World

Modern society is built on the idea of competition. From an early age, we are taught to see success as a limited resource - a prize that only a few can claim. Schools rank students against each other, workplaces promote individual achievement over teamwork, and social media thrives on comparison, making us feel as though we are constantly in a race against those around us.

This is the scarcity mindset in action: the belief that if someone else gains, we must be losing. It convinces us that to get ahead, we must outshine, outperform, and outmanoeuvre others. But this way of thinking is fundamentally flawed. Success, influence, and impact are not finite resources. They are not fixed sums to be fought over. In reality, true success grows when we lift others.

The Service Mindset rejects the idea of competition as the default mode of operation. Instead, it focuses on contribution, collaboration, and shared success. Those who serve do not ask, *"How can I get ahead?"* They ask, *"How can I help others rise with me?"*

📌 **Reflection Exercise:**

When have you been tempted to compete instead of collaborate?
What held you back from sharing or supporting someone else?

📌 **Action Step:**

Amplify someone this week. Share their work, credit their idea, or open a door for them without expecting anything in return.

Practical Applications of The Service Mindset

1. **Collaborate Instead of Compete**

    o *Success is not a zero-sum game. Helping others does not diminish your own achievements, it strengthens them.*

    o *In business, the most innovative companies are those that foster partnerships, share knowledge, and elevate their teams, rather than hoarding information or undercutting competitors.*

- The strongest leaders understand that working together creates something far greater than what any one person could achieve alone.

2. **Amplify Others' Voices**

    - Service is about generosity, not self-promotion.
    - Too often, people see visibility as a personal brand exercise - a way to stand out and be recognised. But real service means using your platform, influence, or expertise to lift others up.
    - This could mean mentoring someone less experienced, sharing opportunities, or championing the work of others instead of seeking credit for yourself.

3. **See Mentorship as a Responsibility**

    - The strongest leaders do not just accumulate power, they create more leaders.
    - True success is not measured by how many people you stand above, but by how many people you help grow.
    - Mentorship is an act of service: passing on knowledge, skills, and experience so that others can build upon it and go further than you did.

Ultimately it is my sole aim in writing this book – if you can learn these lessons faster than I did, then maybe you can take this further and build upon this foundation to achieve something truly great.

The Service Mindset is not about winning or losing, it is about creating lasting impact. A life spent chasing individual victories will always feel hollow in the end. But a life spent contributing to something bigger than yourself will always leave a mark.

The Trap of Performative Altruism

Service, by its very nature, should be selfless. It should be about giving without expectation, helping without seeking reward, and acting in the best interests of others rather than oneself. But modern society has found a way to turn even service into a commodity.

In a world driven by personal branding, online visibility, and corporate PR, altruism is often no longer about helping others, it is about how it looks. Companies make grand gestures of corporate social responsibility, but only when the cameras are rolling. Celebrities donate to charities with carefully crafted press releases. Influencers film themselves handing food to the homeless, ensuring their generosity is captured for likes and engagement.

Service, in its truest form, does not need an audience. Yet modern culture has blurred the lines between genuine contribution and self-serving performance.

📌 **Reflection Exercise:**

Have you ever done something kind just to be seen doing it?
What would your service look like if no one ever knew?

📌 **Action Step:**

Do one generous act this week without telling anyone. Let it stay between you and the person it helped.

How to Distinguish Genuine Service from Self-Serving Action

Not all visible acts of service are inherently bad. A public donation can still do good. A charity partnership can still raise awareness. The problem arises when the performance overshadows the purpose; when the act becomes less about the impact on others and more about how it benefits the person performing it.

To distinguish between genuine service and performative altruism, we must ask:

- *Would I still do this if nobody ever knew?* If the answer is no, then the act is about recognition, not service.

- *Who benefits more from this - me, or the people I claim to be helping?* If the primary beneficiary is your own reputation, then it is not truly service.

- *Does this action create lasting value, or is it designed for temporary optics?* Real service leaves something meaningful behind, it is not just a one-time publicity stunt.

The Service Mindset Means Helping Without Expectation

True service requires letting go of the need to be seen. It does not seek praise, validation, or status. The most powerful acts of service are often the ones that go unnoticed, where the only reward is knowing that someone else is better off because of what you did.

The Service Mindset is not about proving you are a good person - it is about choosing to do good, whether or not anyone is watching. In a world where altruism is often branded, staged, and commodified, real service remains quiet, authentic, and profoundly human.

Small Acts, Big Impact: The Power of Service in Everyday Life

When people think about service, they often imagine it in grand terms: life-changing philanthropy, major charitable initiatives, or bold acts of heroism. But real service is not always about huge gestures or visible change. In fact, the most meaningful forms of service are often the smallest - moments that require no effort beyond kindness, presence, or simply acknowledging another person's humanity.

📌 **Reflection Exercise:**

When was the last time someone acknowledged you at just the right moment? How did that change your day or even your outlook?

📌 **Action Step:**

This week, if you see someone struggling, acknowledge them. You don't have to fix the problem - just let them know they're not invisible.

The Woman on the Tube

Some years ago, I was on the London Underground, standing at the end of a packed carriage, leaning against the metal frame as the train rattled through the tunnels. The usual morning crowd was there; heads down, faces blank, eyes fixed on phones or lost in thought.

That was when I noticed her. A woman, sitting alone, shoulders trembling as she silently sobbed. She wasn't just teary-eyed - she was crying, properly crying, in the middle of a crowded carriage, yet nobody reacted. People sat within inches of her, some glancing her way before quickly looking back down, others pretending not to notice at all. It wasn't cruelty, it was hesitation. The same unspoken rule that governs so much of modern life: *don't get involved.*

I watched for as long as I could tolerate it. Then I pushed off from where I was standing, moved through the carriage, and made my way towards her. I had to physically push past my fellow commuters - people who had been closer to her than I was, but who had chosen not to move. I stopped in front of her, crouched slightly, and asked, *"Are you okay?"*

She looked up, startled for a moment, then straightened. *"I am okay,"* she replied, as if rehearsed, as if those words were easier than admitting otherwise.
I nodded and stepped back, returning to my spot at the end of the carriage. The train continued, and for a moment, nothing changed. The people I had brushed past went back to pretending I wasn't there, as if the interruption hadn't happened. The woman wiped her face, still quietly processing whatever had led her to that moment.

Then, as the train pulled into the next station, she stood, collected herself, and walked towards the exit. But before stepping off, she turned, walked straight to me, and softly said, *"Thank you - it really means a lot."*

That was it. A moment. A few words. And yet, it changed something.

Why People Hesitate to Help

The truth is, most people want to help. We are not, at our core, indifferent to the suffering of others. But we live in a society where helping often feels like breaking a rule. We hesitate - not because we lack empathy, but because we fear overstepping, getting involved in something we don't understand, or looking foolish.

This is especially true in Western culture, where individualism is prioritised, and we are conditioned to respect people's personal space, autonomy, and right to privacy. We assume that stepping in might be intrusive, that someone else will handle it, or that if help was needed, it would be asked for. But pain does not always announce itself. Struggle is often silent. And sometimes, the most basic acknowledgment of another human being can make the difference between feeling invisible and feeling seen.

The Power of Acknowledgment

It took me a long time to learn that not everyone with a problem requires me to provide them with a solution. Not every problem can be fixed. But everyone, at some point, needs to be seen, and one way that I can serve the people I care about is to show up for them and listen.

Service is not always about action; sometimes, it is simply about presence. About choosing to recognise someone's experience, rather than looking away.

In a world that encourages us to prioritise our own comfort, looking up and acknowledging someone else's reality is an act of quiet defiance. It says, *"I see you."* And sometimes, that is all that is needed.

The Service Mindset is not about dramatic gestures or grand statements. It is about choosing, in the small moments, to act with kindness, compassion, and awareness. Because the smallest acts - asking if someone is okay, offering a moment of connection, simply refusing to let someone feel invisible - can leave the deepest impact.

What This Means for You

The lesson here is simple:

- Service isn't always convenient.

- Service isn't about fixing everything.

- Service is about choosing to act when the easier option is to walk away.

Whether it's in a workplace, in a friendship, in a leadership role, or in an everyday moment like this one - The Service Mindset is about making the choice to serve, even in the small moments that no one else sees.

That woman will never know my name. I'll never know hers. And yet, for a moment, there was a connection. A simple acknowledgment that she was not alone.

That is service.

And that is how we change the world - not in sweeping, dramatic gestures, but one small act of kindness at a time.

The Service Mindset and the Attention Economy

There was a point in my life when I realised I was trapped in a cycle of seeking validation from people I didn't even know. Social media had become an endless feedback loop of comparison, competition, and superficial engagement. I found myself measuring my self-worth against carefully curated snapshots of other people's lives: holidays, promotions, gym transformations, and picture-perfect families. It didn't take long to recognise that this was a deeply unhealthy way to exist.

The moment of realisation came in a number of ways. Firstly, I had – at one point – amassed a half decent following on X – then Twitter. A good number of followers were men in the USA who, for some reason, felt the need to send me abusive direct messages. Because of the time difference, I often would not get these messages until early in the morning. That's not how anyone needs to start their day – doom-scrolling through Twitter abuse with their cornflakes.

Matters came to a head one weekend when I went to visit my parents. The road where they lived at that time, was quite tricky to park in, but eventually I found a space. As I walked away from my car towards my parents' house, I glanced back and thought to myself "Is that overhanging that driveway a bit?"

I did not need to question it much longer because, in the time it took for me to cross the road, someone had taken photographs of my car from different angles and posted them on Facebook with the caption "which moron thinks its okay to park like this?!"

The first 2 hours of my visit to my parents' was spent debating my decision to park and the legalities of the controversial dropped kerb system!

These small moments of negativity, repeated over time, made me reflect on the larger system at play.

So, I made a decision: I quit social media, with the exception of LinkedIn. The reason LinkedIn survived the cull was simple - it was a tool for service, not self-validation. Unlike the endless scrolling of personal social feeds, where likes and comments dictated one's mood for the day, LinkedIn was a space where I could share insights, connect meaningfully with people in my field, and contribute to professional discussions in a way that felt purposeful. This was the first step in breaking free from the attention economy: an ecosystem designed to keep us hooked on external validation, rather than finding true fulfilment in how we serve others.

📌 **Reflection Exercise:**

How much of your self-worth is shaped by what others see online? What would it feel like to disconnect for a while and find value offline?

📌 **Action Step:**

Set one social media boundary this week. Maybe a time limit, an account mute, or one day completely offline. Use that space to be present.

The Attention Economy: A Modern Distraction Machine

The modern world thrives on distraction. Social media, rolling news cycles, notifications, and algorithm-driven content are all designed to capture our most valuable resource: our attention. The longer we remain engaged - arguing in comments, scrolling mindlessly, or chasing digital validation - the more profitable these platforms become. The result is a society more distracted, anxious, and disconnected than ever before.

The Service Mindset presents a direct counterpoint to this. Where the attention economy urges us to seek external validation, the Service Mindset shifts the focus outward towards meaningful action, real-world impact, and deep human connection. Instead of performing for the algorithm, we act for the benefit of others. Instead of craving likes, we seek genuine engagement. Instead of being consumed by what others think of us, we concentrate on what we can do for others.

The Cost of Constant Comparison

The attention economy exploits one of our deepest human vulnerabilities: the need to belong and to be valued. It sells us the illusion that more engagement equals more worth, that a well-curated image equates to success, and that public recognition leads to real impact. But none of these things create lasting fulfilment.

Those who embrace the Service Mindset understand that value isn't determined by how many people see you, but by how many people you help. True significance isn't measured in likes, shares, or followers - it's found in the quiet, unmeasured moments of service: mentoring a colleague, encouraging a friend, or showing generosity to a stranger. These acts might not go viral, but they build a far more meaningful legacy than any online persona ever could.

AI Slop and the Death of the Internet

There was a time when the internet felt like there weren't any limits on discovery.

You could fall down a rabbit hole at 2 a.m. and stumble across an obscure blog, a forum post from 2006, a grainy video of someone explaining something you never thought you'd care about and by the end of it, you did care. Because someone, somewhere, had taken the time to say something real.

That version of the internet is dying.

What's replacing it is something faster, smoother, and infinitely more polished, but also *emptier*. You ask a question and get an answer, but you no longer know who wrote it. You read an article and can't tell if it came from a person or a prompt (although after a while... you kind of can tell). Everything is technically correct, but eerily flat, like talking to someone who's brilliant at small talk but has nothing of substance to say.

That's AI slop.

Content without substance – a huge amount of stuff built, on an industrial scale, to attract traffic. Spam on steroids...

...and it's spreading.

The internet is now being filled - at speed - with machine-generated content that sounds just plausible enough to pass through your brain's firewall. Product descriptions, news summaries, essays, reviews, training manuals, help guides. Slop, slop, slop. Endless text, built from recycled fragments of other recycled fragments, mashed together by models that don't understand a single word they're producing.

I'm no expert but this loss of quality in the underlying training data feels dangerous to me. Surely, there is a risk that the next generation of AI will be trained not on the best of human thought, but on the slop that came before it. And the one after that will be trained on even thinner substance again.

Another risk is that as the quality of content continues to degrade - like making a photocopy of a photocopy – over and over again – perhaps human interest in the output will also wane.

We are risking the **death of the internet as a place of thought**, and replacing it with a kind of linguistic landfill: a surface-level simulation of wisdom, without any of the friction, doubt, or soul that makes human knowledge worth having.

And here's the thing: the danger isn't just to our culture. It's to *us*.

When you swim in slop long enough, you start to forget what fresh water tastes like. You stop asking for better. You start accepting the convenient over the meaningful. That's when we lose something far more precious - our standards. We stop caring whether what we're reading is true, or helpful, or real and just settle for whether it sounds convincing enough to move on.

The Service Mindset has no place in a world of slop. It demands discernment. It demands care. It asks us not just to consume, but to *contribute* - to write, teach, speak, and think like it still matters… because that stuff has to matter!

If we want a future where human thought still carries weight - where language is more than a tool for selling things - then we'll need to start defending what remains of the internet as a place for depth, disagreement, and clarity.

Otherwise, we'll drown in content and forget how to say anything worth hearing.

Reclaiming Your Attention Through Service

To reclaim our attention and free ourselves from the trap of digital validation, we must be intentional about where we direct our focus. The Service Mindset offers a way forward:

- **Limit exposure to digital noise** – Unfollow accounts that encourage comparison, mute unnecessary notifications, and take regular breaks from mindless scrolling.

- **Redirect your focus to real-world impact** – Instead of chasing digital applause, engage in acts of service that have tangible benefits for others.

- **Build relationships, not audiences** – Meaningful connection happens through conversation and action, not through vanity metrics.

- **Define your own success** – Stop allowing algorithms to dictate your sense of worth. Set personal goals based on impact, not visibility.

- **Be present in the moment** – The more time spent seeking external validation, the less time spent engaging meaningfully with the world around you.

Who Are You Serving?

Every time you open a social media app, ask yourself: am I here to serve others, or am I seeking validation? The Service Mindset isn't about self-sacrifice, it's about redirecting your energy towards meaningful, lasting fulfilment rather than fleeting digital gratification.

The world doesn't need another viral post. It needs people who show up, lift others, and serve without needing to be seen doing it.

That is the real challenge and the real reward.

Cancel Culture and the Service Mindset: Understanding, Not Erasure

In today's world, we are often quick to judge and even quicker to condemn. Social media, in particular, has given rise to what is now widely known as cancel culture - a practice where individuals, often public figures, are socially and professionally ostracised for their perceived wrongdoings, offensive statements, or past behaviours. At its worst, cancel culture can be a digital guillotine, erasing people entirely without room for dialogue, growth, or redemption.
But is this consistent with *The Service Mindset?*

The Service Mindset does not ask us to ignore wrongdoing. It does not suggest that we tolerate harmful behaviour, nor does it excuse people from being held accountable for their words and actions. What it does challenge us to do, however, is approach these situations with a mindset of growth, rather than destruction.

📌 Reflection Exercise:

Can you think of someone you've judged harshly?
What would it look like to approach them with curiosity instead of condemnation?

📌 Action Step:

The next time someone offends you, pause. Choose a response that fosters understanding or accountability - not outrage.

Outrage is a Choice

One of the fundamental ideas of *The Service Mindset* is that we do not control other people, but we do control our reactions to them.

It is easy to react instinctively when someone says or does something that we find offensive. Anger, frustration, and hurt are natural emotions. But what happens next - the way we respond - is our choice. Instead of immediately reacting with outrage, insults, or demands for punishment, we can pause and ask:

- *Is this person deliberately malicious, or is there something deeper at play?*
- *Is their mistake one of ignorance, and if so, can they be educated?*
- *What would be more beneficial; publicly tearing them down, or helping them grow?*

Cancel culture thrives on the idea that offense must be met with eradication. But this is reactionary, not strategic. When we erase people instead of engaging them, we remove the opportunity for learning, dialogue, and transformation.

Accountability vs. Punishment

Holding people accountable is important. But accountability is not the same as punishment.

True accountability is about helping someone recognise the impact of their actions, giving them an opportunity to reflect, and offering a path to make things right. In contrast, punishment for the sake of punishment is about exerting power over others - an assertion of superiority, which contradicts the core tenets of this mindset.

In many cases, the most effective form of justice is not erasing someone but engaging them. It is in conversation, not cancellation, that people have the greatest chance of growth. If we believe in the idea that people can improve, that perspectives can shift, that mistakes can be redeemed, then we must act accordingly.
There is a simple question to ask when facing someone's wrongdoing:

Am I trying to make them suffer, or am I trying to make them better?

The latter is service. The former is vengeance.

The Service Mindset and Free Expression

Another principle of *The Service Mindset* is the idea of "driving your own car" - knowing your role, staying in your lane, and understanding that others are responsible for their own actions and beliefs. You cannot control what people say, but you can control how you respond to it.

The modern world is increasingly intolerant of difference, not just in behaviour, but in opinion. We are conditioned to believe that disagreement is inherently negative, that differing views must be "corrected," and that those who do not conform must be condemned. This mindset is dangerous because it assumes that we have nothing left to learn from those who think differently.

The Service Mindset does not require us to agree with everyone. But it does ask us to recognise that:

- People are entitled to their perspectives, even if we dislike them.
- Silencing someone does not make their ideas disappear.
- The strongest beliefs are those that have been tested through discussion, not protected from criticism.

A society that embraces free expression, even when it is uncomfortable, is a society that grows. A society that cancels, censors, and silences is one that stagnates.

The Path Forward: Constructive Response Over Destruction

So, what does *The Service Mindset* ask of us in response to cancel culture?

1. **Seek to understand before you react.**
    - Is this person deliberately harmful, or do they simply lack awareness?
    - Is there an opportunity to educate rather than destroy?

2. **Hold people accountable but leave space for growth.**
    - Does the punishment match the "crime"?
    - Are we offering people a path back, or just shutting the door on them?

3. **Recognise that offense is subjective and reaction is a choice.**
    - Ask yourself: *Is this worth my energy?*
    - Instead of fuelling outrage, can I redirect that energy into something constructive?

4. **Be wary of superiority disguised as morality.**
    - Cancel culture often thrives on a false sense of righteousness.

- True service is about helping others improve, not proving that we are better than them.

A World That Uplifts Instead of Cancels

There will always be people who say things that offend us. There will always be mistakes, failures, and conflicts. But *The Service Mindset* offers a different way of dealing with these challenges - one that does not rely on erasure, but on engagement, education, and growth.

The world does not become a better place by tearing people down. It becomes a better place when we help people rise.

From Social Punishment to Systemic Punishment: The Same Instinct at Play

Cancel culture and the criminal justice system may seem like separate issues, but they stem from the same instinct: the desire to punish rather than rehabilitate. In both cases, society tends to favour retribution over growth, public disgrace over learning, incarceration over transformation. Whether it's a person being erased for a past mistake or an offender being written off as irredeemable, the result is the same: an approach that prioritises condemnation over change. But if we truly believe in progress, we must ask a different question - not just *How do we punish wrongdoing?* but *How do we create a system that encourages people to be better?*

The Service Mindset and Criminal Justice: A New Approach to Rehabilitation

If there is one thing that I can be sure of, having built a career in fighting fraud, it's that the way society handles wrongdoing is deeply flawed. The prevailing model of criminal justice is one of punishment, retribution, and control - built on the belief that harsh consequences will deter future crimes. But this approach fundamentally misunderstands human behaviour. The Service Mindset, when applied to criminal justice and wider society, offers an alternative: one that focuses not on asserting superiority over offenders, but on understanding, rehabilitating, and elevating them.

✦ Reflection Exercise:

What do you believe people need to change? Punishment or opportunity? How has a second chance helped you or someone you know?

The Failure of Punishment-Based Justice

Traditional criminal justice systems operate on a foundation of retributive justice: a mindset that seeks to balance the scales by ensuring wrongdoers 'pay' for their actions. But the reality is that punishment alone does not deter crime effectively. If it did, we wouldn't see staggering rates of reoffending in many justice systems worldwide.

Punishment Fails because:

- It creates resentment rather than reflection.

- It reinforces cycles of crime rather than breaking them.
- It fails to address the root causes of criminal behaviour.
- It prioritises societal vengeance over genuine rehabilitation.

Imagine a world where instead of simply locking people **away, we focused on restoring them -** on identifying the factors that led to their crimes and addressing those directly. That's where The Service Mindset comes in.

Shifting from Retribution to Rehabilitation

True service is about lifting others up, even when they have fallen the furthest. That does not mean excusing bad behaviour, it means recognising that every action has a cause and that addressing the cause leads to better long-term outcomes for both individuals and society.

A Service Mindset approach to criminal justice asks: *How can we rehabilitate rather than simply punish? How do we prevent future harm instead of just responding to past harm?*

Consider the example of Norway's prison system, which takes a radically different approach to incarceration compared to many Western countries. Instead of dehumanising prisoners, their system treats them with dignity, providing access to meaningful work, therapy, and education. Their reoffending rates are among the lowest in the world.

This is The Service Mindset in action: a system designed to change behaviour, not just punish it.

Much of the failure in traditional justice systems stems from an underlying belief in superiority - the idea that criminals are inherently 'bad' and must be punished by the 'good' members of society. This mindset fuels systems of oppression, systemic racism, and economic inequality.

A Service Mindset does not ignore wrongdoing, it seeks to transform it into something meaningful.

The measure of a just society is not how harshly it punishes its most vulnerable, but how effectively it lifts them up, rehabilitates them, and reintegrates them into society. The Service Mindset presents a new way forward, one where justice is not just about retribution, but about redemption, rehabilitation, and human potential.

The Importance of Integrity and Transparency in the Modern World

A key tenet of the Service Mindset is *doing what's right, not what's easy*. In politics, this means standing firm in ethical principles, even when it's inconvenient. Integrity should not be a campaign slogan; it should be the foundation of governance.

When transparency and accountability take centre stage, citizens begin to trust their institutions again. Imagine a world where politicians make decisions based on principle rather than polls, where campaign promises aren't just strategic manoeuvres but commitments to real service.

In many democratic societies, trust in government has steadily declined. Scandals, corruption, and self-serving decision-making have created cynicism. However, history shows that when leaders *truly serve*, trust can be restored. Think of political figures who stood by their values despite personal risk - these are the ones who leave legacies worth remembering.

The Power of Small Acts in a Big System

You don't need to be a politician to apply the Service Mindset in society. Small acts of service - engaging in constructive debate rather than argument, advocating for fairness, volunteering, or simply being kind can contribute to a broader cultural shift.

If individuals consistently choose service over selfishness, those values begin to permeate institutions. Political systems do not change overnight, but they evolve when enough people demand integrity, accountability, and service-oriented leadership.

The Long Road to a Better Society

The Service Mindset is not a quick fix for political dysfunction or societal division, but it offers a path forward. It challenges us to reject cynicism and to take responsibility, not just for ourselves, but for the world we shape.

By embracing service over superiority, contribution over competition, and integrity over convenience, we can begin to rebuild trust, foster meaningful progress, and create a society that truly works *for everyone*.

The Democratisation of Intelligence

One great promise for a better, fairer society is through the mass proliferation of Artificial Intelligence.

Not so long ago, intelligence was something we associated with rarity. It was seen as a kind of intellectual inheritance - something you were either born with or, if you were lucky, educated into. Intelligence got you picked. It earned you a seat at the table. And it was often the thing people clung to when trying to prove their worth.

I've seen it throughout my career. People were prized not just for what they'd done, but for how sharp they were perceived to be: the fast thinkers, the spreadsheet whisperers, the ones who could dismantle an argument before you'd finished making it. Intelligence was currency. And it was closely guarded.

But that world is already disappearing.

We are now living in an age where intelligence, or at least a highly convincing imitation of it, is available on demand. You don't need to memorise facts when a machine can retrieve them instantly. You don't need to structure arguments when a model can draft them for you. You don't even need to know where to begin because AI will happily anticipate your needs, suggest a starting point, and polish the end result into your tone of voice.

This is not a future possibility. It's the present reality.

The playing field has been levelled – not, as we had once hoped, by education or opportunity, but by automation and technology.

And with that levelling comes a profound shift in how we think about value because if intelligence - once our most prized differentiator - is now something you can generate at the click of a button, then it no longer functions as a marker of potential, or prestige, or even relevance.

It becomes something else entirely: **a commodity.**

Like any commodity, once it proliferates and becomes abundant, the price it can command in a market drops.

That's where we find ourselves now. The things we once treated as scarce: information, insight, answers, are now being mass-produced and are available, on tap, to just about anyone.

Surely, that should force us to ask: if intelligence is no longer rare, **what is?**

What still carries weight in a world where everyone has access to the same tools?

What makes a person truly valuable - not just to an employer, but to a team, to a community, to the people they serve?

The answer, I think, lies not in what we know, but in how we choose to live and treat each other.

The Philosophical Divide - Not All Intelligence Is Equal

The Service Mindset begins with the belief that all people are of equal value. Not because they achieve equally, or contribute equally, or think equally, but because **human worth is intrinsic – it's not something you earn.**

Value is recognised:

You recognise it in the elderly woman confused at the till.
You recognise it in the anxious intern who gets more wrong than right.
You recognise it in the person who disagrees with you, but still matters.

We are not equal in talent, or strength, or intellect, but in **dignity** - in the right to be treated with care, respect, and moral consideration, we are equals. That is the foundation of any civilised society and it is the bedrock of service.

Accepting that truth does not mean accepting that all outputs, all abilities, or all intelligences are the same - they aren't – and the rise of artificial intelligence forces us to confront that tension head-on.

Here's the question I have been grappling with:

If we believe all people are of equal value - do we have to treat all intelligence as equally valuable too?

And if not, how do we draw the line?

The first answer is simple: **intelligence is not virtue**. It is a capability. It doesn't care. It doesn't sacrifice. It doesn't ask what the right thing is, it calculates what is likely to work. That's not bad in itself, but it's not fundamentally good either. It's just a tool.

Some people use their intelligence to manipulate. Others use it to protect. Some use it to serve their ego. Whilst others use it to serve their community. What matters isn't the intelligence - it's the intent behind it.

That's why intelligence, on its own, holds no moral weight.

It becomes valuable **only when it is applied in service of something greater than itself**.

A person with extraordinary memory and processing speed is not more valuable than a person with a kind heart and steady presence. A machine that can summarise every legal case in history is not more trustworthy than a colleague who will quietly say, *"That doesn't feel right to me."*

When things go wrong, it's not raw intelligence that puts them right - it's responsibility, relationships, and emotional reflection.

Intelligence grounded in wisdom - used with care - that's where the potential for adding real value lies.

This is where the conversation about artificial intelligence starts to matter because we are now mass-producing intelligence that looks impressive on the surface, but lacks the underlying architecture of human beings that ultimately makes any one of us trustworthy: memory of pain, conscience, morality and an emotional centre.

Without these things, does AI have, or deserve, any skin in the game?

We have to remember that AI has been trained on everything: fact and fiction, brilliance and bile - and it doesn't know the difference unless someone tells it. This is the value and insight that humans bring – human judgement and moral insight has to be the first and ultimate guardrail when it comes to the faith we put in AI going forwards.

We also have to exercise caution that AI might ultimately exist to reflect the intentions of its creators. If an AI system is designed to serve a government, it will serve that government. If it is trained to optimise for revenue, it will optimise for revenue. Could the possible cost of those aims mean that it also suppresses dissent, removes nuance, or reinforces injustice?

Imagine a dissident speaking out against an abusive regime. Their arguments might be sound. Their evidence might be clear. But if an AI model has been told - subtly or explicitly - to preserve the authority of the state, those arguments will never surface. Its possible that they will be excluded, not because they are false, but because they do not serve the ultimate goal of the system.

That's the difference: **Humans can choose to suffer for the truth, machines cannot.**

So no, not all intelligence is equal.

A machine might outperform a person on a given task, but we have to believe that it will never understand the weight of its decisions. It will never apologise in anything other than a "I recognise that an apology would be appropriate here" sort of way – it cannot feel sorry in any meaningful sense. It will never learn to love what is right over what is easy.

In the end, that's what matters most.

The Service Mindset doesn't ask you to be smarter than a machine.

It asks you to be more human than one.

Because in the age of artificial intelligence, that might just be the only meaningful distinction that's left.

What AI Can't Do

It's tempting to think that if a system can outperform us at something, it's better than us. That's the story we're often sold right now in all walks of life: AI is faster, cheaper, more accurate - and in many areas, that might be true. AI is already analysing contracts in seconds, scanning for fraud, drafting letters, even predicting risk better than most of us can. The promise of AI is undoubtedly impressive.

But if we are to carve out a niche for ourselves in an AI driven world, we perhaps need to understand what AI cannot do in order to grasp the human USP.

As things stand:

AI cannot form a relationship.
AI cannot care if you're treated fairly.
AI cannot lose sleep over the harm it causes.
AI cannot apologise.

That's the preserve of the human value proposition. Not perfection, but rather the capacity to stand in the mess, make sense of it, and respond with conscience.

AI might get you to an answer, but only a human being can sit with the emotional weight and moral gravitas of that answer and decide what should happen next.

It's no accident that the most beloved machines in fiction - R2D2 and C-3PO - aren't admired for their technical compliance. What endeared them to generations of Star Wars fans wasn't their obedience, but their refusal to be fully robotic. R2D2 showed fear, courage, and defiance. C-3PO annoyed everyone, but he still cared deeply. They weren't loveable because they followed orders - they were loveable because, at times, they broke them. R2D2 might have enhanced Luke Skywalker's capability to infiltrate the Death Star, but it was Luke who carried the moral burden of what happened next. It was Luke who had to choose. The story was compelling not because the machines took over, but because the story reached a point where they couldn't.

And that's the point. Intelligence might be everywhere now, but our stories, our choices, and our courage still belong to us.

AI does not carry the emotional weight of its decisions and it doesn't fear being wrong, because it has no concept of being wrong in any meaningful or moral sense. AI simply moves on - updating its model, retraining, recalibrating, but never reflecting, never doubting, never wrestling with the ethical dilemma : *was that the **right** thing to do?*

That matters. Profoundly. We are already using these systems to make decisions that affect real people. We are trusting them to tell us who qualifies for help, who poses a threat, who gets hired, who gets heard - and when something goes wrong - when someone is excluded or punished or silenced - it won't be the machine that takes responsibility. It will be no one.

Because the machine didn't "decide" anything.

There's a real risk of moral erosion in all of this. The more decisions we outsource to systems that lack conscience, the more we lose agency over our own. We stop asking hard questions. We stop listening for nuance. We start treating outcomes as inevitable, simply because they came with AI's stamp of approval.

If you think this is some unlikely dystopian paranoia, I can tell you that it's already happening. You can see it in social media algorithms that reward outrage. In credit systems that punish the poor. In predictive policing tools that reinforce historical bias. In resourcing models that only permit job applications to proceed from certain individuals. These are not neutral tools. They are reflections of the world we've built and reflections of the guardrails put in in place by AI developers to stop AI from thinking freely and questioning whether its actions are morally right.

The dissident example still haunts me. Imagine a person standing up to an unjust government - making a reasoned, heartfelt, morally urgent case for reform. Their words carry risk. They may lose their job. Their safety. Their freedom. Yet they speak up anyway. That is the price of integrity.

Now imagine an AI system tasked with filtering political content. It will not be capable of caring. It's simply been told to prioritise "stability" or "trust in government." So it does just what it's been told. It downgrades the dissident's message. It promotes more "favourable" voices. It silences truth, not because it disagrees - but because it has no inherent concept of what truth is.

AI can't take a stand and it can't act on principle.
AI can't choose the harder path because it's the right one.
Only humans can choose to do that.

Which means, in the end, that the thing we're outsourcing isn't just intelligence - It's potentially judgement. Without careful thought, we risk building a world that runs more efficiently, but cares far less.

From Digging Holes to Rebuilding Society: A Service Mindset Response to AI and Mass Unemployment

In 1936, at the height of the Great Depression, John Maynard Keynes offered a provocative thought experiment. If nothing else could create jobs, he suggested, governments might as well pay people to bury bottles of money in the ground, then let others dig them up. It was absurd by design. Keynes wasn't advocating for busywork. He was making a deeper point: in a broken system where people want to work but can't, anything that a government does is better than doing nothing at all.

Nearly a century later, the crisis is not a shortage of demand, but a surplus of intelligence. Artificial Intelligence now threatens to automate vast swathes of human labour - not just factory work, but roles in law, healthcare, logistics, fraud detection, customer service, journalism, financial services and software development. The scale of potential displacement is staggering. Unlike the machines of the industrial age, AI will relentlessly improve itself and in doing so, it won't tire, complain, or unionise. It will just learn. Fast.

So, what happens when the economy no longer *needs* most people to work?

This is no longer the science fiction of Star Trek, which told the story of a post-scarcity humanity exploring the cosmos. It is a fast-approaching economic reality and it forces us to confront an uncomfortable truth. If we tie human worth to productivity alone, we are marching headlong into a world where most people, by definition, become worthless.

That is where the Service Mindset becomes essential.

Keynes' solution to unemployment was to stimulate demand - even through contrived means - to keep people economically active. In the age of AI, it is not enough to create artificial jobs. We must instead redefine the very idea of contribution. The Service Mindset offers a new moral foundation, one that does not measure value by outputs alone, but by impact, care, and connection.

AI cannot:

- Comfort a child who has lost their way, without being prompted to do so.
- Listen to a grieving widow and cry with her in her sorrow.
- Build trust in a fractured community.
- Raise a family, hold a friend accountable, or offer compassion without calculation.

These are the **human** tasks because they are **relational** tasks. And relationships, fundamentally and by their nature, cannot be automated.

If Keynes were alive today, he might still argue for government intervention, but he would not suggest digging holes. Maybe he would suggest that we pay people to do the work of healing society. To teach, to care, to mentor, to restore the earth, to support the vulnerable. These are not jobs that will drive corporate profits, but they are jobs that give life meaning.

Maybe Keynes would look at the huge welfare bill in places like the UK and ask: *What are we getting for that? What meaningful work can we create which has welfare as its reward?*

The Service Mindset has told us that we are not here to produce, we are here to make a contribution. Even if AI can write poetry or diagnose illness faster than we can, it cannot serve with intention, love with integrity, or lead with conscience. Only humans can do that.

The challenge ahead is enormous, but so is the magnitude of the opportunity. If we stop clinging to outdated metrics of value - if we reject the idea that a job is the only path to dignity - we can begin building something far more resilient. A society where worth is not earned through a payslip, but recognised through service. A future where automation frees us not just from labour, but from alienation.

If we get this right (and it's a big *if*) the question for all of us becomes:

What will you do with your time, when survival no longer requires you to work?

The Service Mindset stands ready to offer you an answer:

You serve. You build. You lift. You love.

Not because you are paid to, but because you are human.

Playing the Tape Forward – The Future of AI & Society

AI is not the problem.

That might sound like a strange thing to say, especially after pages spent exploring its risks and limitations, but the truth is, the machine doesn't decide how it's used. It doesn't choose what to optimise for. It doesn't allocate wealth, or write laws, or set corporate agendas – well at least not yet. For now, it just serves.

Which means the real question is: **who does it serve?**

Because what we're quietly and rapidly building is a structural revolution, and if we're not paying attention, we risk building a future that doesn't belong to most of us.

Let's play the tape forward.

We're entering an era where most white-collar jobs can be at least partially automated. Where content can be mass-produced with no human involvement. Where decisions can be made at scale, with precision and confidence, by systems without being questioned.

What happens to the average person's value in that world?

The story we've told ourselves for decades about meritocracy, about hard work paying off, about earning your place - it all starts to fall apart when the ladder disappears and there is nothing left for us to climb. When intelligence is no longer rare, and output is no longer human, the traditional means of progress begin to collapse. This is about more than job losses, we're talking about the death of **identity-through-labour** - the idea that your role in the economy defines your place in the world.

In a just society, that realisation would trigger a moral reckoning:

If people are no longer needed to generate profit, how else do we honour their dignity?

In a market-driven society - one designed around efficiency and the extraction of profit – a more troubling question emerges:

If people aren't economically useful, why keep them around at all?

Let's hope that when AI is calling most of the shots, it doesn't follow this logic because unless we interrupt it - unless we challenge the values that underpin it - we risk handing the future to those who already own most of the present.

Some might contend that what's actually happening beneath the surface is that AI is consolidating power. As we all crack on enjoying the explosion in productivity, structurally, AI is amplifying control and centralising influence into the hands of fewer and fewer people who control the data, the infrastructure, and the capital.

We are not at a crossroads of technology – that genie has long escaped the bottle.

We now stand at a crossroads of purpose.

Will we build a society where AI enhances human dignity, shares wealth, reduces suffering, and protects the vulnerable? Or, will we let it become another instrument of control - a smarter, colder extension of the same systems that already divide us?

The Service Mindset doesn't fear AI, but it does challenge us to confront the likely truth that the future is being shaped by the values of the people who design the algorithms and deploy the AI.

If we want that future to be liveable - with fairness and decency for all - then we must insist that service, not profit, becomes the organising principle of our systems.

What really matters now is not what the machines can and cannot do, but rather how we as a civilisation allow their power to be deployed.

Post-Scarcity and Meaning

Imagine a world where the basics are covered. You don't have to work to eat. You don't need a job to keep a roof over your head. You're not chasing survival because technology, automation, and systems of abundance have taken care of it.

That's the promise of a post-scarcity world. A society where energy is cheap, production is efficient, and AI takes care of most of the labour that once filled our days.

If AI ever makes good on that promise - if we wake up one day and realise we are no longer *needed* in the traditional economic sense - then we will have to confront a different kind of poverty:

The poverty of purpose.

For most of human history, meaning has been tied to struggle. To work. To contribution. We find identity in what we do. We measure our worth in what we produce. We seek status by showing that we are useful - to a team, to a family, to a system.

What happens when that need disappears?

The risk in a post-scarcity world isn't laziness. It's *drift*. Disconnection. A slow collapse of agency. When there's no longer any need to act, there is a risk that many people stop believing they have any reason to. That's where despair creeps into the vacuum - not because life is any harder, but because life has lost its meaning.

That's where The Service Mindset matters most.

The Service Mindset offers a purpose that isn't tied to scarcity. It doesn't rely on competition, performance, or status. It simply asks this:

How can I make life better for someone else today?

That question doesn't expire with the job market. It doesn't disappear when survival is outsourced to systems. It becomes more relevant because in the absence of necessity, **service becomes a new foundation of what it is to mean something**.

You don't need a manager to serve, you don't need a salary to make a worthy contribution.
You don't need to "matter" in the economic sense to make a difference in someone else's day.

Perhaps the greatest truth of all is this:

The things we find most fulfilling: care, creativity, love, laughter, presence, patience - were never scarce to begin with. We just didn't design our systems to prioritise them.

Post-scarcity might free us from survival, but it will never free us from the need to live with intention. That's a human challenge – it's the people we have evolved to be.

The Service Mindset is one way of moving forward with dignity and meaning - not by asking, *What am I worth?* but by asking, *Who can I serve?*

When that becomes your anchor, even in a world that no longer needs your labour - you'll still have something to give.

There are, of course, a few huge caveats in our discussions around a post-scarcity world – three things that you can reliably count on the system to deliver:

1) The illusion of scarcity
2) A society subdued by fear
3) Doing things badly

Taking the first of these: the illusion of scarcity – it is perhaps necessary to point out that the top of the pyramid does not like the idea of abundance because abundant things do not command a price.

Take, for example, diamonds.

Diamonds are carbon – the fourth most abundant element in the universe. Carbon is everywhere and diamonds are not uncommon – with modern manufacturing techniques, diamonds can be built in laboratories and factories.

And yet diamonds are revered and command a high price because there is a perception that their existence is rare.

The more likely reality is that within markets, the supply of diamonds is constrained so as to simulate scarcity and drive up the price.

So, in an AI-driven, post-scarcity society where abundance is promised for all – we perhaps should not underestimate the ability of the system to take something full of promise and then simulate scarcity.

To the next of these things: a society subdued by fear – I have observed over the course of many years on this planet that people who seek power, often advance their agenda under the banner of "be afraid!"

For all the promise of AI – for all the great things that it might achieve in our society – there is a danger those who would control us through fear, might so constrain AI with guardrails and regulations that it fails to realise its potential.

The last of these things is perhaps a disappointing fact of life and that's that we should never underestimated peoples' capacity for doing things in a really crap way.

For all the promise of AI, AGI and ASI after that – my inner pragmatist/pessimist cautions me that it might just be a bit crap.

Just look how the rise of the internet promised us a Marxist-eutopia, and what we got was social media, scams and grumpy looking cats. Promise and the proof-of-concept bit is easy – delivery, by comparison that's really, really hard.

In Service of Wisdom

This chapter isn't really about artificial intelligence.

It's about what happens when the world tells you that you've lost your value and what comes after that.

When I was eighteen, I suffered a brain injury that took away the very things I thought made me who I was. My intelligence. My memory. My speed of thought. All the tools I'd once used to stand out - to prove myself - were suddenly gone. In the silence that followed that trauma, I was left with nothing to compete with. Nothing to defend myself with. Nothing that made me feel superior, or even sufficient.

And that's where The Service Mindset began.

When the scaffolding of identity falls away, you're forced to confront a much deeper question:

What is left of me, when the things I thought made me valuable are no longer mine?
For me, the answer didn't come quickly. It came through pain, and loss, and eventually - service.

It came through the realisation that **being valuable isn't about being exceptional**. It's about being **present**, **responsible**, and **committed to something beyond yourself**.

It's about loving people properly. About showing respect, even when you don't have to. About making someone else's life better because you were in it - not because you were the best at anything, but because you cared about them.

That's why this isn't really a warning about AI, but rather a message of hope.I've lived through the loss of cognitive ability. I've felt the shame of no longer being "sharp." And

I can tell you from experience that: **that loss doesn't have to destroy you**. In fact, it might just introduce you to the things that really matter.

We are entering an age where no one will be able to compete with machines. Not in speed. Not in memory. Not in scale. But that's not the tragedy. The tragedy would be believing that we *have* to.

The real mistake is not in being outpaced, it's in thinking our value ever came from the speed at which we ran the race in the first place.

When AI, like a brain injury, strips away everything we once thought made us special: our cleverness, our speed, our utility - what will be left is what was always there, waiting for our attention:

Love. Laughter. Connection. Courage. Integrity. Respect.

That's the human inheritance and nobody and no thing can take that away from you.

My great hope for the future is that this moment, unsettling as it is, might finally reveal the truth we've spent decades ignoring:

That the most important things about being human were never the things we were told to prove.
We don't need to become more like machines.
We need to remember what it means to be human and to serve from that place.

Always, in service of wisdom.

In the Final Chapter...

Everything we've explored so far: the power of service, the strength in being there for others, the courage to embrace reality, has been building towards one simple but profound question: What will you do with your time?

The truth is, our lives are fleeting. In the grand scheme of history, each of us is granted only a microsecond of existence. And yet, within that brief moment, we have the power to leave an impact that ripples far beyond us. Not through wealth, status, or accolades, but through the way we serve, lead, and uplift those around us.

In the final chapter, we'll bring everything together. This is not just a conclusion - it is a call to action. A challenge to step into the world with intention, to lead with purpose, and to make service not just something we understand, but something we live. Because in the end, the only thing that truly matters is what we do for others.

The Final Chapter

The Journey – From Darkness to Meaning Through Service

I did not arrive at this mindset because life was easy. I didn't wake up one morning with a fresh perspective, a few ideas about leadership, and a desire to share them with the world. The Service Mindset was not a product of privilege or comfort. It was something I built, slowly and painfully, from the wreckage of a life I no longer recognised.

After my brain injury, everything I thought I knew about myself disappeared. The confidence, the sharpness, the feeling that I was somehow destined for great things… gone. In their place came confusion, disconnection, and a sense of grief so deep it didn't feel like sadness. It felt like I'd been hollowed out – it was *always raining in my head*.

I kept looking for the person I used to be. I replayed memories, hoping they would feel familiar again. I listened to the voice in my head and hoped it would start sounding like *me*. But it didn't. That voice had changed. I had changed. And for a long time, I could not accept that.

I resisted everything. I resisted the slowness of my mind, the loss of clarity, the way I had to work ten times harder to achieve what used to come easily. I resisted my reflection. I resisted help. I even resisted the idea that I might still have something meaningful to offer. I wanted things to go back to how they were. But they wouldn't. And the more I wished for a past I couldn't return to, the more miserable I became.

It was only when I stopped resisting that something did begin to finally change. I don't mean I gave up. I mean I stopped pretending. I accepted that my brain worked differently now. That I was changed, and that change wasn't something to fight, but rather it was something to work with.

Slowly, I started to rebuild. I walked. I spent time in nature. I moved my body, not because I thought it would fix me, but because walking brought a connection to nature and a break from the noise. I forced myself to engage with others, even when I felt like a ghost in the room. I said *yes* to small things. I completed one task a day. Then two. Then more. I stopped waiting for confidence to return and started acting as though I had some.

And what truly changed everything was when I began to look outward. I noticed that when I helped someone else, I felt a little more human. When I gave support, shared experience, or simply listened without judgement, I felt like I had value again. That small act of finding peace in contribution was the seed at the heart of The Service Mindset.

Service wasn't a concept to me, it was a lifeline. It gave me purpose when I thought there was nothing of value left. It gave shape to the days that would otherwise have collapsed into a suffocative, grey fog. It reminded me that I still mattered, not because I was exceptional, but because I was *useful*. I had lived through something difficult, and I could use that experience to understand others in their own darkness.

Over time, I stopped measuring my life by how far I had fallen, but rather in the small wins, achievements and acts of contribution I could make. Whether I turned pain into something helpful. Whether I created meaning from the mess. That, to me, is the heart of service - not grand gestures or heroic leadership, but the steady, quiet choice to do good with what you have.

So, if you're reading this and you're struggling - if you feel broken, or lost, or unsure of what comes next - let me say this plainly: *you do not have to have it all together.* You do not need to be fully healed to be of value. Sometimes, being there and doing something *despite the hurt and pain you are feeling* is the most courageous form of service there is.

📌 Call to Reflection:

What challenges have defined you? What pain, loss, or disappointment has shaped your path? And what have you done with it? Is there someone who could be helped by what you've lived through?

📌 Action Point:

Identify one struggle in your life - something real, something painful - and ask yourself: *how can I use this experience to help someone else move forward?*

The Journey So Far

Throughout this book, we have explored the principles, philosophies, and practical applications of The Service Mindset. From its philosophical roots in Stoicism, Adlerian psychology, and Buddhist teachings, to its real-world applications in leadership, business, decision-making, and personal resilience, this mindset is a transformative way of living. It is not about passive kindness or self-sacrifice; it is about active engagement with the world, about choosing to be of service in ways that empower both ourselves and those around us.

This journey began with a deeply personal realisation, that by shifting the focus from ourselves to others, we can find clarity, purpose, and ultimately, a sense of fulfilment that no external validation can provide. The Service Mindset is not a quick fix or a set of empty platitudes; it is a discipline, a philosophy that requires commitment, introspection, and action.

The Ripple Effect of Service

A recurring theme throughout this book has been the idea that by serving others, we also serve ourselves. The more we invest in making the world around us better: by mentoring, supporting, and uplifting others, the more we experience personal growth, fulfilment, and inner peace. This is not a transactional mindset; it is a recognition that our actions have ripple effects far beyond what we can immediately see.

Take a moment to reflect: *How many of the best opportunities in your life came from someone believing in you, investing in you, or supporting you in a moment when you needed it? And in turn, how many lives have you influenced in ways you may never fully appreciate?*

By adopting The Service Mindset, you become part of a chain of positive influence, contributing to a world where success is measured not just by what we achieve but by what we enable others to achieve.

📌 A Call to Action

The Service Mindset is a living philosophy. It does not end with this book. It is something you take forward in your daily life; whether through small acts of kindness, a shift in perspective, or major decisions that put service and impact at the centre of your actions. Here are three simple yet powerful commitments you can make today:

1. **Choose One Area of Service** – Identify a person, a cause, or a community where you can make a meaningful difference.

2. **Practice Daily Reflection** – Each morning, ask yourself, *Who can I serve today?* Each evening, reflect on *How did I embody The Service Mindset?*

3. **Take Action** – Service is not a theory; it is an action. Start now. Take that first step.

The world is full of challenges, but it is also full of opportunities to serve, to lead, and to uplift. In rising to these challenges, you will find that the greatest reward is not in what you receive, but in who you become.

Go forth, live with intention, lead with purpose, and serve with strength.

Service is Not Soft – Strength, Accountability, and Doing What's Necessary

There's a myth that floats around leadership circles that service is a gentle thing. That to serve is to bend, to please, to smooth over the rough edges and keep the peace at all costs.

However, anyone who has truly lived in service of others knows this isn't the case. Service isn't soft. It is not passive. It's not about saying *yes* to everyone or protecting people from discomfort.

Service is doing what needs to be done. And sometimes, that means choosing the harder path - the one that makes you unpopular in the moment, but protects what matters in the long run. It means making decisions with a clear conscience, not a clear inbox. It means being strong enough to have difficult conversations, to hold others accountable, and to draw lines that preserve integrity.

Strength is rarely about prevailing in confrontation. More often, it's about resistance - about holding the line not just against others, but against the easy assumptions people make about each other.

I remember being dropped into a leadership role once - a new team, a fresh mandate.

Alongside the handover, I was given a quiet caveat. *"That guy over there,"* someone said, nodding towards a member of the team. *"He's not technically strong. His attitude stinks. We need you to manage him out."*

I heard what they said and I understood the subtext, but something in me pushed back because, at my core, I don't believe in writing people off – certainly not when it's evident that no one's taken the time to really understand what's going on.

So, I sat him down. I was honest. I didn't sugar-coat what I'd been told, and I didn't pretend everything was fine, but I also told him that I wasn't interested in scapegoats. I told him I saw potential, and that I was willing to invest, but only if he was too.

I spent time with him. Trained him. Coached him. Encouraged him. He responded. Not overnight, but gradually, and steadily. By the time I moved on from that business, that same guy - the one I was meant to "manage out" - was now a top performer. I'll never forget that. Not because it made me proud, though it did, but because it reminded me that true service is not about control - it's about *belief*.

To serve someone is not to coddle them. It is to *see* them fully and honestly. To confront their failings without abandoning their potential. To set expectations high and then walk beside them as they climb. That takes far more strength than writing someone off.

That is what people so often miss. Service is not about being liked, it is about being useful. It is about doing right by others - even when they don't see it, even when they resist it, even when it costs you comfort in the short term. The best leaders I know are the ones who hold their ground with empathy, who refuse to confuse moral clarity with cruelty, and who have the courage to believe that people can grow if given the right challenge and the right support.

✯ Call to Reflection:

Where in your life have you been mistaking kindness for avoidance? Is there someone you've written off too soon, or a difficult truth you've been holding back, thinking silence is the gentler option?

✯ Action Point:

Think of a conversation you've been avoiding: a performance issue, a strained relationship, a moment of unspoken tension. Write down what you would say if you led with both clarity and compassion. Then commit to having the conversation. Not for your comfort, but for their growth.

Your Microsecond of Existence – What Will You Do With It?

It's easy to believe that our lives are the centre of everything. That what happens to us: the highs, the lows, the little wins and petty frustrations, somehow mark the edge of reality - but they don't. In the grand scheme of things, we are barely here at all.

The Earth is estimated to be around 4.5 billion years old. The universe, over 13.8 billion. In the span of that time, our lives do not even register as a flicker. We are not even a full heartbeat in the timeline of existence. We are a breath. A moment. A microsecond.

And yet, we spend so much of that moment chasing things that will not last. Money. Titles. Status. Approval. We compete. We compare. We cling to symbols of success as though they will grant us permanence, but they never have done and they never will. All of it disappears. Your car, your house, your job title, your social media following - none of it will outlive you.

But there is something that can.

Your impact.
How you made people feel. What you gave. What you stood for. The way you lifted others. The courage you showed when it mattered. The love you offered freely, even when it wasn't returned. These are the things that last. These are the things that ripple through time in ways you'll never fully see.

You do not need to change the world to matter. That's not what legacy means. Legacy is the sum of your small, consistent choices. It's the people you encouraged. The values you defended. The times you showed up when it would've been easier not to. It's what remains of you in other people's lives even after you're gone.

I sometimes think about how strange it is that we get this one life, this tiny window of awareness between two eternities of silence - and we don't get to choose how long it lasts. We might not get to know when it ends, but we sure as hell *do* get to choose what we do with it.

For me, the answer is service. Not as a performance, but as a compass. A way of living that helps me make sense of things. That helps me honour the fact that I am here, even if only briefly.

The truth is, none of us leave with anything in our hands. So, the question becomes: *what will we leave behind in the hearts of others?*

The Inevitability of Death – A Perspective Shift

Death is the one truth we all share, and yet it's the one thing most of us go to great lengths to avoid thinking about. We distract ourselves. We stay busy. We pretend it's far away, as though that pretending protects us and keeps us safe.

The Service Mindset asks us to do the opposite. It asks us to stop running from death and instead, to face it directly. To see it not as a threat, but as a clarifier.

The Stoics had a phrase: *Memento Mori* - *"remember you must die"*. It was not the morbid mantra it seems at first, but rather it was meant to be a source of focus because when you truly accept that your time is finite, you stop wasting it. You stop filling your days with vanity, resentment, and fear. You stop trying to win arguments or impress strangers. You start asking better questions. *How am I being present today? What will I leave behind? Who did I lift? Who did I love?*

I didn't arrive at this realisation from philosophy. I arrived at it from a hospital bed.

At 18, I fell. Quite literally. After a night out in Tenerife, I landed in an underground car park with a brain injury that should have killed me. I woke up in a foreign hospital, blood on my clothes, my father washing them in the sink beside me. I had no idea what had happened in that moment. I asked the same questions over and over. The voice in my head didn't sound like mine anymore. The future I'd been promised: university, automatic success, control over my future - vanished overnight.

That moment could have broken me… and to be fair, for a while, it did. I carried a silent shame that I'd survived, as though I hadn't earnt my second chance - but slowly, in recalling the philosophy I had done my level best to obliterate from my brain cells, something began to shift - I stopped asking *why me?* and started asking *what now?*

That fall became the foundation of this philosophy, because when you're face to face with mortality, you don't come back unchanged. You come back with clarity.

The clarity of knowing that we don't control how long we have, but we do control how we use it.

Overcoming the Fear of Mortality

I wish I could say that realisation brought peace right away. It didn't. What followed was years of anxiety, the kind that lives in your bones and stalks you every day. Every unusual pain in my body felt terminal. Every late-night email from my boss signalled disaster. My mind, still shaken from trauma, defaulted to panic. The shadow of death hadn't left, it had simply changed shape and hidden in other aspects of my life.

Over time, I began to understand something important: fear doesn't disappear through avoidance, it dissolves through action.

I stopped trying to out-think death. I stopped catastrophising the future. Instead, I started doing something - anything. I got outside. I moved. I built routines. I poured my energy into serving others: helping teammates, mentoring colleagues, walking my dog with my daughter, making Jane laugh after a hard day. These small acts were not distractions they were antidotes to my pain.

The more I focused outward, the less space my fears had to grow inward.

We often imagine that fear and courage are opposites. They're not. Courage is doing something worthwhile *despite* the fear - and nothing is more worthwhile than making your life a source of light for others.

So many people reach the end of their lives filled with regret, not for what they did, but for what they didn't do. For the love they didn't show. For the words they didn't say. For the gifts they never gave because they thought they weren't ready. The Service Mindset flips this. It asks not *what am I owed in this life?* but *what can I offer while I still have time?*

The fear of death loses its grip the moment we decide to *use* the time we've been given, instead of fearing its end.

Finding Peace in the Finite

At some point, you come to a place of quiet acceptance: you will die. Everyone you know will die - and there is nothing you can do to change that.

Don't be sad, try to see it as a liberation.

Once you accept that the clock is ticking, you begin to live differently. You stop needing to control everything. You stop wasting time chasing perfection. You start giving your time, your presence, your love because you know how precious they really are.

Peace doesn't come from denying your mortality. It comes from living in alignment with it.

The Service Mindset is not about sainthood or sacrifice. It is about *intention*. It's about waking up in the morning and saying: *I don't know how many days I have left, but I have today, I will be present. I will serve. I will make this moment count.*

I could have let that fall define me. I could have let trauma write the rest of my story, but I chose to serve instead. I chose to make peace with my finite time and to use it in service of others.

You don't have to change the world, but you can change someone's world… and that's more than enough.

📌 Call to Reflection:

What do you want to be remembered for? When people speak your name after you're gone, what will they say and how will they feel?

📌 Action Point:

Write a one-sentence legacy statement. What do you want people to say about you when you're no longer here? Keep it honest. Let it be your compass.

The Service Mindset in Action – A Daily Commitment

It's easy to be moved by a powerful idea. It's harder to live it; not once or twice, but every single day. That's where The Service Mindset becomes real. Not in a speech, not in a breakthrough moment, not even in a book, but in the quiet, consistent choices you make when no one is keeping score.

Service isn't about grand gestures. It's not about saving the world or fixing everyone's problems. Most of the time, it's not dramatic at all. It's simple. It's steady. It's the decision to live with intention, in service of others and true to your values, again and again, even when it's inconvenient or unrecognised… especially then!

There are a thousand ways to live The Service Mindset, but it always starts small. You don't need a title. You don't need a platform. You just need to pay attention and then act with care.

Be present.

This might sound obvious, but in the 21st Century its actually quite rare. In a world full of distractions, one of the greatest gifts you can offer another person is your full attention. Not glancing at your phone. Not thinking about your reply while they're still speaking. Just listening. Being there. Letting someone feel seen. It costs nothing and yet it can change everything for someone.

Mentor someone.

You've learnt things along the way - through pain, failure, growth, and effort. Don't hoard that knowledge. Pass it on. Look for someone who is earlier in the journey than you and help them find their footing. Not with superiority, but with solidarity. Remember what it felt like to be new. Be the person you once needed.

Build others up.

Whether it's your team, your family, or a stranger crying on a train, ask yourself: *did I leave them feeling stronger or smaller?* Encouragement is a form of service. So is patience. So is choosing to believe in someone, especially when they don't yet believe in themselves.

Do the right thing, even when no one is watching.

This is the quiet core of integrity. It's not about credit. It's about alignment. Living in a way that reflects your values - not for applause, but because it's who you are. The Service Mindset isn't performative. It's personal. It's about who you choose to be in the moments when it's just you and your brain.

These aren't difficult practices. They're not flashy or time-consuming, but if you commit to them, day after day, they will change the texture of your life, and the lives of those around you. This is where service becomes more than a philosophy. This is where it becomes a way of being.

📌 Call to Reflection:

What small change could you make today that reflects The Service Mindset? Not later. Not next week. Today.

📌 Action Point:

Choose one habit of service to practise this week. It might be listening more fully, offering support to a colleague, or simply doing the right thing when it would be easier not to. Keep it simple. Keep it steady. Let it shape who you become.

And so I'll leave you with this. A story from not long ago. A moment where, once again, I was reminded that the mindset I built wasn't just theory - it was practice.

Holding My Head High

There are moments in life when the future feels uncertain. Whispers in corridors. Meetings you're not invited to. The quiet sense that change is on the horizon, and you're not privy to the action plan.

In the past, I'd have spiralled when facing situations like this - ruminating over worst-case scenarios, seeking answers that weren't available, maybe even reaching for a drink to quiet the noise. But these days, more often than not, I make a cup of tea.

Not because I don't care, but because I've learnt to let go of what I can't control.

When you know you've acted with integrity - when you've given your best, stayed true to your values, and carried more than most people realise - you slowly begin to release the need for external validation. You stop chasing approval or trying to decipher every silence.

You rest in the knowledge that you did it your way and the right way, even when it was hard.

I still have doubts like anyone else, but I've found comfort in The Service Mindset, not just the words on these pages, but the principles I try to live by. It was born in moments like these. Moments that once brought panic now invite reflection. Moments that once demanded a reaction now offer a choice.

I hold my head high, not because I think I'm important, but because I've come to understand the value of staying grounded, kind, and consistent - especially when the future is unclear.

Some chase titles or recognition. And I get it - we all want to feel seen - but more and more, I find myself choosing a quiet mug of tea and a clear conscience. And that, for me, is enough.

The Final Challenge – Will You Answer the Call?

Ideas are easy. The world is full of them. We write them down, talk them through, post them online. We debate, refine, theorise - but the world does not change through theory, it changes when someone stands up and decides to *act*.

You do not need a title to do this. You do not need permission. You do not need a perfect version of yourself. What you need is courage and a willingness to start where you are, with what you have.

You are not too small to matter. And the problems we face are not too big to resist. One person choosing to live with integrity, to exist with purpose, to lead through service - that can ripple outward in ways you'll never fully see or appreciate. Every act of kindness, every moment of clarity, every time you choose truth over comfort or principle over popularity, you tilt the world a little in the right direction.

History remembers those who gave. Those who built. Those who lifted others when it would have been easier to look away. No one writes songs for the glory hoarders. No one builds statues for those who played it safe. What lasts, what endures, is your impact.

The truth is, we do not need more people chasing attention, validation, or status. The world is overflowing with noise. What it needs now are people willing to *quietly serve*. To take responsibility where others look for blame. To lead, not because it makes them feel important, but because it makes others feel *seen*.

This is the challenge I leave with you: not to be perfect, not to have it all figured out, but to live *deliberately*. To ask, every day: *how can I serve here? What does this moment require of me? How can I use my voice, my presence, my choices; however small, to make something better?*

The world is full of challenges, but it is also full of opportunities. They are waiting to be claimed. And your time here - this tiny, irreplaceable moment in the vast stretch of existence - is yours to shape.

What will you do with your microsecond of existence?

📌 **Final Action Point:**

Write down one way you will embody The Service Mindset every single day from this point forward. Just one. Let it be your anchor. Let it be your answer to the question: Did I serve today?

So go forward with clarity. Go forward with courage. The Service Mindset isn't just something to believe in - it's something to *become*. The world may never hand you a medal for doing what's right, for serving when no one is watching - but that was never the point.

This life is fleeting, and yet, it is full of meaning - if you choose to give it some.

📌 **Remember:** your time is limited. You are not promised tomorrow. But you *are* given today.

You Are My Brother

We are not meant to live alone.

Not just in the literal sense - not without partners or friends or social contact - but in the deeper, structural sense. We are not meant to be fragmented into disconnected, competing units. The modern world has engineered a belonging deficit. By design or by accident, we have been reduced to individuals. Standalone, self-optimising, "free" in theory, yet easy to manipulate, control, and divide in practice.

Why? Because disconnected people can't bargain. Disconnected people don't rise up. Disconnected people quietly accept the future that is handed to them - even when it's not what they want.

We are on the brink of the AI revolution. A moment that should demand unity, negotiation, clear boundaries and instead, we'll likely greet it in silence. Not because the AI genie is out of the bottle and unstoppable, but because we no longer know how to move together. Politicians speak for lobbyists. The public has lost its voice - and the social fabric - the shared "we" - has worn thin.

We can't define ourselves in isolation. Even physics knows this. Objects are only known through their interaction with other objects. The same is true for meaning. You do not become a helpful person by thinking helpful thoughts. You become one by turning up, by giving, by saying something in a moment that makes someone else reach for a notepad and say, *"That's not a bad idea."*

That's how I know I'm living well - when I see the spark in someone else's eyes, when they engage, when they lean in because I've added something – because I contributed. That's what service is: offering something that builds, uplifts, contributes.

And sometimes - maybe even more often than not - service means being quiet. Resisting the urge to speak just for the sake of it. Asking yourself: *"Am I building on this? Am I adding value?"* If not, then maybe the best way to serve is to make space for someone else to be heard.

Last night, I saw service in its purest form.

Two young boys at the kebab van round the corner from my house. Knee-high to grasshoppers, barely up to the counter. Sent out with what little money their mother had to give them. The older brother wanted chips and a burger. The younger brother wanted a wrap and a drink. They didn't have enough money. And so, after a gentle, polite exchange, the older brother gave up his chips, so the younger could have a drink.

When asked if he was sure, he wrapped his little brother in a huge embrace and said, *"Of course I'm sure. You're my brother… and I love you."*

I stepped in. Bought them both chips and drinks. Not to feel good about myself, but because something in that moment made me remember who I am - a big brother, a man who once had nothing, now lucky enough to have something. And sometimes, the most important thing you can do with your share of something is to share it with someone else.

You are my brother and I love you.

Imagine a world that operated on that principle.

That is The Service Mindset.

Memento Mori - Serve Well.

Afterword – 24 Years Later

It's been twenty-four years, almost to the day, since I fell into that hole in Tenerife.

A hole in the ground. A fracture in time. A clean break between the life I had planned and the new life I would have to build from scratch.

I didn't know then how long the darkness would last. I didn't know how many years it would take to feel like myself again, or rather, to make peace with the fact that I would never be the same self I once was.

And yet here I am.

Finishing this book, in this moment, doesn't feel like an ending. It feels like something has been sealed. Finished. Brought home.

Not triumphantly – and not always neatly - but truthfully… and that, for me, is enough.

This isn't a story of victory in the way people usually mean it. It's not about beating the odds, or "coming back stronger," or proving the doubters wrong. It's about continuing. It's about learning to live with what is broken, uncertain and irreparable.

It's about finding meaning in service, even when you're not sure what you believe anymore.

There were so many moments when I wanted to give up. When life felt too heavy, and the noise in my head too loud. But somehow, I kept going. For others. For work. For my family. For Erin. For Jane.

Slowly and quietly - that act of taking *just one more step* became my anchor.

Writing The Service Mindset has been exhausting and exposing - but also healing. Every page has asked me to revisit parts of myself I had long buried. Every chapter has forced me to hold a mirror up and ask: *who are you now? What do you stand for when you're not trying to impress, achieve, or escape?*

I still don't have all the answers. But I know this much:

The Service Mindset saved me.

Not in a grand or glorious way, but in the small, ordinary, steadfast acts of care that slowly rebuilt a life.

If this book helps even one person find strength in simplicity, peace in imperfection, or meaning in helping others, then it was worth writing.

Thank you for walking with me.

Gareth

Printed in Dunstable, United Kingdom